Eve was Framed

Eve was Framed

Women and British Justice

———————

Helena Kennedy

Chatto & Windus
LONDON

Published in 1992 by
Chatto & Windus Ltd
20 Vauxhall Bridge Road
London SW1V 2SA

A CIP catalogue record for this book is available
from the British Library.

ISBN 0–7011–3523–9

Phototypeset by Intype, London
Printed and bound in Great Britain by
Mackays of Chatham PLC, Chatham, Kent

Contents

Acknowledgements   vii

Introduction   1

1 Eve was Framed   17
2 Playing Portia   32
3 The Fragrant Woman   65
4 The Wife, the Mother and the Dutiful Daughter   82
5 Asking for It   106
6 Naughty but Nice   140
7 And She was Black   161
8 Man – Slaughter   190
9 The Unreasonable Woman   222
10 She-devils and Amazons   240
11 Courtly Gestures   263

Index   280

To women in prison

Acknowledgements

This is a polemic about the law, not an academic exercise. It is written in the belief that we are at a crucial moment in history which, if seized, could bring about real change in the system. My fear is that the legal system, having been rocked out of its resting place like a huge boulder, will readily fall back into position unless it is pushed all the way.

However, a formidable body of learned work does exist to support the view that women are disadvantaged in the law and in the courts. I am very conscious of my indebtedness to the many wonderful women and men who have given me insights into the workings of the Criminal Justice System over the years. I cannot possibly name them all, but I would first like to mention some of the criminologists and academic lawyers in the field because their books, which are still available to inspire others, lent me reassurance that all was not in the mind and provided me with a sound theoretical base for my professional life: Pat Carlen, Rebecca and Russell Dobash, Frances Heidenson, Susan Edwards, Carol Smart, Terence Morris, Jennifer Temkin, Susan Atkin, Barbara Hoggett, Lorna Smith, Kathleen Donovan, Catherine McKinnon, Jocelynne Scutt, Sylvia Van Heysel, Betsy Stanko and Lucia Zedner. A special mention must go to my great friend Albie Sachs, who is renowned as a South African lawyer. He was imprisoned and almost killed in an explosion because of his political commitment to a new South Africa. He also deserves acknowledgement as a leading contributor to feminist jurisprudence.

I also want to thank Chris Tchaikovsky of Women in Prison,

Pru Stevenson of WISP and Southall Black Sisters for inspiration. And I am grateful to many practitioners, whose own experiences mirror my own. Friends and colleagues who provided special counsel include Sally Belfrage, Leora Mosston, Sally Hughes, Geoffrey Bindman, Ronan Bennett, Di Bevan, Frances Crook, Eric Smellie, Sandra Horley, Anita Dockley, Tanoo Mylavagnum, Jalna Hanmer, Constance Briscoe, Nicholas Blake, Angelica Mitchell, Chief Inspector Jackie Malton, Dr Estela Welldon, Anthony Barnett, Caroline Taylor, David Faulkner, Duncan Campbell of the *Guardian*, Bernard Simon, Martha Field, Rosie Gilbey and Debby Taylor. I was given particular help by one of our finest forensic psychiatrists, Dr Nigel Eastman, who has worked with me on many cases. He has a profound understanding of the interface between law and psychiatry and knows how to make that relationship work in the courtroom. I have learned greatly from our collaboration.

My particular thanks go to one of tomorrow's hopes for the law, Quincy Whittaker, who rescued press cuttings and debated ideas.

Faith Evans, my literary agent, was the prime mover behind the creation of this book. She sat on a jury in one of my cases and later wrote urging me to put pen to paper. It took many years before I did put pen to paper but this book would not have been possible without her generous encouragement, friendship and belief that it was possible. Jenny Uglow, my editor, was the midwife to this endeavour: her insight, intelligence, skill and support were crucial. Also, a tribute to Carmen Callil, my publisher, who beat me with a stick and made me create the space amongst my many other commitments to complete this book. Thank you all. And finally, my eternal gratitude goes to Iain Hutchison whose tolerance, encouragement and love have sustained me.

Introduction

I have chosen in this book to look at the treatment of women in British justice as a paradigm of the faults and blindnesses of the legal system as a whole. Women are not a minority within society, even if they are a distinct minority within the courtroom. Yet their treatment is constantly determined by the degree to which they conform to a non-legal mythology shared by judges, lawyers and jurors alike, sometimes regardless of their sex.

'Calumny!' This was the charge that echoed through the Royal Courts of Justice, on 15 April 1992, the cry of an endangered species, defying those who expected concern and self-criticism instead of a closed-ranks defence of the indefensible. The occasion was the retirement of the Lord Chief Justice, Geoffrey Lane, who for two years had borne the brunt of public concern as almost every month brought another entry in the catalogue of miscarriages of justice: the Birmingham Six, the Guildford Four, the Maguires, the Tottenham Three, Stefan Kiszco, Jacqueline Fletcher, Judith Ward and those who had been wrongly convicted at the hands of the West Midland Crime Squad. One horror story after another emerged about prisoners who had spent years maintaining their innocence in the face of disbelief.

The legal establishment came together to praise Caesar, to rally in a public act of fealty. This was a display of loyalty to a man, privately charming by all accounts, but it also betrayed a dismaying arrogance. Loyalty and empathy would best have been shown by sharing responsibility with the Lord Chief Justice, rather than denying that the judiciary and legal profession had any accounting to do. Personal attacks by the press, public and politicians upon him, as head of the judiciary, stemmed largely from a belief that the buck had to stop somewhere. However, others in the legal profession should feel an even greater weight of accountability. The 'how' and 'why' that has racked the public conscience should be sending all judges and lawyers in search of a means of restoring faith in the concept of British justice.

Have the grandees within the law been chastened by the ghosts of trials past? In legal watering holes these miscarriages are too often dismissed as the regrettable mismanagement of criminal investigation by the police, while the campaigns for justice are recast as the manipulation of procedural flaws by the politically motivated, hell-bent on destroying one of our finest institutions.

Cynicism, the enemy of justice, pervades the Inns of Court. Far from being humbled by these recent experiences, there are still members of the judiciary who are resentful and angry that they have come under scrutiny at all. They claim that it was the system that failed, not the personnel, and, like so many 'bang to rights' accused, point the finger at others in the dock, blaming everyone but themselves: overzealous policing or, at worst, police corruption in the face of crimes with a high emotional charge; inadequate protection for vulnerable defendants of low intelligence or with psychological problems who therefore made undetectably false confessions; scientists lacking in rigour and too closely connected to the police for independent professionalism. Judges and lawyers present themselves as innocent dupes believing in the honesty and forbearance of the police and the experts.

The judiciary will of course be seen to respond: new methods will be sought and refined procedures advanced. The public is already being assured that many of the problems have largely been corrected by intervening legislative changes, like the Police and Criminal Evidence Act 1984 which introduced tape-recorded interviews and additional checks on police procedure. A few more legal curlicues, some honing of the rules, a report here and there, mildly critical perhaps but not severe enough to undermine the status quo, and we can all get back to business.

Some concerned lawyers, searching for more radical cures, promote the inquisitorial system used on the Continent as an advance on the adversarial method in the British courts, with its contest of prosecution and defence. But they ignore the failings which haunt that system too. At regular intervals Italian and French lawyers, in despair at the problems that bedevil their courts, come to this country to explore the advantages of the adversarial way of testing evidence against an accused, recognising the strengths of our system if we were true to it.

Complacency, so often the hallmark of lawyers, has fostered the notion that imperfection is an inevitable part of any legal system. But this time the crisis is too great for that indulgence. The whiff of reform is in the air, and a legal establishment unwilling to engage in self-criticism and corrective measures will continue to lose public confidence.

Righting the wrongs within the legal system will require more than a review of methods. The injustices of the past come from something deeper than bad-apple policemen or imperfect procedures. The problem is one of profound resistances to a changing order, failures of perception about people's lives and expectations, and above all a lack of commitment to the meaning of liberty.

The fundamental tenets of the criminal justice system now proudly emblazon the jackets of British and American crime novels – *Beyond Reasonable Doubt, Presumed Innocent, The Right to Silence, Burden of Proof, Trial by Jury* – but they are slowly being eroded in our courts. It is not the principles which have failed us but we who have failed the principles. These articles of faith are the British legacy in a significant part of the world. Graven in the stones of great halls, they are the core and strength of our legal tradition. Yet the system is in crisis because of a failure to adhere to those precepts.

The recent miscarriages of justice should remind us that it is only by keeping the legal tests for conviction very high that the courts can guarantee the protection of the innocent and maintain respect for the law.

In his direction on the law to the jury, hardly a judge now mentions that the standard of proof should be 'beyond reasonable doubt' and that no one should be convicted in our courts unless the court can establish guilt on these terms. However, the wording invariably used by judges today is that jurors must be 'satisfied so that they are sure', an expression more likely to conjure up advertisements for Cadbury's chocolate. Does the concept of satisfaction or 'being sure' drive one to the level of certainty which should be required before we surrender a citizen to sentencing and the likely loss of liberty? For the most part the only people who mention proof 'beyond reasonable doubt' are defence lawyers.

Such erosions are based on the patronising assumption that jurors are incapable of interpreting the classic test sensibly and will introduce all sorts of silly doubts into their deliberations. In fact, juries are capable of very subtle distinctions: they are just considerably less cynical than the case-hardened practitioners on the judicial bench. They appreciate, for example, that the high requirement of 'proof beyond reasonable doubt' is an acknowledgement that an innocent man or woman can be found in an incriminating situation, like some Kafkaesque nightmare, where a truthful explanation is dismissed as implausible.

It is almost as though the removal of capital punishment has brought its own price. The high standard of proof was demanded because of prizing life as well as liberty, but with the removal of the ultimate sanction there came a corresponding relaxation in the vigilance which is so necessary in criminal cases, as well as an undervaluing of the concept of liberty.

Most juries are true to the values of the criminal process, recognising that it is for the Crown to prove the charges, not for a defendant to prove innocence. Although they like to hear explanations and value the opportunity of assessing defendants in the witness box, they weigh those factors against the fears they imagine overwhelming a person who has been arrested and is facing charges.

It is in fact extraordinary that judges should be commenting on the evidence in any manner whatsoever. Judges often describe themselves as referees of the contest, but since they are drawn from the ranks of advocates a number of them cannot be satisfied with the role of non-combatant. They miss participation in the fight and come down off the bench, usually to fall in behind the prosecution, cross-examining witnesses and filling in gaps the Crown might have missed.

When jurists from other countries see the extent to which our judiciary give rein to their own views and try to influence juries in the summing-up at the end of the trial, they are appalled; it appears a usurping of the jury's function, contrary to the principle of jury trial. This has particularly been commented on in foreign reviews of the recent Irish appeals.

The judge's usual linguistic device is to express an opinion and then add the rider that 'of course, members of the jury, it is a matter for you'. But jurors perceive this as the judge tipping them the wink as to how they should be thinking. Sometimes they speculate that perhaps the judge knows something they do not, such as a history of convictions, or has intelligence about the defendant from security sources.

Juries, like most groups of people, are susceptible to every prejudice imaginable: racism, sexism, homophobia, hostility based on class and age, as well as fear and loathing of particular kinds of crime. Usually finer characteristics win the day, the collective product being greater than the sum of its parts. The responsibility of trying a fellow citizen usually fortifies the inner conscience. But occasionally the feelings released by a particular crime are so profound that a particularly high level of vigilance must be shown by all the key players – police, lawyers, scientists, other forensic experts and, most especially, the judge.

In virtually every one of the major miscarriages of justice cases the backdrop was highly charged with emotion. In the cases of the Birmingham Six, the Guildford Four and the Maguires, this was because of terrorist outrages; in the Tottenham Riot case it was because a policeman was hacked to death in a situation of racial tension; and in the Kiszco case it was because the sexually motivated murder involved a child. It was as though in these cases the burden of proof shifted to the defendants. 'Prove to us you are innocent' was the unspoken demand, and the protections which should be there for all of us were absent.

The system must be measured by these very cases. If we fail to do justice in trials where the public's sympathies are engaged, our civil liberties are meaningless. Legal standards must not wax and wane.

Part of the problem has been the failure of the judiciary to acknowledge unacceptable police practices. It has been a recurring source of comment at the Bar that last year's legal practitioner went on the bench and immediately wiped his judicial memory clean of any experience he might have had of police misconduct, as though the weight of the new wig expunged a lifetime's experience. Or, went the joke, it may have been that higher numbers of prosecutors were ending up on the bench, and prosecutors were used to turning a blind eye to shortcomings in the behaviour of police witnesses.

What in fact happens is that, in accepting the judicial role, many judges become unclear as to their function and relationship with the state. They see themselves as protectors of good order against anarchy, even as joined with the police in the battle against crime. Fighting crime is no bad thing, but what happens to impartiality when judges see themselves as allies of the police rather than of the citizen?

Most criminal lawyers like myself have had to make decisions throughout their professional lives on the basis that the judge will always prefer the police account unless the defence case is overwhelming. Like many a lawyer before and since, I have on occasion advised clients who insist that they were assaulted by police, subjected to abuse or incriminated with concocted statements that, unless it is central to the defence, we should avoid mentioning any of those factors in an effort to keep the judge sweet and so have an easier ride, a fairer summing-up, a lighter sentence. Of course, courtroom tactics are essential to the conduct of the case. Knowing what music to play in particular circumstances is a large part of the advocate's skill, but having to cater to a judge's predisposition in favour of police evidence is more serious than appreciating the minor susceptibilities of a given judge.

I have also frequently weathered horrible court experiences where the defence has inevitably involved direct confrontation with or contradiction of police evidence, and the judicial wrath has poured upon my client and upon me. There are some who, for reasons of professional expediency and a speedier rise up the greasy professional pole, will take on, but not really fight, cases that might upset the judge. This has meant the use of a semaphore or code, signalled by questions from the defence lawyer like, 'Officer, I must put it to you on the instructions of my client that you were twisting his arm when he signed his confession statement.' This reminds the judge that the barrister is having to ask the question because his worthless client insists upon it, and is an effort to sooth M'Lud.

If the judges can control the legal profession as well as the courtroom, and can influence the advance or otherwise of barristers, this is inevitably likely at times to have an impact on the conduct of cases. Forceful advocacy is suspect in some parts of the contemporary Bar, but happily most of the young people who enter the profession and practise criminal law are vigorous in championing their clients' cases.

Many cases of perverted justice have involved extracted confessions. As a young lawyer I learned from the best of the bunch at the criminal Bar that there was rarely any point in arguing for the judge to exclude dodgy confessions. They just would not believe that people ever confessed to crimes they had not committed, especially if it meant questioning police conduct. Theoretically the trial judge had the discretionary power to exclude any incriminating admission obtained in breach of what were known as the Judges' Rules. You could cross-examine the police officers and call witnesses before the judge (in the absence of the jury) before making your submission, but success was so rare that you would have needed the Queen's surgeon to testify to the physical assault of your client in order to win the argument. As a result most of us argued the issues out in front of the jury, and found the public were usually more open to persuasion than His Honour.

This was the standard battle in many ordinary, low-level cases in the 1970s, and it remains so today in front of some judges, though the issues are now somewhat different. The Police and Criminal Evidence Act tightened the rules on what was admissible, but there is still plenty of leeway for the miscreant police officer. Challenge the propriety of policing before certain judges and you must face the consequences.

There can be no excuse for the intellectual dishonesty of sections of the judiciary which colluded in the maintenance of the Irish convictions. This quote from Lord Denning, when he dismissed the attempt by the Birmingham Six to commence a civil action against the police, illustrates an attitude which permeated much of the judges' ranks:

> Just consider the course of events if this action is allowed to proceed to trial. If the six men fail it will mean much time and money will have been expended for no good purpose. If the six men win it will mean that the police are guilty of perjury, that they are guilty of violence and threats, that the confessions were invented and improperly admitted in evidence and the convictions were erroneous. That would mean that the Home Secretary would have to recommend they should be pardoned or remit the case to the Court of Appeal. This is such an appalling vista that every sensible person in the land would say it cannot be right that these actions should go any further. This case shows what a civilised country we are. The state has lavished large sums of money in their defence. On their own evidence they are guilty. It is high time it stopped because this is really an attempt to set aside their convictions. It is a scandal which should not be allowed to continue.

That view was not an aberration. It was shared by many less vocal colleagues.

Fifteen years had passed since their original convictions when in 1989 the Home Office, fearing a wrongful conviction may have taken place, sent the case of the Birmingham Six once again to the Court of Appeal. Lord Chief Justice Lane and his co-judges made plain their outrage at the allegations made by the appellants' lawyers against the police, and dismissed the appeal. No one who sat for any length of time in that court doubted that the appeal would fail. Lord Lane's abhorrence of the slightest slur on the police sat heavily with those of us who were conducting the Guildford appeal, which followed some months later.

In that case the appellants' solicitors were encouraged, where possible, to bring in a different line-up of barristers, in an effort to assuage judicial hostilities. The lawyers involved agonised about the plan of campaign for the legal argument, deciding that George Carman QC should run with Carole Richardson's case. This concentrated on the psychiatric and psychological evidence about her condition during interrogation and her susceptibility to suggestion, even if information had been provided innocently by the police. Although there is a high level of judicial scepticism about psychiatry, this seemed a safer avenue to go down than one which even hinted at police misbehaviour. Once Carole's alibi stood up and her confession fell away, it was argued that the other confessions might follow suit, falling like a pack of cards.

However, we were saddled with a serious problem. Our clients insisted that the interviews were not all as they appeared to be and claimed police misconduct. We considered all sorts of formulae which would soften criticism of the police, and discussed the implications of a full frontal assault on the evidence and the risk of riling the tribunal. Our debate continued until, out of the blue, the independent police enquiry into the case led to the discovery of evidence which supported conclusively the appellants' claims.

It is interesting to speculate what would have happened if the appeal had proceeded and the Crown had not withdrawn their opposition. As it was, no apology attended the release of the Guildford Four. No expressions of shame came from the bench that our system had so profoundly failed these people. And those who criticise the judiciary, however tepidly, continue to be rounded upon by the legal establishment as wreckers and iconoclasts.

The attack upon juries, interestingly, is of a very different order. When juries do precisely what they are supposed to do, applying the tests stringently and acquitting when there is a lurking doubt, they are frequently disparaged as unfit for the task. This happened in February 1992 when a man called Kevin Barry O'Donnell was shot in Northern Ireland by the Security Forces whilst involved in IRA activity. The previous year he had been charged with possession of firearms in the boot of a car and acquitted by an English jury. O'Donnell had denied all knowledge of the firearms and the jury no doubt agonised over their oath to try him fairly before they finally gave him the benefit of the doubt and acquitted him – but following the shooting they were vilified in the press. Calls were immediately made for the ending of trial by jury, since only fools could have been so deluded. It is as though sections of the press would prefer rough justice, mindless of the effects upon other defendants.

Such attacks reveal a contempt for ordinary people and a failure to recognise that the jury system is one of the ingredients of democracy. In surveys by NACRO (National Association for the Care and Resettlement of Offenders), of the trial process amongst convicted defendants the jury is subjected to least criticism.

Juries do what judges should at times also be doing. On occasions juries acquit because they are calling the authorities, especially the police, to account. This causes alarm amongst lawyers, who see it as an abuse of the jurors' oath, which is to try the case on the evidence. However, if the judiciary were more stringent about unacceptable police practices and refused to allow evidence to be admitted where there had been any abuse, juries would feel less inclined to doubt them. There would also be considerable incentive for the police to act properly.

In a discussion recently a senior circuit judge, who is particularly fair, told me how perverse he found juries, describing how in a recent case he had summed up for an acquittal but the jury had still 'potted' the defendants. He laughed, and explained that he usually got his own way with his twelve good men and true. I suppose in the daily grind of administering justice everyone has to find their own methods of survival, and there is no doubt that for some judges the device is to weigh up a case and then pit themselves against the lawyers to secure what they believe to be the right outcome. Judges know that the selection of language, the tone adopted, the raising of an eyebrow, which assisted them as advocates, are still valuable resources on the bench. Does training as an advocate best equip candidates for the judiciary? It certainly should not be the only training.

There was much gnashing and snapping amongst judges about the acquittal of Randall and Pottle in 1991. They had, on their own admission, helped the spy George Blake escape from prison twenty-three years before, and it was clear that the jury was more in tune than the judiciary with the public sense that the events belonged to an era which had passed, and that the conduct of the security services had left something to be desired.

The same disgruntlement was felt when Stephen Owen was acquitted in May 1992 of all charges after his shooting of the hit-and-run driver whose juggernaut crushed his son to death. The lorry driver, Keith Taylor, had served only one year of an eighteen-month sentence for causing death by reckless driving. Juries do sometimes take into account factors other than narrow legal evidence. This verdict included an element of criticism of a system where the maximum penalty for causing death by reckless driving is five years' imprisonment.

In 1984 Clive Ponting, an assistant secretary in the Ministry of Defence who had leaked documents concerning the sinking of the *Belgrano* during the Falklands War, was acquitted by a jury which clearly believed that government secrecy was unacceptable on certain subjects and that the public did have a right to know. The view expressed by the trial judge was that the interests of the government of the day were the same as the interests of the state. This revealed either alarming ignorance or a disregard for our constitutional arrangements. It would be interesting to know how he would describe the role of the judiciary within such a system.

Such inadvertent disclosures sometimes offer an extraordinary glimpse of the underbelly, an insight into the attitudes which frame the judges' performances. We have seen this in recent years with their comments about women in rape trials being 'contributorily negligent' if they accepted a lift or wore a mini-skirt. A view of sexuality is presented which has shocked at least half the population.

In the 1991 national census a majority of the public expressed their loss of confidence in the criminal justice system. They perceived the courts as weighted in favour of the rich and privileged and believed that the system did discriminate, particularly against black people. Why are so many people now distrustful of an institution which formerly commanded their respect? One factor is undoubtedly the change in public awareness. We have a more demanding and informed public which expects the professions, including the judiciary, to be accountable. This is already the case in medicine and education, but as always the law is the last to acknowledge the change.

The perception that the courts are simply out of touch with the reality of people's lives poses a serious threat to justice. When the legal system fails, or is seen to fail, in the fulfilment of its practical function, society reaps the consequences.

Civilised men and women adhere to a social contract requiring them to settle disputes in courtrooms rather than with pistols at dawn. That involves the provision by the courts of symbolic retribution, an assuagement for the victims and their families as well as society. But the contract ceases to operate effectively if victims are not dealt with fairly in the courts or defendants cannot be guaranteed a fair trial. There is a constant tension between the needs of those who suffer crime and those who are accused of it, and it is within that tension that justice is defined. There has to be a constant fine-tuning to a changing world and a willingness to shed preconceptions. The question is whether our current legal training and legal arrangements can meet this challenge.

'The law cannot be subject to fashion' is the judicial refrain. No one would dispute this, but it can become an excuse for atrophy and blinkered vision. Real and generous shifts in attitudes are required to maintain confidence in the law.

The law regulates our social relations. In doing so it issues messages which resonate throughout society. Those messages are internalised. Democracy in itself does not always guarantee that we adhere to the highest principles. Simple headcounting democracy, for example, could reintroduce hanging, and would provide little protection to minorities. On the other hand, the law can never be completely out of step with public feeling or it will be held in contempt. This two-step which the law has to conduct, of leading public opinion yet also reflecting it, is a difficult manoeuvre, but what does not work is for the law to lag behind public concerns or to dismiss their value.

The ritual and mystique of court procedure is itself out of date. A recurrent theme, heard from prisoners and witnesses alike when talking about their courtroom experiences, is the terror of the witness box, the intimidation of the procedure, made undoubtedly worse by the paraphernalia of wigs and gowns and a language which obfuscates rather than illuminates. Some people feel they are unable to give a good account of themselves because of disadvantage in the face of articulate middle-class lawyers. Self-consciousness then interferes with their ability to recollect events accurately. They are often unsure of the questions asked, but answer them as best they can because they do not want to be told off. That process makes many defendants and victims, particularly women, feel like children again, undoubtedly because they often are treated as children. This intimidatory experience was expressed by over half of those interviewed in research recently conducted by Birmingham University (*Guardian*, 30 October 1991).

The criminal trial is a terrifying process. Those who are most affected by it, the victims and defendants, are those who are most neglected and alienated by the ambience and the procedures.

I recently defended in a murder trial before a High Court judge on circuit in a rural town. At regular intervals during the trial the judge acquired companions as he sat up on the bench. Not only did he have, as is usual, his own clerk, who is attired in a tail-coat and who sits alongside him (quite distinct from the regular court clerk who was still sitting in front), but he also had the High Sheriff of the County decked out in velvet knickerbockers and a sword. On a number of days we even had the High Sheriff's wife, looking very Harrods with a hat and pussy-cat bow at her neck. Indeed, there were also days when in addition to the forementioned we had the judge's wife as well up there, sitting smartly at his elbow. It was like a day at the races – one almost expected the binoculars to be passed along so that each could get a better look at the specimens in the dock.

This preposterous business happens in varying degrees in different courts, depending on the good sense of the judge and his spouse – although I can hardly imagine a female High Court judge bringing out hubby for the spectacle. Until recently it was said in the north that if your client was up for sentence before a certain High Court judge, Thursday afternoon was your best bet for leniency because his lady wife had a regular appointment then at the hairdresser's.

During the *Lady Chatterley's Lover* trial, Lady Byrne sat on high alongside her husband throughout the trial, and the look on her face when she heard the evidence did not bode well for the defence. At the end of the trial she was overheard to say, 'What a disgusting verdict'.

It may well be that no influence comes to bear on the judicial impartiality, but it is an affront to those on trial that they should be subjected to such voyeurism. One would have imagined that any judge of the new generation would see the offence in such a charade. There is absolutely no place for it in the modern courtroom.

The courtroom mysticism is not unintentional: the participants are supposed to feel in awe of the process for its magic to work. But for many it brings back some of the nightmares of childhood. For the witness or defendant it means having the focus of attention turning on them in an environment which is comfortable only to a small class of people. It means speaking aloud in front of everyone. It means being scrutinised and perhaps being found wanting.

The number of jurors who cannot read the oath is often cited as a sign of our illiterate times; in fact the problem is more likely the difficulty of enunciating the words in public. The performance is the inhibitor. In an important trial with racial overtones the Crown asked for one of the few black jurors to be 'stood by' (released from service) because of his difficulty with reading; it was later discovered that he had no problem at all but was terrorised by the process. The *faux pas* had in the meantime wiped out confidence in the prosecution team, whose insensitivity was seen as an example of biased white justice.

Many people have misapprehensions about how the courts work. Schooled on American films, they do not realise that our system is different. They also fail to appreciate the degree of dramatic licence which operates. To the victim of a crime, for example, it comes as a shock that the person they see as conducting 'their' case never even says hello to them. Because the victim in a case is a witness the code of professional conduct in relation to witnesses comes into force, which means the prosecuting lawyer cannot speak to them about their evidence. Although the defendant is not a witness in the ordinary sense, even here counsel can confer with him or her only in the presence of a solicitor.

Introduction

Obviously prosecutors could introduce themselves, and many counsel for the Crown are now doing this, but there are still a large number of practitioners who feel that their impartiality should not be impugned. They do not want to run the risk of allegations that they said something inappropriate or tried to coach a witness, so the violated woman or child is left bewildered as to who is who amongst the bigwigs.

Even expert witnesses at times complain of their treatment as either patronising or dismissive. Psychiatrists, psychologists and sociologists have a particularly rough ride. They come like lambs to the slaughter if their reports are full of references to 'cycles of deprivation' or 'cognitive dissonance'. We have our own arcane language in the courtroom and we do not want anyone else's creeping in.

Justice is compromised because people who are caught up in an already flawed legal process are often judged on grounds which have nothing whatsoever to do with the facts of the case. Those who are most susceptible are the young and the working-class, the immigrant, Irish, black, homosexual or female: when we look at the problems facing women, we should always keep these other groups in mind.

In reviewing cases within these chapters I have avoided including my own, save occasionally in the most general of terms: the Bar rules forbid counsel to discuss their own cases in detail. I have concentrated on women and crime because this is the field in which I practise, but the same fundamental problems operate in the other areas of the law in varying degrees. I have also restricted my ambit to the courtroom and reflected on my own branch of the profession, which until recently had a monopoly of rights to conduct trials.

It is often the way with discriminatory practice that its victims know full well what is happening whilst those who perpetrate it are oblivious. Denying women their experience is one of the ways in which male power is maintained – which brings us back to the central issues addressed in this book. Is the criminal justice system sensitive to the reality of women's lives? If this happens to women, are other citizens similarly disadvantaged?

Blame for the crisis in the law cannot be placed at the door of judges or any one group of people. Nor is there any conspiracy afoot. It is the nature of the beast that needs reassessment, and the attitudes which support the survival of the status quo. Creating a legal framework which is truly equitable means a fundamental overhaul of our legal thinking. For too long the legal system has escaped scrutiny and resisted criticism because of its mystical position at the centre of our social order, but the recent miscarriages of justice have called its role into question. The institution itself has to change. Only then will the law be just.

1

Eve was Framed

Law does not spring out of a social vacuum. My maternal grand-mother had her own line in moralising, and one of the old wives' maxims that fell from her lips was that there would be no bad men if there were no bad women. This world view, which would usually be expounded as she swept vigorously around me whilst I attempted homework on the kitchen table, filtered through our days and was certainly absorbed by my mother. As we struggled through Glasgow Central Station past a group of well-soused merrymakers on our way home from paying the rent, she would tighten her grip on my hand and mutter that there was only one thing worse than a drunk man, and that was a drunk woman.

Even as a child it seemed to me that if there was one body of people who were tougher on women than on men it was other women, a puzzling contradiction given the strength of the female bonds in my community. However, for the most part I just accepted that there were higher expectations of women. At every point in my Catholic girlhood the Virgin Mary was presented to us as our role model. Men were simply victims of their own appetites, hardly capable of free will when it came to sex or violence, and it was up to us to act as the restraining influence. After all, woman was responsible for the original sin. It was only later that I came to the conclusion that Eve had been framed.

I swallowed the idea that women should generally be expected to behave better than men, since there seemed ample evidence that they did so anyway, and I could see no harm in keeping up the standard. However, my sense of natural justice balked at the idea of holding women responsible for male transgressions. Why should women be considered the moral cornerstones of society? Does motherhood really carry with it such an overwhelming obligation? Transportation from Paradise is one thing, but a sentence of eternal damnation when the conviction had to be based on the uncorroborated testimony of a co-accused must surely constitute a breach of international standards on human rights. Poor old Eve. I wonder if she would have done any better with a good defence lawyer. Here is the speech for the prosecution:

> To me a thoroughly criminal woman is a most repugnant creature. Although male criminals largely outnumber females, there exist many more of the latter than appear in published statistics. That is to say, women are the cause of, directly or indirectly, a large amount of crime in men for which they receive no statistical credit. Personally I feel quite convinced that some women wield an hypnotic influence over men, and it is invariably a malign influence . . . obeying that instinct for working mischief to the opposite sex which women would seem to have inherited from Mother Eve . . . Speaking generally, women have less willpower than men and therefore less self-control upon emergency. One of the most staggering and repugnant attributes to man exhibited by bad women is their perfectly fiendish cruelty. It is all the more startling by being displayed by one who is supposed to be gentle by nature. It is certainly a matter for meditation that the cruellest forms of crime are invariably committed by women. The only consolation is that they are not women in the ordinary acceptation of the word and something malign happened at their begetting which sets them apart from ordinary human beings.

Who could resist Hargrave L. Adams? I fell upon his *Woman and Crime* in a bookshop just off Chancery Lane, and read it aloud for the entertainment of friends in my early years of practice at the Bar. His Gothic descriptions of the devilish power of women and their abject wickedness were supplemented by photographs of women looking for all the world like pantomime dames. Traces of moustache visible around some of their mouths supported his hinted contention that an excess of male hormone had to account for their behaviour. Others were flagrant in their seductiveness, heavy-lidded temptresses who lured good men to their doom.

Adams wrote his book around 1910, and his parade of poisoners, baby farmers and vitriol throwers seemed a long way from the female offenders who crossed my path in my first years of practice. By and large, these women had come before the court because they lacked money and the opportunity to live a decent life. In the cells cigarettes were exchanged like salt in the desert, and we would talk the hours away in the long wait for cases to be called on.

A probation officer at Holloway prison told me she thought that most women were in jail either because of a man or because of not having a man. This sounded like the flip-side of holding women responsible for male misdeeds, with men this time carrying the can. However, she was highlighting the reality of many women's lives, where involvement in crime arises out of doing something at the behest of a man, or as a result of the hardship of dealing with children alone when the man has left, or of the mess created by sexual abuse suffered when they were children or their experience of violence at the hands of husbands.

One of the main reasons why men commit crime is because it enhances their sense of masculinity, but the reverse is not true; far from it. Femininity is diminished by crime, and women who commit crime are reduced as women by the process of criminalisation because they know that they are perceived differently from their male counterparts.

Why is it that we feel differently about women committing crime? It always seems to me that crime is seen as an inevitable extension of normal male behaviour, whereas women offenders are thought to have breached sacred notions of what is deemed to be truly female. There is also a sense that criminal women poison the fount of youth. Rather like the old aphorism that educating a man means just that, whilst educating a woman means educating a whole family, the phrase 'criminal woman' induces fears of little potential criminals cowering behind her skirts.

All this was new to me. I did not come to the Bar as a feminist looking for slights against women. Indeed, I was not particularly conscious of women's issues at all, except inasmuch as they were part of my general concern about what happened to working-class people when they sought justice. I felt extreme irritation at the lengthy discussions about chairpersons when I wanted to get on with whatever was the business in hand. I did not know then about the power of language and the subtle means used to maintain control. I knew about the power that came with hiring and firing, owning and letting, having an education and being unschooled. I also knew about powerlessness in the face of that.

Powerlessness has inevitably meant that women have had to secure advantage by less crude methods than men, and – not just in the area of crime – have as a result often been labelled devious and Machiavellian, as though such traits are never present in the chaps. Female criminals are also portrayed as a rare species, and rarity quickly becomes translated into abnormality.

One of the major criminology studies conducted in the nineteenth century, by Lombroso and Ferrero, described women as congenitally less inclined to crime than men. However, it seems that they make up for this by the excessive vileness of the crimes they do commit. 'Rarely is a woman wicked,' wrote Cesare Lombroso, 'but when she is she surpasses the male.' Believing that the female criminal could be identified by certain physiological features, the two men examined the skull of Charlotte Corday, murderer of Marat, and pronounced it a truly criminal type. They did not seem to apply rigorous scientific standards to these tests and would most likely have said the same about the skull of a canonised nun if fed suggestive information. The fantasy of cross-examining them with a trunkful of skeletons at the ready brightens the odd moment.

A more recent student of female crime, the American Otto Pollak, contended in his study *The Criminality of Women* (1950) that women manipulate men into committing offences while remaining immune from prosecution themselves. That women are intrinsically cunning is exemplified by the passive role they assume during intercourse, a passivity which allows them to fake orgasms in a way that men cannot. This ability, it seems, endows women with the master status of liars and deceivers.

When it comes to 'economy with the truth' my own experience

is that men are quite as good at dishing out the phoney baloney as women. Women are rare amongst the ranks of confidence tricksters. Yet if you listen to a judge directing the jury in a rape case, you would think most women suffered from an inherent defect which he is reluctantly compelled to spell out. We are not always trustworthy, whatever other value we might have.

As I continued to practise throughout the 1970s and 1980s, it became increasingly clear to me that women in court still had less credibility than men. As soon as it was announced that the alibi witness was a wife, girlfriend or female family member, eyes would often roll to the heavens in tacit agreement that her testimony would be worthless.

I used to think that women police officers would be seen as especially worthy of trust, given that they have not been tainted by police corruption scandals and are portrayed in television drama as *Juliet Bravo* characters, clothed in the feminine appeal of *The Gentle Touch*. However, women in the police force tell me this is not true. It is assumed that, like women in the family, they will lie to save the skin of male colleagues.

Wherever they stand in the courtroom, women are not deemed to have the same authority or credibility as their male counterparts. Female lawyers often describe being patronised and marginalised, their legal arguments given greater weight when repeated in the mouths of male colleagues.

The debate about rape has opened many people's eyes to the workings of the legal system. If such incredible stereotyping of women works against them when they are victims of crime, what happens to women who appear in the dock charged with offences? The answer is not simple, and it is not heartening either. Some would have you believe that judges fall prey to the charms of women and are soft on them out of misguided chivalry. An article in the *Evening Standard* in June 1990 maintained that women were getting away with murder and that a snub nose, high cheekbones and a shapely pair of legs would probably be of more benefit to the accused than an able defence lawyer.

The attitude of the court to a female accused will depend on the kind of woman she is perceived to be. In itself this is no different from the conscious and unconscious approach to any defendant, who is judged according to all sorts of hidden criteria, such as whether they are employable or whether they show enough respect to the court. But for a woman, the assessment of her worth is enmeshed in very limiting ideas. If she challenges conventions in any significant way, she is seen as threatening or, at the least, disappointing. A mere hint in court that a woman might be a bad mother, a bit of a whore or emotionally unstable, and she is lost. And whether she is victim or offender it is very hard to withstand the attack of an inventive cross-examiner. There is, for instance, a double edge to the seemingly uncontroversial question about how long before the alleged rape a woman had sexual intercourse. A long time before implies sexual frustration, a reason for seeking out intercourse with almost anyone, whereas an active sexual life implies a voracious, indiscriminate, appetite. There is no winning.

The chivalry hypothesis has little substance: when their crimes are the same, sentencing does not vary much between the sexes. However, women are actually imprisoned with fewer convictions than men: 53 per cent of women have two or fewer convictions when they first go to prison as against 22 per cent of men (NACRO, 1992). Yet in the gamut of crime women usually commit less serious offences. They also tend to play supportive roles, harbouring and handling stolen goods, providing safe houses, cashing stolen cheques. As in the world of legitimate enterprises, they are still on the payroll but are rarely the pay-master, a syndrome that is reflected in the way that they are sentenced.

Women also hold homes together, and if a female offender on a minor charge seems to perform her domestic functions well it makes no sense to the state for her to be imprisoned. This can be translated as chivalry but is really expediency; women often suffer the consequence of a misguided concern for their welfare and that of their children. Research by the National Association of Probation Officers in 1991 shows that significantly higher numbers of women are pushed up the sentencing tariff and inappropriately given probation for a first offence because they are deemed to be in need of welfare. In the West Midlands 27 per cent of female first offenders were placed on probation as against 13 per cent of men. Probation is an intrusive sentencing option and should not be used instead of conditional discharges or fines. It also means that if the probationer re-offends, prison is a likely option.

The Government's Inspectorate of Probation found in its 1991 report that women, ironically, sometimes receive harsher sentences than men because they are mothers. They may be deemed unsuitable for community service because they have young children, but then the courts, unable or unwilling to come up with an alternative punishment, send them to jail.

I happen to be of the currently unfashionable school that thinks that crime for the most part has its roots in social or emotional deprivation, whether you are male or female. But there is much greater willingness to adopt this view in the case of women, and this in turn feeds into the notion that women are mollycoddled. And because we feel differently about women committing crime, we go to lengths to avoid defining them as criminal, preferring the idea that they have emotional problems; they are mad rather than bad.

The truth is that our desire to seek psychiatric explanations for women's crime is a way of trying to make it invisible, a profound expression of our worst fears about the social fabric falling apart. Women are still the glue that cements the family unit, providing cohesion and continuity, and we do not like to admit to the possibility that there is a potential for crime in Everywoman. There is much less willingness to invoke the workings of the psyche to explain male wrongdoing. Scepticism about the role of the psychiatrist creeps into courtroom discussions, and judges adopt the tone of Lady Bracknell as soon as you dare to mention the unhappy childhood of the brute in the dock. With women the attitude is noticeably different.

The mystery of women's birthgiving properties obviously plays a part in sustaining judicial attitudes, and any disorder or disability linked to childbearing or the menstrual cycle has traditionally been treated sympathetically: post-natal depression or menopausal blues, post-abortion tristesse or premenstrual tension. However, medicalising and pathologising women is a way of perpetuating the myth that they are victims of their own physiology and that the function of all women might be intrinsically impaired. A recent planning appeal was mounted in Australia on the grounds that the presiding member of the Appeals Tribunal was pregnant and, according to the appellant's affidavit, 'suffering from the well-known medical condition (placidity) which detracts significantly from the intellectual competence of all mothers-to-be'.

In the nineteenth century menstruation was a prominent explanation in cataloguing women's crime, especially if the offences were atypical or if the woman was not lower-class. Most women who stole could not afford a lawyer who would have her diagnosed as a kleptomaniac, but for any woman with enough funds for a lawyer and a doctor, nymphomania, pyromania and all manner of manias were invented to explain their aberrant behaviour. Hysteria was the Latin word for the womb.

The suffragettes met with the same insistence that their behaviour was due to menstrual dysfunction, problems with their ovaries or chronic spinsterhood. In recent times the exaggerated attention given to premenstrual tension has fed into the theory that women's biology may be to blame for their behaviour; most defence advocates will be happy to exploit PMT, leaving aside the impact of this for women generally: it is the lawyer's imperative to prevent people going to jail.

In circumstances which defy this simple psychiatric labelling and where the offence is heinous, there is a very different response. Women not only become 'unsexed' in the way that Lady Macbeth felt was necessary to steel herself for crime, but take on monstrous proportions in the collective mind.

Myra Hindley's name is one that comes to everyone's lips as soon as criminals come into the conversation, regardless of sex. Crimes involving children always engage our deepest emotions and we all feel a particular empathy with the families of the victims. But although the Moors Murders must come near the top of any catalogue of atrocities, public horror has concentrated more and more on the female of the two offenders, and I think that, while this is partly because she has not sought to avoid visibility, it is largely because of her gender. Even if women do not themselves have children, society expects them to embody the nurturance and protectiveness associated with mothering, and there is a heightened outrage when they run in the face of those ideas.

Given the nature of our legal system and the history of its development, it is hardly surprising that women have special problems in our courtrooms.

The Common Law upon which our legal system is based developed in the Middle Ages when, drawing on the Roman law tradition, women and children were placed under the jurisdiction of the paternal power, the head of the household, and were deemed to be his property.

As communities grew in size and as the nature of the state changed, legal proceedings became formalised. The records of the previous decisions of the courts were called upon to declare the state of the law, and it was this body of cases and the principles inferred from them which became known as the Common Law.

The main tribunal in which women initially figured was the ecclesiastical court, where allegations of witchcraft were tried. All sorts of behaviour thought to be aberrant for a woman were defined as sorcery and contrary to canon law. The Church had a low opinion of women at the best of times, and those who seemed to have abandoned the control of men or who were licentious or of independent mind rarely survived to sell their story to the local minstrel. In time the jurisdiction over witchcraft transferred to the Assizes, the ordinary criminal courts, and like other serious felonies was met with execution.

As the law developed it began to flow from other sources: the writings and opinions of legal commentators and statutes passed by Parliament. Until comparatively recently women played no part at all in the construction and content of the law, and even now their role in lawmaking is barely significant.

Until the late nineteenth century, under the Common Law a husband and wife were treated as one person and marriage meant the surrender of separate legal rights for a woman. From this unity of husband and wife sprang all the disabilities of the married woman. She could own no property in her own right and commence no legal action because either would imply she had a separate legal existence. Wives then and until very recently could not be raped by their husbands, because they were supposed to have contracted to provide sex whenever their husbands wished it. Women had no custodial rights of the children they bore in wedlock; rights of custody belonged to fathers alone. They were long excluded from being witnesses, save in exceptional cases, and even after it became acceptable for women to testify they could not give evidence against their husbands. They were generally deemed to be under the control of their spouse. In the words of one legal commentator quoted in Radcliffe & Cross's *The English Legal System* (1964).

It was a doctrine of elegant simplicity and one capable of remarkable results. It was a doctrine that removed, in theory, the burdens of responsibility and the sanctions of morality from any woman who entered the holy state of matrimony. Logically considered, all her crimes and all her sins emanated from the duplicated brain of her husband and her lord. Not only did she convey to him her person and her worldly goods, but she added the entire responsibility of her personality to the weight of his own. The creator took from Adam a rib and made it Eve; the common law of England endeavoured to reverse the process, to replace the rib and to remerge the personalities.

The nineteenth century saw a revolutionary change in women's status, brought about (as is always the case), not by the generous bequest of the powerful, but by the pressure of women's demands. The Married Women's Property Acts of 1870 and 1882 were historic victories, allowing married women a legal identity and removing in part their invisibility. But the task of pulling the weight of this legal monolith into the late twentieth century, when people have very different roles and expectations, seems Herculean, especially when well nigh all of the powerful positions within the law are held by the kind of men who explode with laughter or implode with rage at the very mention of gender bias. Most legislation and case law nowadays has the semblance of neutrality, and some legislative changes are designed to improve the position of women, but the letter of the law can too easily become a cloak for the reality.

*

Discriminatory practices surface with regularity in many areas of the law. In the Family Courts, despite enormous improvements, there is still too little value placed on the woman's contribution to the family over the years. The courts are often ignorant of the kinds of jobs and salaries available to women, the costs of child-care and the particular employment problems of the displaced homemaker. I recently attended some judicial training sessions in the USA in which a group of judges were asked to put the value on a bag of groceries. Few were able to do so. It would be interesting to run a similar experiment in this country.

When I did my stint at family work I saw decisions being made about custody in which women were penalised if they had left the matrimonial home, leaving children behind, even when they did so to escape abuse. This was particularly true if a woman had found a boyfriend. It was the same test which had been applied over a century before to Annie Besant, the pioneer of contraception, who was prosecuted for publishing pamphlets on family planning in 1877. Her sexual politics were seen as a sign of her unsuitability as a mother, and she too suffered the slings of court-room bias, by being denied custody of her daughter.

Women have problems in obtaining realistic damages for personal injuries, because awards are so closely tied to wage earning and those who work in the home often receive ridiculously low sums: the real economic value of housework is never explored.

The whole area of damages and compensation is in need of reform. At present inflated damages are awarded by juries in libel cases for the hurt feelings of public figures, as an attempt to call into line a press which is impervious to the idea of privacy; compensation for the loss of a child or the loss of a limb is negligible by comparison. But in civil courts we have mostly done away with juries; in the vast majority of cases, judges without juries award damages for civil wrongs. The courts are still sceptical about psychological harm, and when women sue their abusers the damages are often derisory. In the space of months in 1992 a television star received £50,000 for being described as boring; the former lover of a politician received £105,000 when described as a bimbo; an 18-year-old who had been sexually abused by her father for a year when she was a child was awarded £10,000; and another young woman abused from the age of 11 to 15 by her stepfather received £12,500. And when women sue convicted rapists for compensation, they have had difficulty securing the level of damages that are awarded in road accident cases.

This dichotomy was highlighted in the case of a man called Christopher Meah, who sustained serious injuries in a car crash. As a result of brain damage he suffered a personality change and a latent propensity for sexual violence was unleashed. He committed two exceedingly brutal sexual assaults on women with whom he was acquainted. In the first, a woman was in her East London home alone with her 2-year-old son when Meah arrived, threatened her with a knife, forced her to strip, smeared her with butter and for five hours made her submit to degrading sexual acts in the presence of her child. In the second attack, Meah again made his victim strip, after which he sexually humiliated her, trussed her up like a chicken, raped her and stabbed her several times with a knife.

After his trial in 1983 Mr Meah was imprisoned for life, but the following year he received £45,750 compensation for his motor accident. His first victim received £1,000 from the Criminal Injuries Compensation Board, his second £3,600. The women, not surprisingly, felt a degree of chagrin at the value placed on their suffering by comparison with the award made to their attacker. They decided to sue in the High Court, a rarity in English law because, since those convicted of crime rarely have money in the bank, it is usually a pointless exercise.

After describing in detail the nightmares they still experienced long after the ordeal, the fear of being alone and the irrational guilt so often felt by those who are raped, the two women received £7,080 and £10,480 respectively. There was an outcry in the press. As one woman columnist wrote:

If these women had been facially scarred, they would have got lavish compensation. Instead they have been emotionally slaughtered. Their suffering can't be seen but it is probably for ever. Most women say that for weeks afterwards they scrub their bodies raw but they never feel clean. They find it difficult to return to normal sexual relationships ever again with any kind of innocence, joy or trust.

A *Times* leader compared the award to that of a male plaintiff who had lost his libido after a road accident and had received £100,000. What price a woman's sex-life? Around the same time a man received £12,000 because leg scars would prevent him from wearing shorts and a woman £24,000 for scars which would inhibit her from wearing a bikini.

In many areas of the law women still suffer from antiquated views. Most of the time it is quite unconscious, and therefore hard to challenge. In this book I have concentrated on the criminal justice system, partly because it is the area in which I have now practised, woman and girl, for nearly twenty years, but also because, affecting as it does the liberty of the subject, it is an area of the law which needs to be addressed with the greatest urgency.

The web of prejudice, privilege and misinformation that affects women is, of course, compounded for the poor. The experience of women is a paradigm of that which faces any person, male or female, who is not part of the dominant culture. There is no conspiracy. Often the assumptions arise simply from a lack of insight into the lives lived by people of a different class. A woman who practises in the field of child-care says that over the years, whenever judges have expressed concern about working mothers not spending enough time with their children, she has always made the simple comparison with children who are sent to boarding school. She says that the discomfort can be tangible.

Judging is not an easy task, and in the face of criticism some judges wonder whether it is worth the candle. In the case of press reports that cause uproar after a trial, complex details are often overlooked. But because it is considered undignified and unproductive, judges are encouraged to say nothing in the face of public criticism, even when there may well be good reasons for some of their remarks. That is why open explanations for decisions should, in my view, almost always be given in court. Judges also suffer from being misreported and having their words taken out of context.

If any single category of human being is unaccustomed to being treated as inferior or subordinate, it is a white, male, British judge. In broad terms, four out of five full-time professional judges are still products of public schools and of Oxford and Cambridge. Very occasionally the less privileged have joined the ranks, and that number is slowly growing. It is barely possible to mention the narrow background of the judiciary now without some fellow jumping up and informing you that his father was a coalman or at the very least a mere doctor. Products of the grammar schools will become somewhat thicker on the ground as the beneficiaries of expanded university education in the 1960s progress through the Bar. The retirement age for judges has only just been reduced to 70. The average age of judges in this country is between 60 and 65, which coincides with the time when most other people are retiring. In March 1991, according to statistics presented by the Lord Chancellor's Department, only one judge out of 550 was black. One Lord Justice, two High Court judges and nineteen circuit judges were female.

Being told that you may be unfair, even unconsciously, is not something any of us welcome. The Lord Chancellor, Lord Mackay, who is sensitive to these issues, tells a story about his days as a lecturer at Edinburgh University when he was required to mark a register of student attendance. For the most part he would call out the names of students, but on a number of occasions he marked off the name of the one black student without calling it out, partly because he was well aware of the student's presence but also because he was hesitant about the pronunciation. The student challenged him about it and Lord Mackay was wretched to think he had been hurtful to a student whom he liked and regarded well. It must be emphasised that there are many decent judges who are keen to take on board new learning and who think deeply about the power and authority they wield.

The law mirrors society with all its imperfections and it therefore reflects the subordination of women, even today. But holding up a mirror can never be its sole function. The law affects as well as reflects, and all of those involved in the administration of justice have a special obligation to reject society's irrational prejudices.

The law is symbolic, playing an important role in the internalising of ideas about what is right and natural. If the men of law say sexily dressed women have it coming to them, they reinforce that view in the man on the street. The law constructs beliefs about roles of men and women in the home and at work which feed back into generally held attitudes about women.

True justice is about more than refereeing between two sides. It is about breathing life into the rules so that no side is at a disadvantage because of sex or race or any of the other impediments which deny justice.

It is no answer to make a simple call for equal treatment. Dealing equally with those who are unequal creates more inequality. Justice is obtained by giving a fair and unbiased appraisal of each person and situation, without relying on preconceived notions, whether the defendant is black or white, male or female. Justice recognises the tension between the ideal of equality and the reality of people's lives. There are those who claim that the true classical symbol of Justice has her wearing a blindfold of impartiality, but I prefer the image of an all-seeing goddess, as she appears above the Central Criminal Court at the Old Bailey.

2

Playing Portia

Myths are tent pegs which secure the status quo. In the law, mythology operates almost as powerfully as legal precedent in inhibiting change. Women are particularly at its mercy, although men do not escape its force, especially when issues of class and race emerge.

Sometimes the myths conflict. The myth that women are arch deceivers, prone to making false allegations, blights many rape trials – unless the defendant is black, when the myth of his rampant sexuality emerges in competition. The old belief that it is only working-class men who abuse their wives sits comfortably with the belief that women are masochists anyway. The assumption that men do women's thinking for them, prevailing on them to provide false alibis and bail, does battle with the myth that it is women who incite criminal enterprise.

Mythology is a triumph of belief over reality, depending for its survival not on evidence but on constant reiteration. Myths are not the same as lies, in that they do not involve deliberate falsification. They endure because they serve social needs. The notion that judges are invariably impartial is also pervasive and unreal, but it is supposed to sustain our faith in the legal system.

Mythologies do change. They also vary between different groupings, but what matter are the dominant myths which receive institutional reinforcement daily in the administration of justice.

I had not been in criminal practice for long before I realised that special rules apply in, for example, rape cases. I saw some male jurors winking their support for my male client before the alleged victim had even finished her evidence, and I learned very quickly, like every other lawyer worth her salt and a brief fee, that the nearer I could get to painting my female client as a paragon of traditional womanhood, the more likely she was to experience the quality of mercy. If a woman with a weakness for bother-boots could be persuaded into wearing pearls and a *broderie anglaise* blouse she might just tip the judicial scales in her favour. Of course, male clients are also encouraged to present themselves smartly, but for women the purpose is much more complex.

The first case I ever did was for a woman who was pleading guilty in the Magistrates Court to shoplifting. The items were children's clothes, and I was reassured by all the old hands in chambers that nothing much would happen to her: women always got off lightly and she would probably be fined, even if she did have a couple of previous convictions. I arrived at court and found my client in a state of great anxiety because she had not been able to make any arrangements for her children. It turned out that she had a suspended sentence of imprisonment outstanding which, in some bid to deny the inevitability of going to prison, she had failed to mention to my instructing solicitor. Like so many poor women she had no resources to pay a fine and the courts had on previous occasions run through what they saw as the alternatives: a conditional discharge, then a probation order, then a suspended sentence and now the full McCoy. In this miserable first experience, as I watched my despairing client being taken off to Holloway, weeping for her children, I saw what we all now know from the research. Because their lack of resources makes financial penalties unsuitable, women go to prison far earlier in their criminal activity, despite the often trivial nature of their offending. Three times as many women as men go to prison for a first offence (*Guardian*, 21 November 1991). Currently many women are in prison for non-payment of fines, sometimes relating to non-possession of a television licence. Most are single parents for whom a television is a staple in their existence.

It does not do wonders for your confidence when your first client is packed off to jail, however hopeless the case, but I hung on in there, doing a particularly active trade (which I thoroughly enjoyed) in my early years representing fellow Scots, marauding

Tartan-clad supporters who had been involved in displays of male camaraderie after Cup Finals. I suppose I was instructed on the assumption that I would be able to translate. While every other woman in the law tells stories of being taken for the solicitor's secretary, I was generally taken for the defendant's sister. Young black women in the law tell me the same assumption is made about them. I also had a significant clientele of Glaswegian prostitutes, whose families all thought they were down south working with the civil service. Some of them sent home money for babies their mothers were rearing for them; others had children living with them whom they looked after perfectly well, despite all belief to the contrary.

The early years of every barrister's practice are spent gaining experience in the lower courts. As a woman intent on criminal work I often found myself in the Juvenile and Magistrates Courts representing women and children, because in the dispersal of legal crumbs by solicitors or more especially chambers' clerks the soft end of offending went to the girls. Even as I have progressed up the ladder into serious crime I have always represented a proportionately higher number of women and young people, because in the expectations of the courtroom it is an appropriate role to play.

Women are also often sought to act for men in rape and other sexual assaults, because of the involuntary endorsement they give to the male defendant. Inevitably I have been able to watch the dynamics of the court as well as participate in them, and I have no doubt that sexuality and reproduction play a role in the judging of women which is not only irrelevant but unequalled by anything that happens to men.

For me, coming to the Bar was almost an accident. It was an escape route from the original plan to study in Glasgow, and was devised after weeks of panic in London. I was doing a summer job and had breathed the air of other possibilities, a world beyond. But the pleasure my family had taken in the first of us going to university meant that any proposed alternative had to satisfy their anxieties about the unknown, and fulfil their hopes that I might end up with a good job.

The only professional women they or I had ever known were school teachers, who in those days seemed to have a better material life than any other women we knew. For my own part, doing an English degree seemed like the most wonderful chance to read as much as you wanted without anyone accusing you of shirking. I had spent my childhood hearing aunts rebuke my mother for failing to take my nose out of a book and insisting that too much reading made you ill. Yet there was a certain predictability in heading towards teaching which made me want to resist it. I wanted to do what was not expected of me. The only other person I knew with a degree had read law, and its mysteries had caught my imagination.

My father, a soft-hearted, intelligent man, had left school, like my mother, at 14. He worked as a dispatch hand in the print industry and was active in his union. I remember his passionate belief in the Labour movement and his pride in the changes which had been won in his lifetime. He thrilled to the idea of my doing law, especially when I said I wanted to be a trade union lawyer. I'm not sure where I picked up that idea from, but it seemed like a way of being professional without sounding too high-falutin'.

When some of my relatives were told I had joined 'Gray's Inn' and was studying for the 'Bar' they imagined I had gone in for hotel management or catering and could not understand why anyone would pass up Glasgow University to do such a thing.

The Inns of Court – Lincoln's Inn, Gray's Inn, Middle Temple and Inner Temple – are the four old-established centres for barristers which act both as colleges which you have to join and workplaces where groups of barristers have chambers (offices). The Inns of Court have since the beginning of their existence in the fourteenth century enjoyed the sole right to admit, train and, in general, control the professional life of the barristers. The constitution of the Inns has been described by Sir Frederick Pollock in his *Essays in the Law* as 'a survival of medieval republican oligarchy, the purest to be found in Europe'.

The Inns are governed by the Benchers, who are not elected but who themselves choose their fellows and successors. They act as landlords of the Inns' properties. The Inns are also responsible for the education and training of barristers.

The prospective barrister must be admitted to one of the Inns before undergoing a period of training at the Council of Legal Education, which is the Inns of Court law school. As a requisite for being called to the Bar, the professional body of practitioners, the student must eat 24 dinners in the Inn's Hall.

If a barrister practises in London, he or she will usually do so from chambers which are located in one of the four Inns. When not doing a case out of London, many barristers continue to eat regularly in the Inn, which runs on the lines of the best London clubs – no trouser suits for women.

The arrangements and language would bemuse any bystander, and when you add to that the whole complicated system of courts, divided into different divisions and ranging from the local Magistrates Court to the Court of Appeal, it was no wonder my relatives were bewildered. Their confusion was not helped by my father trying to explain to them that for some reason I had to eat all these dinners in order to qualify. It sounded like a queer way to learn a profession, something only the English could have thought up.

The mysteries of the legal system in Scotland, let alone England, had rarely impinged on our lives, save for shamed references to cousin Bertie, who had ingeniously wired up his electricity to the street-lighting and seen the inside of Barlinnie.

My mother was surprisingly quiet at my decision. To her, London was purgatory, if not hell, and she muttered about things coming to a sorry pass. She had had her own run-in with lawyers when she tried to get compensation for a head injury after a falling slate had nearly blinded her. She had gone to a solicitor only after much cajoling, sure that just asking questions would cost her money and that lawyers were not for the likes of her. She had much more faith in holy water than the legal system, and merely getting involved in that world frightened her. Her line was that any normal person would be thrilled at the chance of being a lady teacher, and she ignored my refrain about not knowing any boys who had that ambition.

Against this well-meaning resistance I just had to succeed; however miserable I was, there could be no complaining. And was I miserable! Like childbirth, nothing had really prepared me for it.

I stepped from the equivalent of a comprehensive school in no mean city into the pages of an Evelyn Waugh novel. Like a foreigner abroad, I smiled a lot to cover my bewilderment, and my benevolence was totally misread by hoards of public-school boys who did not know what it meant to have a girl as a friend.

Lectures were the least of my problems, providing a happy respite from social contact. The Inn robing room, where we put on a legal gown for dining, was the real class divider. Here, like the Queen, women carefully knotted silk headscarves in front of their chins rather than under them, and talked about weekend houseparties and 'cockers-pees', which after enough eavesdropping I realised were nothing more vulgar than cocktail parties.

Sixties radicalism had certainly not had its way in the Inns of Court. Down the road at the London School of Economics, students were in revolt about the way the school was governed; everywhere young people were demonstrating – against the war in Vietnam, then at its height, and against apartheid, demanding disinvestment in South Africa. Meanwhile at Gray's Inn, except amongst a very few, the main topics of conversation were the Field Club Ball and the Fencing Club. There was even a Smoking Concert after dinner during each Trinity Term, from which women were excluded because of the ribald nature of the proceedings. I remember a great uproar when Clarissa Dickson Wright, disguised in a bear outfit, gatecrashed the event. The wrath of one Judge Thesiger was wrought upon her and she was expelled from the Hall.

Hall was supposed to represent the heart of life as a Bar student. Here, in the rarefied atmosphere of the beautiful wood-panelled hall, dining was to present the opportunity for exchanging learned legal footnotes and scholarly opinions on case law. It was all supposed to be made real by our sitting alongside fellows who were actually doing the business of practising in court, though in reality anyone who had a halfway decent practice and a reasonable family life was not whiling away his nights eating Gray's Inn dinners.

The idea behind the anachronistic process of dining is that it creates a camaraderie amongst the profession in which familiarity will help in the maintenance of high ethical standards, somewhat in the nature of the college spirit at Oxford or Cambridge. It is also expected that these events will provide the opportunity for new entrants to a profession to make contacts which will serve them well throughout practice, and may help them in securing a place in Chambers as a pupil or as a tenant. Patronage is an insidious feature of life at the Bar.

Across the refectory tables trainee lawyers are meant to imbibe the barristerial ethos along with their port, hearing courtroom anecdotes, Inns of Court gossip and, if they are very lucky, learned legal exchanges. For most students, 'dining in hall' or 'keeping term' is an inconvenience, to be endured rather than enjoyed.

For me, Gray's Inn was another planet. I remember taking my place tentatively in Hall as one of relatively few women studying for the Bar at that time. I had been forewarned to avoid the seat at the farmost corner of the Hall, as a special rite fell upon the person placed there. As soon as the plates were cleared a clamour went up, remnants of bread rolls were jettisoned towards the corner, spoons were rung against the glasses and the call of 'Up, junior!' resounded through the Hall. The unfortunate student seated at the end of the last row was expected to request permission to smoke from the 'Senior in Hall'. Projecting the voice above such a din in this cavernous room was all part of the oratorical practice for some future advocate as great as Edward Marshall Hall, the Victorian supremo. But woe to the woman who unsuspectingly arrived last and was required to sit in this hellish place. The noise levels were then insurmountable. The demand was that she stand on the table to be heard above the ribaldry and catcalls. I remember expressing my horror to a more worldly table-mate, asking him what was wrong with these people. He laughingly warned me that if I started calling such ancient tradition into question I would be accused of having a chip on my shoulder. I suppose, impervious to his advice, I have continued doing just that ever since.

My avoidance of this seat did not save me from humiliation. Gray's Inn maintained another strange formula for giving students the opportunity of practising their skill as advocates. Prissy rules of etiquette obliged diners to square themselves off into sets of four along the lengthy trestles. Within your 'mess' of four you had to toast each other in a special order and pass the port according to ship's rules. Breach of this etiquette entitled a diner to act as plaintiff and bring a charge against his colleague, who was then required to defend himself. The Senior in Hall sat in judgement.

I unwittingly became the recipient of such a charge, made by a blustering public-school boy. Fingers in his lapels, he denounced me for entering the hallowed halls inappropriately dressed; what was more, he confided conspiratorially, he could 'see through' my 'little scheme'. This attempt at wit was directed at the black crocheted dress I was wearing under my student gown. It was the one black garment I possessed and fulfilled the colour requirement for dining. Appropriate to the fashion of the time, it was several inches above my knees, but it was worn over a black petticoat. I still remember my puzzlement and then mortification as the thundering cacophony built up in the Hall. Spoons hit the table and feet stamped the floor for what seemed like an eternity as they demanded a display of my clothing. Finally, quiet was called for by our 'judge', who asked if I wished to defend myself.

I sat motionless, not recognising the court, and maintaining my right to silence. Calls of 'bad sport' went up, and then the Senior suggested that this was a case where the judge should have a view of the *locus in quo*. He requested that I come up to the front and, after hesitating, I obligingly mustered as much dignity as I could and complied. I was made to parade in front of him with neither of us exchanging a word. On my returning to my place he chivalrously found for me and awarded me a decanter of port. At what a price. For months I tossed in my bed re-creating those events, and in my dreams I did not play the game but made the perfect crushing statement and resisted the pressure that is always applied to women to 'see the fun'.

Like everyone else I completed my dinners. I became engulfed in practice at the Bar and, apart from the occasional lunch in Hall, returned to dine only ten years later. The occasion was a debate, and I was responding to a request from some young women students who felt a motion put before the House was offensive. I can no longer remember the exact wording – something like 'A woman's place is on her back' or 'Woman is her own worst enemy'. In solidarity, I turned up to oppose the motion, optimistic that the majority of male law students would have changed. As the evening wore on my heart sank. All the same old ritual persisted. The buffoon who proposed the motion had a huge claque of puerile supporters in the audience who thought it enormously funny to say rude words usually found in relation to women's secondary sexual characteristics. When one woman student in the Hall expressed indignation, Mr Proposer's response was, 'What's the matter with you, Stephanie, are you having your period?' Visions of him and his cronies got up in full-bottomed wigs and judicial robes flooded my brain. If this was the flower of tomorrow's legal profession, the problem required more than hope and a prayer.

Before long I began gravitating towards other outsiders, many of whom were carefully referred to as 'Commonwealth students', and found a happy home in their midst. Some had interesting political backgrounds and were studying law during periods of enforced exile. Whenever there was a coup in some African state my father would expect the ousted leader to end up at the Inns of Court, and he was often right. Amongst these men and women there were white and black South Africans, people from the Caribbean, Malaysia, India and Pakistan, who opened my eyes to the world and its wider politics. The only time there was ever any real political action amongst the students was when there was an organised student sit-in in resistance to a ploy by the Inns of Court which would have prevented overseas law students staying on after they qualified to get experience in pupillage; they were being asked to undertake to leave as soon as they passed their exams. The campaign was successful, and I have a lasting sense of the solidarity which developed. I became actively involved in the Debating Society, which in Gray's Inn substituted for the student politics you find in other academic institutions. The ticket we ran on for election as office-holders of the society was mildly progressive, and succeeded only because of the general lack of interest of most of the students. I was eventually elected vice-president of the society and found a niche in this 'foreign country' that was the forcing house for tomorrow's legal establishment, but I had to fight damned hard for my foothold. Pity any child of the lower orders who does not have a mother sitting in Glasgow waiting to remind them that they had been warned about taking up with Sassenachs and fancy things like law.

In this world of insiders and outsiders I was often content to be a watcher, a student of social mores, which I suppose explains why I see so much of what goes on in the law through the eyes of the consumer. When people criticise the law or lawyers I rarely feel defensive, because I do not feel they are talking about me. Yet for many within the profession it is an unforgivable betrayal to criticise one's brothers in law. You may be allowed to do it with restraint within the profession, but woe betide the fool who breaks rank. I suppose it is one of the lessons that lives on long after public school, that whatever happens you owe it to your House to defend its good name, even if there is the odd bully or pederast in it generally making life hell.

In the insider/outsider scenario there is often no one more desperately protective of the legal environment than the outsider who now belongs, just as there is no one who loves the Garrick more than the tabloid editor, or the House of Commons more than the member for Wigan-under-Lyme. You should always worry about the barrister who wears the black jacket and pin-striped trousers or who carries one of those cloth bags with their kit in it. It is a sure sign he has only just qualified or that he rarely gets a brief but desperately wants the world to know he is a barrister. Those who need the comfort of a bruderbond insist on the little rituals which set the barrister apart: the silly refusal to shake hands on introduction because we barristers are part of a fraternity where such a formality is not required.

The Bar can be a very seductive place. Once you have got over the hurdles and have established yourself in practice, and once your colleagues know that, despite all those awful views you hold, you are not really that bad after all, it can be wonderful. There is a general tolerance of the other view, and certainly at the Criminal Bar the camaraderie is one of the most pleasurable parts of the job. The fight in court can be tough and the locking of horns can be serious stuff, but only rarely does the wrangle live on beyond the case.

However, there are hurdles, and these should not be forgotten.

Sadly, too many people do forget, or did not encounter them because of the oil of privilege, which works a treat in most institutions and to which the law is particularly susceptible. I did not know anyone in practice at the English Bar when I started, which is the experience of most ordinary folk, and I did not know where to begin when it came to finding pupillage. Fortunately, there is now much more help from the Inns than there used to be, and sponsorship schemes which effect introductions, but anyone whose family had no professional connections was then at a serious disadvantage.

Once called to the Bar, the new barrister is still not fully qualified but must embark on a twelve-month period of pupillage, during which they are attached as an apprentice to a practising barrister. The pupil will go to court with their master to learn how to conduct a case, and will read all his briefs and have a try at writing opinions or drafting pleadings; the pupil will also look up points of law for the master and prepare notes for him to use in court.

I persuaded a friend who qualified the year before to introduce me to his pupil master, whom I then bludgeoned into taking me on, despite his warning that I would hate it in his Chambers. He was absolutely right.

Chambers are the rooms in which barristers work, traditionally cloistered within the Inns. There is an architectural coherence about these male institutions: public schools, Oxbridge colleges, Inns of Court, Houses of Parliament. They combine opulence with austerity. The entrances to many sets of chambers resemble the closes of Scottish tenements, stark and bare-boarded. The conditions within are usually cramped like a book- and leather-bound womb. The lavatories might interest the public health inspectorate.

Within sets of chambers, as the rooms are called, each barrister is self-employed, but there is a unity and interdependence particularly in the early stages of practice, with work switching between barristers. Chambers, therefore, means more than shared offices and involves embracing the corporate identity of your brethren.

The clerks in my pupillage chambers did not like women and acted as though I were a piece of flotsam that had drifted in by mistake. Standing in the clerk's room trying to secure their attention was like trying to get served in the Harrods perfume department when you are wearing your old anorak. There were no other women, and the male barristers minded the invasion of their all-male sanctum. The discrimination was blatant, and sets of chambers openly declared a no-women policy.

The story for black barristers was even worse. In 1979 there were only 200 ethnic minority barristers in independent practice (Royal Commission on Legal Services report). Most of those practised, as they do now, from chambers entirely comprised of those from ethnic minorities, and their work came largely from the minority communities. It was as a result of that Royal Commission's recommendation that a committee was set up to look at racial discrimination. A survey commissioned by the Bar Council in 1989 showed that in multi-racial Britain more than half of the total of all chambers did not have a single black or Asian tenant and that 53 per cent of non-white barristers were located in sixteen sets. This empirical research led to the fiercely debated Bar policy of setting a target of at least 5 per cent ethnic minority lawyers in all chambers.

No research has ever been undertaken into the class background of barristers, but it goes without saying that still too few working-class men and women find their way into practice; although a reasonable proportion of Bar students are now coming from polytechnics, that is not an indicator of social background. While there has been an increase in the numbers of those entering further education, particularly of women, the numbers of students from lower socio-economic groups has not increased. Indeed, after years of campaign by some of us for pupils to receive grants or payment so that those without private incomes could survive, we are now finding that the scheme which was introduced has backfired. While chambers are obliged to provide financing for a number of pupils, which they do by way of scholarships, the effect of this has been to reduce the numbers of pupillages because of the cost to chambers, and since conventional criteria are used in assessing ability the few places there are are going to conventional candidates.

I survived pupillage by doing odd jobs, but there is less casual employment available today. When I ran into financial problems in 1972 I wrote to my MP, Dr Jack Cunningham, to complain about the unavailability of grants or other support, and he in turn raised the matter with the then Minister of Education. Having herself qualified at the Bar, she suggested I might turn my hand to a bit of freelance journalism to see me through the lean times. She herself had apparently had a column in the *Daily Express*. She failed to mention her millionaire husband, whose name was Denis.

It was clear to me that I was not likely to be taken on as a tenant, a fully paid-up member who has his name on the door and thus officially becomes one of the barristers practising from those chambers. Obtaining a tenancy is extremely difficult, because the number of those emerging from pupillage and looking for tenancies considerably outstrips that of available spaces.

I had moved chambers for my second six months and my pupil-master was about to leave the Bar to become an MP. Rather than begin the miserable process which faces young barristers of applying endlessly to different chambers with constant rejection, I joined forces with five other novice practitioners and decided to establish a new set of chambers. A notice appeared on the information board in Middle Temple Lane advertising three tiny rooms in Lincoln's Inn as available for a large set of chambers to use as an annexe. We purloined the notice and became the only candidates for the tenancy, found a very junior clerk to manage our work, and innocently launched into practice, servicing by and large the newly emergent law centres, to which we were very committed.

Many of the problems women and others have faced in the legal profession are similar to those encountered in any occupation. The law is not the only profession in which people get jobs through having the right social connections, or knowing the right people. Nor is it the only activity in which style, appearance, demeanour and self-confidence play a large part in success. However, as well as the traditional legal and cultural handicaps, there are also structural problems within the profession itself. Women have to overcome the handicaps created by the already established tracks which divide the profession into élite and non-élite areas, and find themselves, as I did, more readily functioning in areas that are undeservedly less prestigious, such as family law, child-care and low-level crime.

But change has taken place. It became too silly and unfashionable to keep certain chambers as bastions of chauvinism, and there are now few without one woman barrister. The days are gone where the majority feared that the male sanctum would be destroyed by high-pitched voices and repositories for sanitary towels. I laughed out loud a couple of years back when I found a letter from Inner Temple in my pigeonhole telling me that women's personal hygiene was causing a problem for the ancient sewage system of the Inn, which had never been designed to deal with women. Could we legal women desist, or insist on suitable bins being introduced into the lavatories? I saw it as a victory for women that we were here in sufficient numbers now to block the drains, but pitied the isolated female souls who would have to be very brave indeed to raise the issue at a chambers meeting.

However, despite protestations from older women that discrimination is a thing of the past, change has not gone to the core. One of the problems is that chambers now have a small quota of women, often huddled down at the most recently recruited end, and are reluctant to take on more, even if they are the best candidates. They think they are doing well if, out of twenty-five or thirty barristers, they have four or five women. The accounting of progress, under the tutelage of the public relations experts, is done through a number count rather than through any profound shift in established thinking. There is rarely any question of chambers working towards 50 per cent women, and on the solicitor's side of the profession still too few women become senior partners in major firms.

The heads of chambers know that it is important to claim that chambers have an equal opportunities policy, but further questioning shows that no structures exist to make that a reality. In the Law Schools there have been almost as many female law students as men for a number of years now, and they are coming through with excellent qualifications. As one Head of Chambers announced at a Bar Council meeting in 1991, 'My chambers has just taken on a candidate who has a first in Greats from Oxford, was top of the Bar exams and, what's more, she is a cuddlesome little blonde'. They are clearly not cuddly enough, because women are still not being taken on in commensurate numbers in sets of chambers.

In 1991, 82 per cent of practising barristers (or counsel as they are called) in England and Wales were men. Some of the women now coming to the Bar are mature women making a courageous career change, and several of them have come to me specifically about the problems they have faced in getting established. The problems do not lie with the women themselves but with those who influence selection procedures: one suspects that older women pose even more of a threat than 'girls'.

The Bar is not an easy choice for women, for reasons other than the old prejudices. It can be very hard to compete publicly and enter into open debate with men. We are still not educated adequately for it. There is no reason why men would fully understand that fear of the public forum because, although most advocates, regardless of gender, have anxiety attacks, that is very different from standing up in a predominantly male environment and finding your voice.

Confidence and skill in advocacy come from doing it repeatedly, but irascible old men don't make the going easy. I am no oratorical genius, but I try to encourage female pupils to watch other women in court, just to reassure them that they do not have to behave like men or function in any way that feels unnatural.

The days of jokes in Latin had largely passed by the time I was called to the Bar. It is during the early days of pupillage that the mysteries of legal practice are fathomed and the strange language of the courtroom is learned. Out of the mouths of the babes who are new barristers came learned incantations – 'May it please, My Lord' and the like – taken from some bygone era and fed into the mouths of old Etonians. They seemed a wholly inappropriate means of communication for me, a Glaswegian who spoke with the voice of the people. I decided that I could live without some of the verbal ritual and perhaps still achieve a measure of *gravitas*.

The whole business of deciding who is any good as an advocate is fraught with value judgements. As in the theatre, styles change, and nowadays Marshall Hall would be considered a terrible old ham. Advocacy is about communicating and persuading, something women are not only as good at as men, but often in fact better – more down to earth and less pompous. It requires the marshalling of material, research, the ability to charge your argument with imagery. It involves an interplay of the cerebral and the emotional, with a shifting of emphasis between the two, depending on your recipients. You have to be quick on your feet and have a good memory.

The extraordinary thing about the Bar is that large numbers of practitioners rarely do the thing which most members of the public imagine must be their daily bread and butter – i.e. persuade a jury that someone is innocent or guilty. Many are civil practitioners, whose days are largely spent behind a desk working on a brief, advising in the capacity of consultant and only occasionally making a foray into court. Criminal advocacy is to my mind crucial work in the courts because the liberty of the subject is at stake, but there are parts of the Bar which are quite sniffy about crime, as though there is something unpleasantly contagious about the clientele.

Every barrister is asked regularly by perplexed laymen how they feel about representing someone they know to be guilty. I am told that each profession elicits a parallel classic enquiry: doctors are asked if they ever feel squeamish about blood; actors are quizzed about being able to learn their lines; dentists about being sadists. For my own part, representing clients who are probably guilty is rarely a problem; it is representing those you think are innocent which induces sleepless nights. However, the polite answer we all give is that it is not our role to judge guilt or innocence; we concentrate instead on evaluating and testing the evidence and putting our clients' cases as they would themselves if they were acting in person.

The reason, of course, for the question is the public feeling of distaste for the 'hired gun', the courtroom mercenary who will defend the indefensible – the challenge is invariably about representing terrorists, child abusers and rapists. What is misunderstood is the moral basis for advocacy; it is somehow assumed that representing those who are charged with terrible crimes is a mark

of amorality. If every lawyer refused to act for those whose conduct is reprehensible, many unpopular people might go unrepresented or be represented by a limited section of the profession.
But there is another important consideration. If a barrister was
able to pick and choose his or her clients, endorsement would
follow from having a certain counsel and, conversely, failing to
secure eminent counsel would emit a damning message. The principle was expounded by Erskine when he represented Tom Paine
on a charge of sedition in 1792.

> If the advocate refuses to defend from what he may think of
> the charge or of the defence, he assumes the character of the
> judge; nay, he assumes it before the hour of judgement; and in
> proportion to his rank and reputation puts the heavy influence
> of perhaps a mistaken opinion into the scale against the accused.

Alternatively, if the 'cab rank' principle of taking all-comers did
not exist, advocates might avoid a case for fear that acting for
particular clients may identify them with the allegations. Even so,
when Lord Hooson defended in the Moors Murders case some of
his political opponents (not the candidates he hastened to add)
tried to use it against him in an election campaign. Those of us
who have acted in the Irish cases have always been subjected to
allegations of being terrorist sympathisers.

The longer I practise the more whole heartedly committed I
become to the cab-rank principle, not only because of its constitutional significance in protecting civil liberties, but because of the
incoherence of any other course for criminal practitioners. Picking
over the horrors of crime to settle for those which are least offensive is hardly a worthwhile pursuit. In any event it is by no means
always possible to tell whether your client is indeed guilty. Often
I read the papers in a case and think it sounds ridiculous until I
meet the client, whose personal account is so compelling that my
original view changes. And there are also occasions when I think
a case is terrific – until ten minutes into the consultation.

The criminal courts also demand a rather different style, because
here barristers are trying to persuade a jury rather than a judge.
The pleasure of working with a jury is hard to describe, and for

those who are addicted there is nothing like it. It is one of the reasons why good advocates often make lousy judges. As I have already indicated, they continually want to step down into the ring and spar with one side or the other (usually the other), and they grieve for the old days when the adrenalin surged. The Court of Appeal was compelled to quash a conviction last year because a trial judge at Southend Crown Court took over the role of prosecutor and cross-examined the defendant. The Appeal Court held that his behaviour was undesirable and left him vulnerable to proper criticism (*R v Simbodyal, The Times*, 10 October 1991).

But criminal advocacy can raise a particular problem for women in that it is the most adversarial arena in the court system. You have to enjoy the taste of blood and some men on the bench feel uncomfortable with assertive women, an ambivalence that becomes very clear when arguments are heated. If there is a woman on both sides, interventions of the 'Come now, ladies' variety are common, said in a tone which suggests that some kind of catfight is breaking out. Passivity is still the expected role; aggression is considered phallic, certainly unattractive in a woman. Those messages are in the air and can be very undermining for young women struggling to feel comfortable as professionals. It is particularly hard on those whose femininity is still dependent on approval from male authority figures. The way we socialise girls means they are taught to avoid confrontation and encouraged to please. Both can be useful skills in advocacy, but in courtroom battles you also have to be bold, and having a cross Daddy figure up there on the bench can create a real identity problem.

Quite unjustly, women are still not rated highly as advocates. Johnson's old adage still holds: like performing dogs, the surprise is not that they might do it well but that they do it at all.

'Show me the woman barrister who can laugh a case out of court,' was the challenge made to me by one of the men at the Bar. I was pushed to think of one – but nor could I think of many men with the power and control to mock a whole state prosecution. That particular abandoned style is not available to most advocates, least of all to women.

Fortunately, women are becoming much less vulnerable to the criticism that only tough old boots survive in the criminal courts or that female criminal lawyers have to be as hard as nails. I am constantly told by colleagues that the word amongst certain judges is that I am a terrible harridan who eats small boys for breakfast. Whoever this woman was that filled them with terror, she became particularly confusing when she became pregnant. The contradictory myths about women are profoundly in conflict when a woman advocate fighting her corner is also a symbol of fecundity. There is a tangible difference in atmosphere. Juries are bemused and interested; judges are benign, and worry about being seen to argue with you. I have been tempted to consider making it a permanent state in the interests of my clients.

Stereotypes are more likely to emerge when women are scarce than when they are common. For women lawyers they tend to eclipse demonstrations of competence and make it harder for them to show professional strength. To some extent the examples of stereotyping are trivial and have little to do with one's performance as a lawyer. But to the extent that women have to learn to ignore the comments they elicit, or to respond to them, or are made to feel trapped in uncomfortable roles, the prevailing images are handicaps which men do not share – unless they are black.

The casting of a woman as the protagonist lawyer in films of courtroom dramas has established a fashionable new persona: the message is that we can be tough, assertive and all-woman as well. A lawyer's womanliness is shown by giving her a sex-life, children and snazzy little suits nipped in at the waist, and she shows signs of being compassionate about her clients as well as passionate about winning. But never far behind is that terrible female giveaway: over-identification with her clients. Women face this accusation much more frequently than men because explanations have to be found for why they fight so hard to win. Men performing with the same vigour are merely described as passionate advocates.

Over-identification is a charge rarely made of corporate lawyers: after all, it's hard to over-identify with a trust fund or the Credit Union. And while committed and zealous prosecutors do exist, I do not imagine that there are many who would be described as identifying too closely with the Queen. It is only ever said of defence lawyers who fight hard for their clients; and it is never a complaint from the customer. In my experience, professional distance is often used as an excuse for having no bedside manner. It is also a way of excluding women's values from notions of professionalism: caring is interpreted as partial; it is impartiality that is the male, legal, ideal.

It is however perfectly possible to feel for a client's anguish without losing the ability to judge the appropriate tactic. In fact the opposite – denial of the ways in which their cases affect them emotionally – is the problem with most male barristers and judges. You cannot remain unaffected in a criminal case involving child sexual abuse which goes on for several months, with detailed and repeated evidence from damaged children, in a courtroom awash with pornographic evidence. It may be that learning to acknowledge ways in which they are touched by different kinds of cases would enable lawyers to function more effectively as professionals.

Many barristers love the wig and gown. They are part of the élitism of the profession. Although the Commercial Bar are keen to abandon the wig, and the new Lord Chief Justice, Peter Taylor, is happy to see it go, the suggestion has created an uproar amongst many criminal barristers, who came to the Bar for the outfit. I would certainly be thrilled to see an end to the wig, which is ridiculous and uncomfortable but especially liked by men who are going bald. It is maintained that the wig provides a degree of welcome anonymity, apparently not needed by our friends in the Chancery division, who have a better class of clientele, unlikely to seek them out if they lose the case.

The wig will probably be clung to the more earnestly now to distinguish the barrister from that mere mortal the solicitor advocate, who as a result of a challenge to the Bar's monopoly rights of audience is able to conduct cases in most courts.

However, although I think the wig should be relegated to ceremonial occasions, I think that some sort of robe which covers clothes is probably very useful for women, and would favour a closed gown like that worn by French advocates. This provides a protection against the conclusions drawn from women's dress or the constant commenting on appearance which can blight the lives of American women lawyers. When I was a novice at the Bar, I had a judge ask me to put my hair up in a chignon because he thought I was flicking my ponytail at the jury and gaining advantage. Only recently, another wrote to my head of chambers to complain about my bracelets, which he considered inappropriate for court. He said not a word to me, but using the insidious mechanisms which operate at the Bar, was making an attempt to bring me into line. (Male barristers festooned with gold watch-chains would never raise an eyebrow.) I can well imagine the problems there would be for women more fully exposed to view.

There is far too much pomp and circumstance in British courts, but after discussing courtroom experience with female attorneys in the USA I can appreciate that there are clearly certain benefits to be gained from some degree of formality. It is a question of getting the balance right. One of the major complaints by American women lawyers is that they are often undermined in court by being referred to as 'honey' by their male colleagues, and even by judges – not a problem I have ever encountered in the Old Bailey, where the hardship is much more likely to be about being acknowledged at all, lawyers being collectively referred to as 'gentlemen'. Women in Britain complain that, even when they are first in an indictment and therefore ought to be the person addressed first by the judge, there are times when this does not happen because the judge instinctively addresses his remarks to one of the men in the line. This is felt to be the case more often with some of the older judges, and they probably do not even know they are doing it.

Language generally is a problem. Perhaps with too much accommodation, I learned to live with the assertion that the male pronoun includes the female before realising that, if the law and courtroom analogies are always couched in male pronouns, it is more difficult for juries to see women embraced by their application. Language may perpetuate hidden values, and a conscious effort has to be made to make professional language include women. Studies have shown that when women read job advertisements which use the male pronoun they do not see themselves as applicants. In the United States, Canada and Australia there is now a commitment to ensuring that legislation is drafted in neutral language, while existing legislation is being updated and revised. Judges in all these jurisdictions are now coming to accept the symbolic affect of language, and according to Jocelynne Scutt, the eminent Australian lawyer and academic, the late Lionel Murphy, one of Australia's senior judges and a champion of women's rights, successfully converted many of his colleagues to the use of the term 'Ms', since marital or single status was of no relevance. Most attempts to do this in British courts are met with ridicule. When it was attempted before Mr Justice Harman, he was reported by Marcel Berlins in his *Guardian* column in 1991 as having denounced such nonsense. The judge apparently went on to explain that there are only three types of women: mothers, wives and whores.

It is also hard for men who have been used to male-exclusive environments to stop addressing people by their surname. I have a personal abhorrence of people in the dock being referred to by surname alone, and refuse to do so for men or women, even when it is the procedure adopted by the court. I was once corrected by a judge for always referring to my client by her full name. It may not feel demeaning to men, who refer to each other in that way from school, and do so even to professional colleagues, but it is not a normal form of address for women, and most hate it.

One of the main pockets of change in the courtroom is in the composition of the jury. Until the sixties women made up a comparatively small proportion of jurors because there was a requirement that the twelve persons good and true should be householders, and few women were registered as such. Now the jury panel is taken from the voting register and women are called for service as readily and randomly as men. While some women excuse themselves because of young children and the difficulty in making provision for them, far fewer women excuse themselves because of important professional commitments. Unlike their male counterparts, few seem to believe their workplace will collapse without them. As a result, there are often significant numbers of women on juries, playing an important part. It is difficult to know whether this has made any significant change in the decisions of juries, since women are not necessarily easier on their own sex, but the articles about rape, for example, in the pages of women's magazines, have raised understanding about the nature of sexual offences, and I am convinced that this has affected the discussions which take place in jury rooms.

Fifteen years ago I was a co-author of a book about the profession which, because of a typographical error on the spine, read as *The Baron Trial* (rather than *The Bar on Trial*). People who thought they were buying a thriller were in for a serious disappointment, but they would at least have been enlightened as to the inner workings of the Bar. It makes very interesting reading now, because our agenda for change could be seen as the groundplan of the discussions about reform which are taking place today. It perhaps says something about the law that gestation takes so long.

My chapter in the book was about discrimination in the profession, and it documented the very real problems that faced women then. I interviewed countless women about their experiences, most of which were pretty ghastly, but, as is still the case, few wanted to be identified. They knew that it is not possible to talk about prejudice from a position of weakness, either as someone who has not ridden it out or who is herself at the receiving end. It is one of the reasons why women who have made it and men who understand the problems have such a responsibility. The women who told me their stories were fearful that, if it were known they had complained, they would never get on, the Bar being too small a place to be saddled with a reputation for having a grouse. Little has changed today: young women corner me now in robing rooms with tales of blatant discrimination which they feel powerless to confront in case it reflects badly on them. They do not know how to deal with sexual harassment, because they fear they will be accused by male colleagues of making an issue out of nothing and that it will be used as an excuse for not offering them a permanent place. They still face unacceptable questions in interviews about whether they have marriage plans and intend having children. The new loaded question is whether they are feminists: women who have strong views about equal opportunities are perceived as extremists and are not likely to fit into chambers.

In 1981 there was a tribunal case in Liverpool which decided quite emphatically that this kind of interviewing was contravening the sex discrimination legislation, but for some reason the legal profession seems to consider itself immune from this law. Of course, refusing to answer the questions rarely endears the woman to her interviewing panel. My advice has been to say they intend putting babies off until as close as possible to the menopause. The very mention of anything to do with the menstrual cycle will change the subject instantly.

Most persistent of all, I am told, is the attitude still held by some clerks that you only pass a brief on to a young woman in chambers if you have run out of fellows. Chambers administration depends on the clerks system, which functions on a good day like a theatrical agency and on a bad one like an office of the Department of Social Security. The clerks are supposed to organise your practice, make sure you are in the right court at the right time, and generally sell your skills to the solicitor client. They also have to manage your books and financial relationships and get your money in from errant solicitors. Unfortunately, few people manage to combine these skills, and those who succeed on the public relations side are rarely any good at the administration.

Clerks often talk about themselves as if they were successful bookmakers. They refer to their 'guvnors' as if they were about to run the next race at Newmarket, and use expressions like 'horses for courses', 'my stable of barristers' and 'backing a particular young gentleman'. Women do not get too high a rating against those odds until they have already proved themselves.

Traditionally, clerks earned 10 per cent of their barristers' earnings. Over the years this has slowly been eroded to 7 per cent or even 5 per cent, but a high earning potential is still involved. Others earn a percentage of their chamber's turnover, which still means they can make as much as Queen's Counsel; this can involve sums in excess of £100,000.

Reconstructing clerks has not been easy, but the cold winds of the marketplace could be the eventual undoing of the old breed. They have always operated a strange sort of masonic closed shop, which bitterly opposes entry to anyone from outside their ranks, but they are now being forced away from the quill pen and into intimacy with new technology. Their sinecures are no longer safe. They are increasingly being replaced by salaried practice managers and chief administrators who come from experience in the City and marketing and who are only too willing to realise the potential of women in the law so long as it is a money-spinner. We are also beginning to see more women becoming clerks, although the speed of that change is about as ferocious as a mild breeze.

Women who make it into chambers still drift away in significant numbers because of the inadequacy of fair arrangements for maternity leave. Many chambers think that when women take time out for childbirth they should continue paying their full rent despite not using the facilities. Resistance to the provision of any rebate or special discount is one of the central issues now affecting equal opportunities at the Bar.

Changing attitudes is a hard and slow process. It is now seventy years since the first woman was called to the Bar, yet the profession has never had women in the House of Lords and only has one now in the Court of Appeal. There are only three women on the High Court bench, and out of 426 circuit judges nineteen are women.

When I was researching the history of women's arrival on the scene I could scarcely credit the intellectual somersaults the judiciary went through to keep them out. The myth of judicial neutrality was certainly exploded in the cases which came before the courts at the beginning of this century.

A series of nineteenth-century statutes provided that access to public office, entry to the professions and entitlement to vote should be granted to any 'person' who possessed the right qualifications. The judges bent over backwards to uphold the male monopoly by deciding that women could not be included, even if they were qualified, because they were not 'persons'. All the previous case law interpreted 'persons' as being male, and naturally our courts bound by precedent could do no more than follow suit. What else could a poor chap do?

The idea that women had anything positive to offer the justice system has always been a hard pill for men of law to swallow. As early as the thirteenth century legal commentators were holding forth on the inappropriateness of women on the bench. According to Andrew Horn in his thirteenth-century treatise, *The Mirror of Justices*, 'Women . . . serfs . . . those under the age of twenty-one, open lepers, idiots, attorneys [i.e. solicitors], lunatics, deaf mutes, those excommunicated by a bishop [and] criminal persons' were ineligible for appointment to the bench. In 1915 all the judges were members of the Athenaeum, a gentleman's club which to this day excludes women. The then Master of the Rolls wrote to a new Lord Chancellor suggesting it would make sense for him to join. Membership of the judicial club is exclusive and remains so to this day, although it is no longer confined to a particular leather-bound watering hole.

Bertha Cave, by some mistake, was allowed to join Gray's Inn in 1902. This should have been the first step in her legal career, but when the Benchers who ran the Inn realised their error they called a special meeting to make sure it was the last, rescinding the decision on the grounds that there was no 'precedent' for letting women in. An appeal before the Lord Chancellor and a tribunal of eight other judges confirmed her ejection.

In 1913 Miss Beeb, a brilliant Oxford scholar, applied for admission to the Law Society with a view to entering articles, the vocational training course for solicitors, but the courts denied her the right. Christabel Pankhurst tried to join an Inn but was excluded. The arguments presented by the judges were internally inconsistent, confused, and a disturbing resort to discriminatory practices in the application of the law.

By 1919, following the First World War, the tide of public opinion had changed and male exclusiveness was beginning to seem absurd but the only way to force change upon the legal profession and the judges was by statute, and the Sex Disqualification (Removal) Act 1919 was passed accordingly. There were already women practising law in other common-law jurisdictions like the United States, Australia and New Zealand; in Britain, Ivy Williams was at last called to the Bar by Inner Temple in 1922. The first woman solicitor also qualified in that year.

It was another forty years before we saw a woman on the bench, however, when Elizabeth Lane was appointed a County Court judge. A few years later, in 1965, she became the first woman to sit on a High Court bench. Trumpets sounded heralding a new era, yet we have had only five more women in the ensuing twenty-five years. In Scotland, albeit a smaller jurisdiction, there are no women sitting in the higher courts.

The women who reach the upper echelons usually have to prove themselves in ways different to their male colleagues. Their routes to success are often circuitous. When Elizabeth Lane came to the High Court bench she had already proved herself as a judge in the County Court. This is despite the fact that she had first argued an appeal in the House of Lords, the first woman to do so, in 1946. She was generally considered a good lawyer, albeit 'not an advocate who would set the Thames on fire'; as we have seen, however, advocacy can be a poor qualification for judging.

Dame Elizabeth Butler Sloss, now a Lord Justice of Appeal, was not a practising barrister when appointed to the High Court bench either. She was one of the Registrars of the Family Division – one of the 'back-room' judges that keep the procedural wheels turning – when her considerable judicial skills were recognised. It is almost as though the leap of imagination required in recognising judicial potential in women is rarely possible unless they are seen in action for some time at a more lowly level. Of the three current High Court judges who are women, Joyanne Bracewell also came from the County Court and Mrs Justice Ebsworth, the latest recruit, came from the Circuit bench. Only Margaret Booth came up the way most men do, directly from the ranks of the Queen's Counsel.

As in other professions, there is a glass ceiling for women which means that getting to the top floor involves a detour out through the window and up the drainpipe, rather than a direct route along the charted corridors of power.

In the scramble up the professional ladder, becoming a Queen's Counsel is an important milestone. A successful barrister will consider applying after about twenty years, but the transition is not automatic and only a small proportion of practising barristers 'take silk', as donning the new robe is called. The procedure, like everything in the law, is wrapped in secrecy and involves applying to the Lord Chancellor to be considered by him for appointment. As with judicial appointments, soundings are taken from the judges to assess your standing – and the sound might be a raspberry if you are a rocker of boats or a person of unsound political opinions. No reasons are given for refusal; some barristers may wait several years before being appointed.

Applicants are very secretive about whether they have applied, considering a refusal a vote of no confidence. I was open about being refused on my first application, and spoke about it when asked on *Woman's Hour* in 1990 because I believe that furtiveness feeds into unacceptable practices and secrecy is far too rife in the law. I suspect the powers that be feared I would go on to make an annual announcement over the airwaves about being turned down, which is why they relented in 1991.

If you are successful in your application, it does not mean that you, in fact, sup tea with the Queen and advise her on her legal affairs. (My own children think I will be the person who represents the Queen if she is arrested.) The silk system is a way of singling out for solicitors and lay clients those who are deemed to be the cream of the profession, at the height of their powers. It has considerable cachet and does wonders for your earning potential, as well as being a recognition of expertise. However, it involves secretive and therefore questionable assessments of a barrister's ability, and these days, where chambers are allowed to publish professional brochures and the professions exchange information readily, there is little need to signal to the solicitor or client who is any good. If the market is to be extolled, then why not let excellence find its own level?

In October 1990, according to Bar Council statistics, 1,163 (18 per cent) out of 6,645 practising barristers in England and Wales were female, but the wastage as they proceed within the profession is only now being monitored by the newly created Bar Committee on Sex Discrimination. Out of 682 silks, twenty-nine (4 per cent) are female, statistics which speak for themselves. In Scotland there are two women QCs, and in Northern Ireland one. Having more women on the top rung of the practitioners' ladder is as significant for women as increasing the number of judges.

It is the old question of who defines excellence. Who are the gatekeepers? How many women are involved in the vetting procedures? Since the head of every circuit, every specialist Bar association except one, and every division of the courts is a man, there cannot be many women involved in any formal consultation. Women will not figure in the high table gossip much either.

Merit is presented as a neutral concept, an apolitical criterion of personal worth, when in fact it involves subjective judgements made by a very narrow band of people. Like other institutions, the law uses the meritocracy argument to immunise itself against any challenge about how it makes its appointments. The merit test is rarely mentioned for jobs of low status. Merit is a concept designed to regulate the allocation of highly paid, prestigious positions, and the grander the appointment the more elusive and invisible the evaluative process becomes.

Ironically, as soon as any attempt is made to introduce awareness about the ways women and black people have been disfavoured in this process, there is an assumption that the merit principle will be violated. The port will be diluted. There is far more whispering about the rationale for the appointment of women and blacks than there ever is about white men. Sadly, the beneficiaries in any merit system, male and female, usually support that system simply because of the personal endorsement it affords them; thus they will defend the grossest interpretations of merit on the basis that they themselves got there because of outstanding ability.

Sally Hughes, the journalist and barrister, conducted sound research on behalf of the Law Society which was published in 1991. This showed that women did have less chance of becoming judges, and in the South-East wait on average two years longer than similarly qualified men. Indeed, over 60 per cent of male barristers can look forward to some kind of judicial appointment as a natural professional progression, rather than as any mark of exceptional merit. This means that many unexceptional men become judges, a factor they would not like to be widely known. The study also challenges the view that, because women are now entering the profession in larger numbers, it is only a matter of time before this is reflected in the make-up of the judiciary.

In the studies of Dr R.M. Kanter, reported in the *Harvard Women's Lawyer*, whenever people of any social type are proportionally scarce (i.e. less than 20 per cent of the total), the dynamics of tokenism are set in motion. Token appointees are more visible and worry about being seen to fail. They are also faced with the choice of accepting comparative isolation or becoming a member of the dominant group at the price of denying their own identity and accepting a definition of themselves as 'exceptional'. The flattery of being labelled in that way can be quite intoxicating for women – the 'queen bee' syndrome – but it also creates a pressure in that, while in that role, she is not able to fight for her rights as a woman or to stand up for her sex, but rather is inclined to turn her back on other women, either literally or figuratively, in order to protect her place. It is perhaps not surprising that it has taken until 1991 for the creation of an Association of Women Barristers, and regrettable that so few senior women participate.

In a 1991 television programme, *Judge for Yourselves*, which questioned the absence of women from the Bar, Mrs Justice Bracewell dismissed the idea of taking positive steps to promote women, as it would reduce the quality of judges, and asserted that it was irremediably difficult to combine a family with a career at the Bar. This was 'a fact of life'. The idea that it was the institution which should change was not considered.

Lord Justice Butler Sloss unfortunately made a conscious choice to keep the title Lord rather than Lady when she was appointed to the Appeal Court. She is a woman of considerable talent for whom I have a special admiration. She outshines most of her male colleagues because of her ability and humanity. However, at the launch of the Association of Women Barristers she explained that she could not accept the role of President because it would be too political and she felt it necessary to advise the women not to rock the professional boat too strenuously. Stealth was the old way forward.

It is important to recognise the extent to which male values and perceptions are adopted by women. In 1985 an American experiment published in the *Harvard Law Review* involved randomly assigning an essay to 150 male and 150 female academics with the author's name indicated variably as John T. McKay, J.T. McKay and Joan T. McKay. The subjects were asked to rate the essays on such qualities as persuasiveness, intellectual depth and style. Although the essays were identical, those believed to be written by Joan consistently received lower ratings from male and female readers than those believed to have been written by John or J.T.

Some women say they never experience discrimination and they may be the lucky few. However, there are women who sail through the process having made a conscious decision to identify with their male colleagues and become 'one of the chaps', albeit a feminine version. They see the world through male eyes and remain happily blind to the inequities of the system. These women can be a particular drawback to progress.

However, more and more women understandably ask whether their skills are undervalued in a system where merit is defined by men. They question whether account is taken of the differences in the career patterns of women, particularly if they have had children and have tailored their practices accordingly. Is there any recognition of the considerable skills involved in running a home, caring for children and having a career at the same time? Few women with young children will travel away from home for extended periods to conduct cases, or will take on such a quantity of advice work that they cannot spend some time in the evening with their children, and these factors inevitably affect their earnings, one of the criteria for evaluating success and 'standing'.

Women also participate less in the interstices of the law – the circuit dinners, the cricket matches, the golf, the wine committees, the Bar Council and specialist Bar associations. If they have children, they certainly do not stay around for the drinks in El Vino's or other places, where solicitors and clerks are wooed for briefs by male members of chambers and where career-advancing gossip is exchanged. They know fewer judges socially and, given the male ethos of the profession, will not be championed in their career rise in the same way that men are. A Conservative woman MP, acknowledging similar problems in the House of Commons, described it as men 'talking-up' an aspirant male colleague in a way that would rarely be done for a woman. The lubrication of patronage is not as readily available to facilitate the rise of women. Male judges also invoke the decisions of their own wives who have withdrawn from careers, either permanently or for substantial periods, and who would never dream of expecting special consideration.

Opponents of positive action often assert that the problems start at an earlier stage and that it is not the function of the legal system to correct failures in education. But the cycle is only ever going to be broken if white and black schoolchildren, male and female, see that the legal system is not just administered by white men. My own small daughter currently thinks that all lawyers are women, and does not understand why everyone laughs at her assumption.

The courtroom is still an arena where men, for the most part, play the dominant roles. The women are largely ushers or clerks or solicitor's representatives, spear-carriers or extras in the drama. Having women at the top in significant numbers would change the nature of the discourse. Chambers too would function differently: men would ease up on many of their attitudes, and myths would be shattered. If judges during their luncheon recess were sitting round a table talking about their cases with women and being ribbed for their arcane views, they might start taking stock of a different kind of experience.

It is important for people to see women in positions of power. We have to stop sending out the message that only a special breed of person can get to be a lawyer or a judge, and that they all wear dark suits and talk with marbles in their mouths. We can only hope to gain the public's confidence if that kind of remoteness from the real world is addressed.

No doubt methods of male networking exist in other professions too, but the smell of the gentleman's club permeates every crevice of the Inns of Court. The odour of exclusiveness, like most personal smells, never offends its owners – indeed, they are usually quite impervious to it.

'Rubbish. Show me the proof!' I can hear the cries of protest echoing down the corridors of the Royal Courts. It is hard to find evidence to satisfy those who have no interest in change. As we have seen, most discrimination does not happen at visible levels. As Mary Robinson, the President of Ireland and an eminent lawyer, said in the Allen Lane Foundation Lecture in February 1992:

Every society maintains an invisible life where attitudes and assumptions are formed. Every society is hostage to this unseen place, where fear conquers reason and old attitudes remain entrenched. It is here that the chance phrases and small asides are made which say so little and reveal so much.

If we are to go forward we need to look at attitudes and the language which expresses attitude . . . If we are to strike a balance, if we are to readjust participation and enrich our society with dialogue, we have to revise this way of thinking.

3

The Fragrant Woman

There was a little girl, who had a little curl
Right in the middle of her forehead.
When she was good, she was very, very good
But when she was bad she was horrid.

When Jeffrey Archer, the former Conservative Party Chairman, sued the *Star* for libel in 1987 over his alleged association with a prostitute, his wife gave evidence on his behalf. She indicated discreetly that she and her husband enjoyed a full married life, speaking with delicacy about the indelicate. She was the exemplar of the Good Wife, standing by her husband as the wives of John Profumo and Cecil Parkinson had done before her. She was dressed unassumingly but with great care, attractive without being striking.

Mr Justice Caulfield was moved to lyricism when he dealt with Mary Archer's evidence in his direction to the jury. He suggested to them that their vision of her in the witness box would never disappear. Indeed, His Lordship became quite rapturous. 'Has she fragrance? Would she have, without the strain of this, radiance?' His personal view that Mrs Archer's scent could expunge any whiff of scandal was undisguised. Here was the flower of woman-hood, whose moral worth shone like a flame in the murky world of tabloid newspapers, sex and call-girls.

Monica Cogland, the prostitute, was Magdalene to Mrs Archer's Mary in this morality play. Her evidence did not evoke much sympathy and in the view of judge and jury was probably untruthful. Here was a woman who sold her body to the next buyer and who might lie for the right price.

Polar examples of the female sex, these two women created a contrast which was orchestrated by the press and which enabled Jeffrey Archer to recede from the centre of the courtroom drama. Mary Archer's evidence was not of great consequence *per se*. Why should anyone need to know whether the plaintiff slept with his wife? Establishing this did not preclude the possibility that he might also like to have sex with prostitutes; nor was the issue of whether he had spots on his back, as described by Ms Cogland, of great moment in the total scheme of the case.

Many lawyers would say that the issue here was one of the credibility of witnesses, but underlying the assessment is a catalogue of assumptions about good and bad women.

The good wife features regularly in our courts, though usually as the other half of a male offender. For, as the songs and stories tell us, the love of a good woman can be the making of a man, and any hope of redemption is often deemed to lie with a criminal's wife. Wives are also brought forth as a measure of whether the man has reason to mend his ways. Hidden victims of the criminal justice system, they and their children, as well as their spouses, have sentences passed upon them. Every year of a term of imprisonment means for them the loneliness of separation, bringing up a family without support, suffering financial hardship and the misery of long journeys and unfulfilling visits to remote prisons.

The Home Office decision to remove the right of remand prisoners to have food brought to them daily from outside was greatly criticised by many of us as an additional hardship for those who were still not convicted of a crime. Yet the wife of one client sighed with relief. Having to get up every day to cook the *boeuf bourguignon* that was her man's favourite dish (bank robbers often have a particular interest in gastronomy, acquired from reading James Bond novels in the long waits), ensuring that she had prepared enough to feed everyone else on A wing as well (status-enhancing within the prison population, like standing the whole pub a round), then blow-drying herself into a *Dynasty* lookalike and getting down to Brixton prison with the smaller children in tow all before 11 a.m. would be a burden to the most devoted wife. Enough was enough, and the removal of this particular liberty seemed perfectly civil to a whole body of women whose views are rarely canvassed.

On the rare occasion when 'the good wife' does appear in the dock it is usually because she has allowed her love for her husband to 'seduce' her into crime, helping him to escape custody, harbouring him from the forces of law or concealing stolen items. Wives are rarely indicted for being the passive beneficiaries. If a husband indulges in unconventional means for bringing home the bacon, it is accepted as unlikely that she will be able to prevent it. She usually has to play an active role before the police will charge her, though her safe passage can often be the bargaining counter used effectively by the police to get the husband to 'cough'. If a woman can show that her will has been suborned by her husband it provides potent mitigation. The time taken off her sentence will be added to his. The *Daily Telegraph* on 22 September 1987 reported that:

> The wife of burglar Brian 'Raffles' Reddington walked free from court yesterday after pleading guilty to handling £20,000 worth of stolen jewellery. Her husband was jailed for 8 years last month when he pleaded guilty to raids in which goods worth more than £1 million were taken. Beatrice Reddington, who is still living in the house she shared with her husband, admitted handling stolen goods. She was sentenced to 12 months' jail suspended for two years. During a police raid on her home, Mrs Reddington hid a bag containing £20,000 of jewels, which had been stolen by her husband. However, she handed over the jewels the next day after a phonecall from her husband who was being held by the police.
>
> 'Gone now are the fur coats, the expensive jewels and the Rolls-Royce. Mrs Reddington is struggling to bring up her two children on her savings,' said counsel for the defence.

Judges and juries alike have a soft spot for the good wife, and when she is in the dock charged with playing some ancillary role she is often acquitted. This is what gives rise to claims that women benefit from chivalry, but it works only if she fulfils the stereotype.

Because the image of the faithful, supportive, albeit misguided, wife is so powerful, lawyers always try to turn a female client into just such a one. The use of the term 'common-law wife' is insinuated into proceedings precisely for this purpose. It is intended to communicate the positive aspects of wifeliness rather than the negative connotations of adulterous relationships: 'mistresses' do not fare so well in trials, though the smallness of their part may also be reflected in the sentences they receive. When the politician John Stonehouse was charged with fraud in 1976 his secretary, with whom he was having a love affair, stood trial for lending him minimal assistance. Like others before her, she failed to secure the sympathetic acquittal which might have been obtained by a wife. Sympathy is not a commodity often granted to women who break the rules.

Bad wives are also women who break the rules. They do so by being dissolute or unfaithful, or by not fulfilling the wifely functions.

Wives who betray their husbands offend against the notion of women as keepers of the hearth. Fidelity was of course originally based on the need to secure the succession, to ensure that those who carry a family's name are entitled to do so – hardly pressing considerations today. Yet male indignation at betrayal is not paralleled when the shoe is on the other foot. In earlier times this female betrayal was exemplified by the women poisoners who, before the strict regulation of drugs, disposed of their tyrannical or inconvenient husbands by the subtle spicing of his food with arsenic or strychnine, obtained from pharmacists on the pretext of wanting to lighten their skin or get rid of vermin. Adelaide Bartlett's lover obtained the supply for her in 1896. That a wife who should nurture her husband and care for his domestic needs might abuse that very function, and on the pretext of ministering to him should feed him his own destruction, was an outrage which brought down the foulest condemnation. As a crime it was the perfect symbol of the deceitfulness of women.

Half of all female murder victims are killed by a husband or lover.

In the majority of these cases male defendants mount a defence of provocation: that their wives' conduct drove them to a sudden loss of control. Within the male stronghold of the court it is all too easy to create the feeling that a woman had it coming to her. Pictures of nagging, reproachful, bitter termagants who turn domestic life into a hell on earth are painted before the jury. Man-haters skilled in the art of cruelty are summoned up to haunt the trials of men pushed to their limits. One dead wife who became known as the Lady in the Lake was described by defence counsel as 'an aberrant piece of humanity'. He meant that she had committed adultery and did not make the beds.

Families and friends listen in horror from the public galleries to descriptions of those they know and love that bear no relation to reality. Unless the groundwork has already been done, which is rare, prosecuting counsel is in no position adequately to cross-examine the defendant about the allegations, or to call evidence of rebuttal, challenging their truth. The very people who could give evidence are often sitting there in court, frustrated that they cannot be called to counter the stories being told against their dead friend or relative. Their confidence in the legal system is often shattered by what is seen as the collusion of weak prosecutors and ruthless defence lawyers.

It is almost inevitable in murder trials, regardless of sex, that the conduct of the deceased is called into question, but attacks upon the character of women victims often have a particular quality, and of course the denigration is not confined to homicide trials.

Even a fictional character, Lady Chatterley, came in for this kind of vilification when Lawrence's book was tried under the Obscene Publications Act in 1960. In this trial, counsel for the Crown famously asked the jury whether they felt the book was one they would allow their 'wives or servants' to read, displaying the outmoded attitudes of sections of the Bar in the era of the Beatles and the swinging sixties.

The case was not going well for the Crown, who were sounding sanctimonious and philistine in the face of the evidence of so many eminent literary figures. There came a point in the trial where the prosecution switched tack and focused their assault on the morality of Lady Chatterley herself, knowing this was likely to have more sway with a jury. They seemed to be maintaining that whatever she did and wherever she did it might have been acceptable had she been doing it with her husband. A wife's adultery with a servant was particularly objectionable to Mervyn Griffith-Jones, who prosecuted the case, and his view was echoed by Mr Justice Byrne, who tried it. It was of no consequence that the marriage was loveless and the husband impotent. Such situations call upon stoicism from dutiful wives, who are not licentious slaves of their sexual appetites.

Reminiscing about the trial in 1990 Lord Hutchinson, one of the counsel for the defence, said in conversation that he felt he was having to defend an adulterous woman.

Judges are not aware that they allow preconceived ideas about 'good' women to affect their decision-making. When I took part in a radio discussion in 1990 with Sir Frederick Lawton, the retired Appeal Court judge, about the locking up of a woman by Judge Pickles, he honestly and sincerely asserted that he had never allowed the sex of a person in the dock to affect his decision. I am sure he was speaking for the majority of his colleagues. Few judges consciously subscribe to discriminatory practices: they all believe in approaching the individual facts in a case in an individual way. However, hidden expectations creep in unawares. Judicial aberrations are always explained away as exceptional, maverick or isolated, but they are more likely a matter of the game being given away by the less sophisticated participants.

Our current Lord Chancellor has shone some light into corners of our legal machinery which had hitherto remained obscure. By lifting some of the restrictions on judges speaking out publicly he has allowed us, in a small way, to get a better sense of the men who administer justice. Few judges avail themselves of this new found freedom, recognising the pitfalls. However, James Pickles, who was a circuit judge in Leeds until 1991, has merrily engaged in public debate, expounding views, many of which his colleagues share but would never be caught dead uttering aloud.

A judge like this gets it in the neck from all quarters: from women decrying his anachronistic attitudes, and liberals horrified at his punitive sentencing, to the establishment, which is none too happy about his weakness for plain speaking on matters they would prefer left unaired. The Bar see him as a loose cannon liable to bring the judiciary into disrepute; what they are really taking issue with is his vulgarity in parading his views. Though one or two judges have explained their rationale for performing public duties on our behalf, the usual procedure when the proverbial hits the fan is for the judiciary to keep their heads well down below the bench until the public outcry has died away. Very often there was a degree of sense in Judge Pickles's decisions, but he, and others like him, failed to take account of the reality of people's lives. It is not an easy task to find the correct balance between the objective principles of the law and the subjective conditions of individual lives.

Two cases in 1989 particularly focused the limelight on Judge Pickles. In one, he sentenced Michele Renshaw, a young mother, to imprisonment for contempt of court for refusing to give evidence against her former boyfriend, whom she maintained had assaulted her. Her imprisonment as a single parent involved separation from her young child. On oath, she explained to the court that in the run-up to the trial she had received frightening phonecalls which she believed came from friends of the accused. Judge Pickles defended his action by claiming that the interests of justice were best served by bringing offenders to book. If people invented allegations in the knowledge that at a later stage, without any repercussions, they could withdraw their evidence, it would be an abuse of the criminal justice process and could involve serious harm to the accused. He could equally have said that it is an abuse of the system for defendants to feel that they can with impunity threaten witnesses, with the consequence that the case has to be dropped and justice denied. Judge Pickles failed to resolve this dilemma because he gave insufficient opportunity to the woman to consider the implications of her decision and to receive counselling. She was describing a familiar pattern of domestic violence in which everything is stacked against the woman attempting to secure justice. His decision probably compounded her experience of being repeatedly punished by men.

The Court of Appeal ordered Michele Renshaw's release and

rebuked Judge Pickles for his insensitivity. This exercise was repeated soon afterwards when he sentenced a pregnant woman, Tracey Scott, a cashier, to prison for a first offence of dishonesty: she had allowed friends to pass her till without paying. The offence involved 'a betrayal of the employer's trust', and it is certainly not unusual for judges to send people to prison for this kind of offence, even if they have never done it before and even if the offender has a young child. But Judge Pickles's turbulent romance with the press meant that he did not benefit from the oblivion that protects many a sterner colleague. He made comments to the effect that, in his view, he should not be influenced by the existence of the baby because if judges showed themselves to be susceptible in this way young women would be tempted to get themselves pregnant to avoid prison. This is not a unique view; judges tend to think that wily defendants will contemplate anything to shirk punishment, and lawyers are always worried that new developments in a defendant's life between arrest and trial will look like a calculated effort to influence the judge, and that he will view it as 'holding a gun at his head'. Pregnancy is a particularly loaded event, and combines with a belief in women's deviousness to operate against many defendants. This is particularly true when the woman is black because of the common view that young black women enter into motherhood much more casually than their white counterparts. Some feel that women in these days of equality should have no special advantage over men because of their biology.

Judge Pickles's attitudes are often quite conventional judicial opinions. Only weeks after the pregnant cashier was imprisoned, Judge Brian Woods, with little publicity, sent a seven-months' pregnant woman to prison, saying, 'The law does not entitle me to draw genteel distinctions between the sexes. The fact that she is pregnant is really not relevant.'

Where James Pickles separates from his brethren is in his belief that open debate is beneficial rather than detrimental to the bench. He is an advocate of greater public accountability by judges and wants to see the system working in a less secretive way, especially in the appointment of judges. Whilst these are views with which most of the public would agree, it is undoubtedly this strand of his thinking, and his telling tales out of school, which rattled his colleagues – not, unfortunately, his punitive attitude to women.

The sociologist Pat Carlen has produced some wonderful work over several years (*Women's Imprisonment: Study in Social Control*, 1983; and *Criminal Women*, 1985) on the attitudes of Scottish magistrates and judges to the women who come before them charged with crime. In an attempt to discover why women were sent to prison when most of their crime was so trivial, she asked a representative selection of the judiciary the question, '*What affects your final decision when you are uncertain whether to send a woman to prison?*' The following are some of the answers she received:

'Women who live more ordered lives don't commit crime because with a husband and children to look after they don't have time.'

'It may not be necessary to send her to prison if she has a husband. He may tell her to stop it.'

'Women with steady husbands or cohabitees don't commit crime – they are kept occupied.'

'If she's a good mother we don't want to take her away. If she's not a good mother it doesn't really matter.'

'If you discover a woman has no children it clears the way to send her to prison. If she has children but they're in care then I take the view she is footloose and fancy-free and I treat her as a single woman.'

'If they have left their husbands and their children are already in care it may seem a very good idea to send them to prison for three months.'

When I first read Pat Carlen's material I found the endorsement of everything I had felt in my bones and witnessed in court. Here it was, from the very mouths of those who sat in judgement. There is nothing peculiarly Scottish about these attitudes: they have confronted me daily. Women whose children are in care, women who are divorced or separated, women who do not fulfil their appropriate role, all encounter unmatched prejudice. The work of criminologists like Frances Heidensohn, Susan Edwards or Russell and Rebecca Dobash added further texture and colour to my own picture of the criminal courts.

Magistrates and judges bemoan the limited range of possibilities when it comes to sentencing women. Yet another conditional discharge may seem too lenient a disposal, fines perpetuate the vicious circle of poverty, community service has been inadequately developed and is insufficiently geared to women, particularly if they have small children. In the trap of having to go down-tariff or up-tariff – the tariff being the mean sentence for the type of offence – because no really appropriate penalty is available, our judiciary plays the sugar and spice game of deciding what this little girl is made of. The tests are always the same, revolving around how our clients function as wives, daughters and mothers. Single women without those labels pose special problems. Here the issue is whether they lead orderly or disorderly lives, hold down jobs and have community or family ties. So long as they conform, they are dealt with in much the same way as men.

Good mothers get credit with the court. The equivalent for men used to be a good service record, a mention in dispatches or boxing for the regiment. Yet the principles applied in deciding whether or not someone is a good mother are essentially middle-class. The emphasis is less on how many hours women spend prattling with their children or rolling together on the floor than on cleanliness and homemaking skills. Social enquiry reports, written by people who know the market with which they are dealing, make references to the spick-and-span council flat, the well-kept home, the neatly arranged ornaments and the scrubbed children. If a woman's children are in care her failure is already established, and whatever circumstances led to the separation are largely ignored.

Transcripts of criminal proceedings abound with questions from the bench which are in no way relevant to the issues but which are used as indicators of the kind of woman who is before the court. In 1988 a 35-year-old woman appeared on charges of armed robbery with her husband, who was only 22. The usual Bonnie and Clyde references were made in the press. In her early teens the woman had given birth to a baby which had been fostered, a fact which had only been referred to in passing. But the judge wanted to know whether she had maintained contact with the child, and whether she had ever tried to offer the baby a home once she herself was settled. Defenders of the judge could maintain that he was just endeavouring to obtain as much information as possible about the person before him, regardless of sex, but the personal history of the male accused was never explored (although it could have exposed his sexual abuse when a child). The judge's questions were clearly his litmus test of the nature of the woman. Such examples are endless. The men in our criminal courts, particularly the older generation, have a romantic view of motherhood. Perhaps the haze of time passing has affected their memories of parenting, so that they no longer recollect the penetrating cries of their own children – or perhaps they were protected from them by their wives and other domestic help. And, of course, the stereotyping of women extends to jurors, lawyers, experts and all the other participants in the process.

A male robber, however, is rarely thought of in terms of fathering. The good father is unlikely to stir the compassion of a court by portraying himself in the bosom of his family. He should be out working, lawfully providing for them.

The compulsion to make women fulfil accepted criteria of decent womanhood is a great temptation to lawyers, who in colluding with it succumb to a paternalism which effectively marginalises women. A case which struck me forcefully at the time was that of Sarah Tisdall, who was charged in 1984 under section 2 of the old Official Secrets Act because she sent the *Guardian* information about the deployment of American missiles in the UK. Here a grown woman, who as a matter of principle and moral indignation had divulged classified information to a national newspaper, was infantalised in the court process. She was described as 'misguided' by the prosecution, a view which was in turn endorsed by her own counsel, and as a 'silly girl' by the police. Her own counsel said, 'There is no suggestion at all that we are dealing here with an unbalanced or insecure young woman or one so politically inspired as to be intent on a personal political crusade.' The counsel representing her was anxious to distance her from the peace movement, insisting that she was basically nonpolitical and pro-nuclear defence. The intention of all the men involved was to turn a seriously meant act, based on the moral conviction that governments had a duty to inform and the public a right to know, into something of little significance. This was done with the best will in the world, and was aimed at securing the sympathy of a court which it was hoped would function in a paternalistic way. As in the trial of Clive Ponting, the issue as to whether this was indeed a crime could have been left to a jury, and Sarah Tisdall might also have been acquitted. However, even though all the players, prosecution, police and defence combined to a man in presenting Sarah Tisdall as a politically innocent soul who followed her heart rather than her head, and who did not realise the implications of her actions, Judge Cantley was having none of it. The opportunity to make an example of those who divulge secrets, even at the expense of a rather minor civil servant, was one which could not be missed. Sarah Tisdall was sentenced to six months' imprisonment. The *Sun* was particularly concerned that this daughter of well-to-do doctor parents, who had been brought up amidst upper-class respectability, should be locked in with murderers, lesbians and drug addicts. It reported a detective as saying, 'I shudder to think what the little angel will go through. It's going to be hell for her.'

The sentence did seem ludicrous, given the Crown's concession that no serious consequences flowed from the offence, and must have left Sarah Tisdall, a highly principled and courageous woman, feeling she had copped it both ways: losing dignity in the way that she was patronised, and not getting a better result.

Duncan Campbell, the investigative journalist, gave me an interesting account of the arrests of Sarah Tisdall and Clive Ponting. His views are instructive because he himself has had experience of the criminal justice system as it deals with issues of official secrecy. Having been one of the defendants in the ABC trial, which was also about disclosing material which was supposed to be secret, he is well aware of the special pressures which apply in cases about the public's right to know. He contacted both Tisdall and Ponting when they were arrested and gave each the same advice about what he thought was possible for them within the courtroom. Ponting, he reports, was immediately interested in challenging the charges, taking 'a pro-active stance' and wanting to weigh all the options. His reaction was followed through in the way that he and his legal team took on the courtroom battle. Duncan Campbell's view was that precisely the same options were available to Sarah Tisdall. Her response was one most women would adopt when confronted by an attack on their integrity and values: to retreat to a non-combative position. Clearly the status of the two was different, and their experience and training probably equipped them differently for the public clamour and the role as defendant, but in many ways Sarah Tisdall's case was likely to be more appealing to a jury, and the outcome of her case fills me with regret. Perhaps the instinct for gambling is not as well developed in women.

The double standards experienced by women in the courts are also prevalent in the juvenile justice system. The remit of the Juvenile Courts goes beyond that of adult courts because it is concerned about the well-being of children and young people. This means that sanctions can be brought into operation for behaviour that is not technically criminal but likely to affect a young person's development. Children can be brought there for truanting, for being neglected or in 'moral danger' or beyond parental control. Many girls are thus brought into the system and harshly sanctioned for non-criminal offences or trivial misdemeanours when they are not conforming to notions of proper behaviour.

Girls are referred to the Juvenile Courts for different reasons than are boys, and are dealt with differently. A son's overnight absence will earn him a knowing wink, and drunkenness will be seen as a natural part of his growing up – boys will be boys – but the same behaviour by a girl calls down very different responses. There is a clear preoccupation with the sexuality of teenage girls and an over-emphatic concern with their moral welfare. If she fails to come home on time, hangs around the wrong part of town or adopts dubious friends, a girl is far more likely to be declared in moral danger, for which, at the instigation of her parents, school, social worker or the police, she may be taken into the care of the local authority. The same behaviour in boys does not evoke the same response from the courts. These young women often start off in the penal system having committed no crime at all, but once it is on their record that they have been locked up, a cycle of imprisonment begins, and offending often follows.

In 1986 there was a short-lived scandal when a 17-year-old first offender was remanded in custody to Holloway for three weeks for stealing a pint of milk. It was perfectly clear that the magistrates had not liked her punk appearance and disapproved of her living in a squat. And in *Justice of the Peace* a magistrates' magazine, a judge was quoted as saying that he would be more likely to place in custody a child or girl whose behaviour was 'unchildlike or unfeminine'; unmanly behaviour was not on his list. Being boister-ous and getting into scraps is not inherently deviant for young men, but fighting by girls is anathema to the bench, and offences which contain violence or the threat of violence often invite heavier responses when committed by girls. Burglary by girls also often meets with heavier sanctions. Chris Tchaikovsky, the director of Women in Prison, has no doubts about the different criteria used in assessing women and in dealing with their perceived aberrations. Rebellious girls are, in her words, 'disciplined, infantilised, femin-ised, medicalised and domesticised'.

Imprisonment is used as a means of social control, and that is particularly true in relation to women. The 1990 report from the National Association of Probation Officers gave an account of a 19-year-old woman charged with a social security fraud which involved thousands of pounds by the time it was discovered. She was a single parent, badly in debt, trying to manage on her own without parental support. Instead of taking the obvious course and providing this mother with the resources of the probation service, the court separated her from her baby and sent her to prison for eighteen months. She was described as a promiscuous young woman as sentence was passed. That sort of story is by no means unusual; the thinking behind such a course is that the amount of money involved is too great to order probation – the woman will think she is 'getting away with it'. Instead we have another person incarcerated with little likelihood of its doing her one jot of good. The money will never be recovered anyway, and worst of all a child is separated from its mother. The damage produced is enormous.

In our Family Courts the philosophy is that the child comes first in any dispute. Children need their parents, and only in the most extreme circumstances do we break that bond. Yet in the criminal courts officials wash their hands of responsibility by saying that if her children suffer it is the criminal woman who is to blame. The family is presented as the foundation of society, to be supported and preserved. Women who transgress accepted roles and fail 'the family' unleash punitive responses, yet a veil is drawn over the sacred institution when the ritual of sentencing takes place. The report on Holloway prison's mother and baby unit for the Howard League for Penal Reform by Dr Dora Black, the eminent child psychiatrist, explains that the trauma of separation of young children from their mothers frequently leads to mental illness or at the least to profound emotional problems when they reach adolescence. In England and Wales a maximum of thirty-nine mothers can keep their babies with them in prison; even then, children cannot stay beyond the age of eighteen months. This limit on places means that keeping your baby is a privilege. Some states in the USA now recognise the right of every mother of an infant to have that child with her unless she has a history of child abuse or the child would suffer. We have recently managed to introduce the idea of more open access for children to their mothers in prison, but it is extraordinary that this issue of children's rights has been so long in being addressed.

The Inspector of Prisons, Judge Stephen Tumin, described the unsatisfactory conditions at the Holloway unit in his April 1992 report: poor nutrition, staff untrained in child-care, lack of stimulation for the babies, inadequate facilities. These findings echoed an excellent multi-disciplinary inspection of all the prison facilities for Mothers and Babies in Prison, conducted by the Department of Health and reported in March 1992. The provision being made is wholly unacceptable. However, some prison campaigners fear that improving conditions will encourage courts to send more women with children to prison.

In September 1991 Susannah Jackson was convicted of defrauding her employer and friend the dress designer Lindka Cierak of £20,000 and of stealing some valuable clothes. His Honour Judge Anwyl Davies sentenced her to immediate imprisonment, although she was a single parent with a new baby which she was breast-feeding. Anthony Scrivener QC, who was Chairman of the Bar, immediately appealed her case, without waiting for the grant of legal aid, to prevent separation from her baby. The Court of Appeal replaced the sentence with a suspended sentence.

On one of my own recent visits to Holloway Prison's mother and baby unit, a young woman told me of the nightmare of being remanded in custody for reports from Isleworth Crown Court when there was no place on the unit to accommodate her baby. She was released after twenty-four hours on an application for bail to the High Court. In the meantime she was separated from the baby, which she was breastfeeding, and suffered the agony of engorged breasts and desperation at how the baby was coping without her. In the end she was sent down for nine months. Her offence was a cheque-card fraud valued at £700, and although this time she was able to bring the baby into prison with her, her other child, a toddler, was left in the care of her father and was seriously disturbed by the separation. Imprisoning mothers should be a last resort, but judges have different ideas as to what that means.

Where a parent, male or female, has primary care of a child, the criminal courts should be required to obtain social enquiry reports on the impact upon the family of imprisonment. The hypocrisy of lauding the family and motherhood on the one hand while refusing adequately to acknowledge the social and economic supports necessary to sustain women in their motherhood role is a shameful reflection on the values of the justice system. For men and women alike, as was shown in the Woolf Report (1991), separation from the family is the worst aspect of imprisonment, but for women the guilt of failing their children exacts a special burden. Their offence is seen as being against more than the criminal law, and that is how they themselves feel it. I am not blind to the inhumanity some women wreak on others, nor to their criminality. Women can be ghastly, but the majority of those who are in prison should not be there. What is needed is the creation of real alternatives, such as appropriate community service, hostels and rehabilitation units. If the modern spirit of sentencing policy behind the new Criminal Justice Act 1991 is truly that prisons are places for dealing with serious crime, particularly violence, then it should be translated into reality by the judges, and our female prisons particularly could virtually be emptied.

4

The Wife, the Mother and the Dutiful Daughter

Cases involving domestic violence are an important gauge of entrenched attitudes about the proper roles of men and women. Violence is still seen as a legitimate response to certain kinds of female behaviour.

One of the problems for women has been the split between what is perceived as public, and therefore the law's business, and what is private, which shouldn't concern the law at all. Most of us are content that the law and the power of the state should be strictly limited so that their encroachment on individual freedom is kept to a minimum. The way in which people choose to conduct their private lives should be regulated as little as possible by the state and we have been happy to incorporate the ideas of liberal philosophy into our jurisprudence. Normally, it is only where private behaviour harms others that we condone the intervention of the law, and we use this as the basis of our argument for the legalisation of adult homosexual behaviour. Yet this separation of the private and public has worked against women, whose major sphere of activity is in the private domain. And so those who apply the law often fail women in the areas where they are most vulnerable.

The issue of domestic violence has gradually been tackled since the late 1970s after years of turning a blind eye, failing to prosecute and taking little action against its perpetrators. Marital behaviour behind closed doors was for a long time deemed a 'no go' area for law enforcement. This reluctance of the law to become involved accounts for much of the past difficulty in pursuing legal remedies for child abuse, both physical and sexual, and for rape, unless it involved being jumped on in an alleyway.

The arguments which are used to explain the failure of the criminal law in these areas always turn on the evidential problems, but in fact the private/public dichotomy is an essential element which has not been recognised because lawyers cannot see that not regulating is as significant as regulating. But finding remedies in law for the protection of women and their children poses a problem, because it inevitably involves greater intervention by the state and the possible erosion of defendants' rights. Policing the bedroom is not a course we should readily advocate, but there should never be any qualms when it is done at the behest of those who are being abused themselves, or on their behalf by concerned parties. The police, who would have no problem entering premises believed to contain explosive substances, become very sensitive to the rights of man when the information relates to domestic violence. But it is not fair to confine criticism to the police, who are trying to change their approach. Many forces are now establishing domestic violence units with specially trained officers conducting the investigations. The spotlight must move to the courtroom, where the problems are still considerable. American research showed that when members of the public witnessed violence between two people they were more reluctant to report it if it was between a man and a woman. In answer to questionnaires, the majority of people felt that there were situations in which it was acceptable for a husband to hit his wife – not necessarily when she was being violent to him.

The legal difficulties when offences take place in private are considerable. Usually there are no independent witnesses, deep and complicated emotional turmoil often surrounds the events, motives for making allegations are questioned and, if the allegations are of a sexual nature, the law has developed rules seeking evidence from some independent source. In the case of domestic violence, women are unsatisfactory complainants, fearful of, or ambivalent about, pursuing a prosecution because of the potential implications. Minimising is a coping device used by those who are abused, adult and child, but it is still misunderstood by those who investigate and by the courts.

Many excuses given for failing to prosecute lack substance. Police officers fail to look for evidence that would support the complaint, particularly of a forensic nature, once an assault has been labelled 'domestic'. The reluctance of victims to pursue a prosecution is often exaggerated. In the waiting areas of courts, ushers and court staff have frequently expressed the view to me that it is six of one and half-a-dozen of the other, despite the fact that in the majority of cases it is the women who bear the scars, literally, and who have called the police. The historical fallacy that women are usually equal and active participants in domestic violence lives on. The alternative line is that many women invite beatings because of nagging, or that they are masochists. The nagging wife is put on to the scales as a counterweight to the violent husband, although few die in direct consequence of a tongue-lashing, and indeed most battered wives cannot afford the luxury of a grinding whinge.

Police, lawyers and judges often regard prosecution as inappropriate because it might harm family relationships, and see their role as helping to preserve the marriage. In a *World in Action* programme shown on television in 1990, about rape as part of the pattern of domestic violence within marriage, Sir Frederick Lawton, a retired Appeal Court judge, explained that if it were open to wives to bring prosecutions for rape, albeit against a background of domestic violence, it would prohibit any chance of rehabilitation of the marriage and would have a deleterious effect on children – as though rape itself, rather than the prosecution, might not already have had that effect. Precisely these arguments about 'irreparable damage to the family' have been used to counter the introduction of every piece of reforming legislation for the benefit of women in the last hundred years, whether it was allowing her to divorce, hold property in her own name, gain the vote, or obtain the right to enter the professions and public life.

Time and again following an assault men are given a 'talking to' rather than being arrested. Frequently when the police are called out to these situations they do not even record the incident, so that if a prosecution does proceed a history of previous violence is not available. Domestic violence is also charged as a minor common assault, even where there are visible injuries which would amount to actual bodily harm. This means that the cases are assigned to magistrates courts, processed quickly, and treated less seriously than other types of assault, and in the spirit that such a course is more likely to lead to the couple making it up. In the few cases where they do go for trial, acquittal rates are high and fining is by far the most common disposal. Imprisonment is the least frequent outcome. At a time when judges are being called upon to treat violent offences with severity, those labelled as domestic violence still seem to attract a different approach.

Women at magistrates courts can meet a hostile environment. If their husband is on bail, he often sits in the hallway feet away from her, harassing her and coercing her into dropping the charges. If he is in the cells, the same pressure may be exercised by his family or mates. The initial questioning of the woman is sometimes antagonistic, justified by those who are supposed to be on her side as testing the strength of any case they could bring and letting her see what is going to come from those who will represent her husband. Many victims internalise the blame implied by authority figures and, naturally enough, often decide not to go through with a court case. Such failure to proceed can be met with irritation. If she does steel herself to go through with it, it is precisely then that she needs support. This is when further violence might occur, because involving the police and the courts is a declaration of the right to control her own life, and if there is one thing that upsets a wife-beater it is a wife who asserts herself.

One of the appalling courses taken by courts under pressure to get through the list is to bind over both parties to keep the peace. This is seen as a nice speedy disposal, which dispenses with the need for a contested case. The rationale for mutual bind-overs is the same as that used in the civil courts when a woman has gone to seek an injunction but is fobbed off with mutual undertakings. It is maintained that it neutralises the hostility, but what it means in effect is that the woman who comes to court for help is now on record herself as violent, despite the fact that there is no evidence of her having done anything wrong. By supposedly creating equality between the parties the court reinforces inequality. The message to the defendant is that he is not accountable for his violence and the cycle is perpetuated.

That women accept abuse for so long without complaint seems barely credible to courts and jurors, and is in turn interpreted as a tolerance of the violence, detracting from the need to provide a tough remedy. In the Nussbaum/Steinberg case which was tried in New York in January 1989, Hedda Nussbaum not only accepted violence against herself, but also against her adopted children, culminating in the death of her little daughter. This threw the debate wide open. Hedda Nussbaum did not fit the public perception of the downtrodden battered wife. She had had a good education, worked in publishing and lived with a lawyer. After the death of their child, Nussbaum was granted immunity from prosecution on condition that she gave evidence against Joel Steinberg, promoting allegations that the law was soft on women who aided and abetted crime. However, the spectacle of Hedda Nussbaum in the witness box was of a woman beaten into submission, undeniably the victim of domestic violence and incapable of standing up for herself. Steinberg was convicted of manslaughter.

Nussbaum was a middle-class woman for whom alternative accommodation must have been available. What her case demonstrated were the psychological effects of an experience – effects which are often so severe as to render women incapable of taking the necessary steps to end the relationship. In the early stages women believe the violent incidents are isolated events. The male partners are remorseful and the women believe everything will improve. They usually rationalise the abuse as the result of excess alcohol or the effects of stress on their partner because of overwork, no work, a new baby. Eventually the excuses are no longer convincing but by that time the cycle is so established it is impossible to break. In almost every case in which I have been involved the women present themselves in a very flat, unemotional way which can fail to arouse, in a judge or a jury, a full appreciation of her partner's behaviour towards her. Psychologists describe it as lack of 'affect'. They are also often so filled with shame at the public exposure of what they see as their private failure that they sometimes minimise the extent of their suffering.

Women with children often stay in such a relationship in the interests of their children: they fear that if they leave they will set up a situation which might lead to their being taken into care. If they leave their children they will fail as a mother; if they take them, they may face homelessness. Leaving thus becomes a monumental step. In court no reason is good enough to justify a woman leaving her children. The hostility towards a mother who contemplates doing this, even where she can no longer survive her husband's cruelty and has nowhere to bring children if she takes them with her, can annihilate her cause in a trial by jury.

When the playwright Peter Flannery and I were working on the television drama *Blind Justice* in 1987 we were posed with a similar dilemma in the creation of the character Katherine Hughes, who was a radical woman barrister. We had to create a scandal in her past which the press could dig up and use in an attempt to discredit her. Peter was keen to invent a child left behind with a previous husband but I balked at that because the character of Katherine ran in the face of most stereotypes of women, and I felt that to have her abandon a child, however good her reasons, would completely lose her the audience sympathy we needed in order to lend credibility to her arguments. I won the day, but I know I was pandering to a negative reaction.

The Home Office has now issued a circular to the police emphasising the criminal nature of attacks on women by husbands and boyfriends, and the issue is being taken much more seriously, though with varying rigour. The Law Commission has also recommended stronger powers for the courts, which will mean courts can make non-molestation orders, forbidding pestering, harassment and violence, and occupation orders, excluding men from the matrimonial home or ordering the return of the victim. If the protections are made law, they will extend to engaged couples, former spouses and cohabitees, lovers and ex-lovers and other family members. The commission also suggests that courts should be given the power, as in Scotland, to transfer a tenancy from one cohabitee to another, whether or not the couple are joint tenants. This idea is taking some swallowing because it interferes with the law's insistence that an Englishman's home is his castle – even if it is a prison to his wife. Prescriptions for improving the position of women clearly go beyond the ambit of the law and involve providing social and housing options so that women do not feel required to accept the unacceptable, but there are a myriad ways in which the law itself can be reformed. Unfortunately, the knee-jerk response of most lawyers, even those with progressive attitudes, is to resist any change which might affect the position of a defendant.

The unwillingness to welcome innovations which would ameliorate the experience of victims in our courtrooms has been based on legitimate concerns to prevent unfair conviction. However, at times it is just about a resistance to change. We saw this in the initial opposition to introducing video links for the giving of evidence by child victims who are afraid and inhibited by the presence of the accused and a courtroom full of observers (Pigot report, 1989). We have also seen it in the dismissal of suggestions that the victim might have separate representation, even of a limited nature in appropriate cases.

There are clearly cases such as child battering in which the quality of a woman's care for her children moves to centre stage. The evidence can make sickening reading and I am not without my own rage at the child's pain. Feeding children heroin or turning adolescent daughters on to the streets for prostitution can rarely be viewed in a sympathetic light.

In some cases, however, where women have harmed their children, class divisions **as well as** gender expectations are at the root of the court's inability to understand how the offences were committed. A mother of four children was convicted of cutting her son with a breadknife. The woman's children had different fathers, none of whom was around, and two of the children were of mixed race. The family were living on the breadline and the oldest boy, who was 8, was already showing signs of problem behaviour. Social services confirmed that a change of personnel had meant a period with no social work support. The family was living in a flat without electricity. A doctor testified that the injury to the boy's head was not serious and would have involved little force. A school teacher wrote to the court to describe the effort the woman was putting into helping her children to read. She had minimal previous history of offending. She was sentenced to eighteen months' imprisonment.

There is a chasm of misunderstanding between the privileged

professionals who work the system and the offender bringing up children alone without financial and emotional resources. The misery of that existence and the toll it can take is rarely appreciated.

With horrifying regularity, cases of child-killing come before the courts. The components have surprisingly few variables. The couple are usually young. In the majority of cases the child is a girl and the male partner is a stepfather. The death is usually preceded by protracted neglect and abuse before a final brutal assault. The cases which stand out in our minds are, of course, those where Social Service departments, underfunded and under pressure, are severely criticised and formal inquiries follow. Among these are the cases of Jasmine Beckford, whose stepfather, Maurice, was jailed in March 1985 for ten years for her manslaughter, and whose mother, Beverly Lorrington, received eighteen months for wilful neglect; Heidi Koseda, whose stepfather, Nicholas Price, was sentenced to life imprisonment in September 1985 with a recommendation that he serve a minimum of fifteen years and whose mother, Rosemarie Koseda, pleaded guilty to manslaughter and was detained under the Mental Health Act; and Kimberly Carlisle, whose stepfather, Nigel Hall, and mother, Pauline, were both charged with murder. On 15 May 1987 Nigel Hall was convicted and sentenced to life imprisonment for Kimberly's killing, whilst Pauline Carlisle was not held responsible for her death but was jailed for twelve years for cruelty. The wicked stepmother is the spectre that has haunted us all since childhood. Yet in the courts it is the male equivalent who appears with greater regularity. However, natural fathers appear in the dock with frequency too.

Public anger towards the men who commit these crimes against defenceless infants is matched by bewilderment and disgust at the role of the women. The questions which spring into the minds of us all are repeatedly asked in court. Why didn't you protect the child? Why didn't you leave? Why didn't you seek the help of police, doctors, health visitors, social workers or even just a friend? Why did you cover up your partner's behaviour? Why did you protect him rather than your own baby? How could you allow him to harm repeatedly the child you had borne?

The women themselves do not know the answer to these questions. They have usually been beaten or emotionally battered by their men and are the passive partners in volatile relationships. Often they are grateful for the attentions of the men in their lives, however abusive that attention might be. Their low sense of their own worth often emanates from childhood experiences. The children they bear become extensions of themselves, and I suspect this is particularly the case with female children. The apparent collusion in violence towards their offspring has often seemed to me to be a consolidation of what they have come to expect for themselves. The whole cycle is a paradigm of the worst kind of power imbalance.

Others have become incapable of taking action. The effect of long-term abuse, physical and mental, on otherwise capable, strong women is devastating. The abuser's control can become so absolute that he no longer has to use physical violence. The threat is ever present: even when women go out of doors or go to work the spell is not broken. In the pattern of abuse it is a common feature that the women are isolated, forbidden to have visitors or friendships or much contact with members of their families. Possessiveness and jealousy, which had been flattering at the commencement of the relationship, becomes oppressive and controlling. A psychological freezing means they lose their ability to take the protective steps that another mother could initiate. Their partners are perceived by them to be omnipotent, so that any move out of line will invoke punishment and avoidance becomes paramount, even if it means failing to protect a child. They learn to be helpless and hopeless, convinced that any attempt to escape will invoke the infliction of more torture on them all.

Not only is it misunderstood that the woman's own reality becomes so distorted that she believes nothing will prevail upon her husband to stop, and that any challenge to him will destroy her, but it should also not be forgotten that in very many cases nothing does stop abusive men, and battered women end up dead. In the majority of domestic murder cases, men kill women, and there is usually a history of abuse on his part. The case of Jayanti Patel (March 1992), where the accused managed to murder his battered wife in a police station, testified to the reality of her fears.

Evidence of his persistent violence to women came out during the trial. In 1980 he had been convicted of stabbing his first wife. In 1984 he had poured boiling water over her, stabbed her in the throat and battered her, for which he was sentenced to just twelve months' imprisonment, which at least enabled his first wife to divorce him.

Understanding domestic violence is a challenge to the courts. To onlookers the response of the battered woman seems abnormal, but to her it is a rational response to her abnormal circumstances. Misconceptions litter the court and are reflected in the verdicts of juries: women have ample opportunities to leave; in some perverse way they like the pain; no real woman becomes so crushed by her abusive partner that her maternal instinct could be extinguished.

Cross-examining of women in such cases frequently operates on the premise that a certain level of violence is acceptable. One prosecutor's recent questioning of a man who battered his wife and child began with the assertion, 'Whatever your relationship with your girlfriend, the one person who did not deserve to be hit was the baby.' In another, where the woman had agreed that she was only ever slapped, it was suggested that the physical violence could, therefore, be put on one side.

In their lives with battering husbands, women themselves invariably minimise the extent of the violence to which they are subjected because of self-blaming and their own sense of shame. Or they cover up their man's behaviour because they fear the consequences of exposing him. They avoid going to the doctor, and cover their bruises. They provide innocent explanations to outsiders for injuries and concoct elaborate stories to distract attention from the abuse. They also cannot face up to the horror of what is happening, and part of the pretence is to delude themselves.

Finding physical evidence of the abuse is difficult when the matter becomes material in a court, with lawyers for the other side claiming recent fabrication or exaggeration. In every contested criminal case I have conducted over the years involving the battering of a woman she is accused of inflating her account. Corroboration of less than a handful of assaults is par for the course, and those often become the only instances of violence which are accepted.

The constant theme in the accounts of battered women who come before the courts is that they had lived in hope that everything would come all right, that if they had a proper home, or a baby, or the baby was older, or he had a job, or his job had fewer pressures, or they had more money, then the relationship would return to the romantic idyll of the courtship. This is the sustaining factor in the early stages of the abuse, and thereafter the control is too well established for them to feel able to challenge it. However, continuing to live with the tormentor is seen as a testament to the acceptability of his behaviour.

A constant refrain in the questioning is 'Why did you not leave?', something the mother herself can never answer coherently. Because it can induce responses which are counter to common sense, I currently seek to call expert testimony in these cases as to the effects of cumulative abuse on its victims. This is still new terrain in Britain but is a practice which has already developed in Canada and a majority of states in America. The test for admissibility of expert testimony is whether the matters into which the testimony goes are outside the experience of the jury:

> It is aimed at an area where the purported common knowledge of the jury may be very much mistaken, an area where juror's logic drawn from their own experience may lead to a wholly incorrect conclusion, an area where expert knowledge would enable the jurors to disregard their prior conclusions as being common myths rather than common knowledge. (State v Kelly, New Jersey Supreme Court)

Traditionally, judges have taken the view that experts should be kept out of cases wherever possible and have felt there is nothing complicated about domestic violence. Everyone is supposed to know the effects of a hard clout. Until the psychological effects of domestic violence are fully understood, experts should be allowed to give testimony, and my argument is that the question 'Why don't they leave?' is proof of our failure to understand the problem.

In the cases where experts are called, it is not their function to usurp the jury's role in the trial. They are able to state what effect the abuse would have if the history given by the woman were true. It is then for the jury to determine the truth or otherwise of the account. I have found judges increasingly willing to permit the inclusion of this evidence, but there is strenuous resistance from some quarters of the Bar, where it is seen as special pleading for women. Ideally a situation will develop where the effects of cumulative violence will be so widely understood that courts will need no assistance. It will not be necessary for psychiatrists and psychologists to 'loan their experience' to the jury. We have yet to reach that stage.

In the United States the pattern of behaviour exhibited by abused women is labelled Battered Woman's Syndrome and is a sub-category of Post Traumatic Stress Disorder, recognised by the World Health Organisation in its classifications of mental disorders.

The gravity, indeed the tragedy, of domestic violence can hardly be overstated. Greater media attention to this phenomenon in recent years has revealed both its prevalence and its horrific impact on women from all walks of life. Far from protecting women from it, the law has historically sanctioned the abuse of women within marriage as an aspect of the husband's ownership of his wife and his right to chastise her 'with a stick no thicker than his thumb'.

A woman who comes before a judge and jury with the claim that she has been battered and suggests this may be a relevant factor in evaluating her subsequent actions still faces the prospect of being condemned by popular mythology about domestic violence: either she was not as badly beaten as she claims, or she must have stayed out of some masochistic enjoyment of it. Although society has abandoned its formal approval of spousal abuse, tolerance of it continues in some circles today.

The leading case for this expert testimony, with a superb judgement by the Canadian Supreme Court judge, Bertha Wilson, is that of Lavallee v Regina, which was decided in May 1990. It is now an authority cited internationally, and must be the finest legal exposition on domestic violence. The court of seven judges had three women on it:

If it strains credulity to imagine what the ordinary man would do in the position of the battered spouse, it is probably because men do not typically find themselves in that situation. Some women do, however. The definition of what is reasonable must be adapted to circumstances which are, by and large, foreign to the world inhabited by the hypothetical reasonable man . . . Where evidence exists that an accused is in a battering relationship, expert testimony can assist the jury in determining whether the accused had a reasonable apprehension of death when she acted by explaining the heightened sensitivity of a battered woman to her partner's acts. Without such testimony I am sceptical that the average fact-finder would be capable of appreciating why her subjective fear may have been reasonable in the context of the relationship. After all, the hypothetical reasonable man observing only the final incident may have been unlikely to recognise the batterer's threat as potentially lethal.

Frequently, the judgement refers to the work of the pioneering clinical psychologist Dr Lenore Walker, the author of *The Battered Woman's Syndrome*. She describes in her research the recurring theme of abusive behaviour being intermittent, alternating with normal acceptable conduct, and this inconsistency being the means by which the traumatic bond is established.

The designation 'battered woman syndrome' is one that causes me some disquiet. It seems more sensible to avoid gender-specific labels like this because of the pathological cul-de-sac they create for women and also because of the hostility a special defence engenders in men. Furthermore, the features are also present in other relationships where there is a power imbalance: hostage and captor; battered child and abusive parent; cult follower and leader; prisoner and guard. I have acted for a homosexual man who was physically and emotionally abused in his relationship with his male partner, and, hard as it is to imagine, there might occasionally be men who manifest the same surrender of control in response to abuse from women. It also concerns me that an acceptance of a rigidly defined syndrome can exclude those who do not completely conform to the criteria. Women find such varied ways of surviving that behavioural checklists do not always work. What is clear from the now extensive research is that all sorts of women are subjected to abuse, deal with it in a multiplicity of ways and put up with it because complicated dynamics are set in motion. However, putting the name to one side, it is crucial that the principles of 'battered woman syndrome' should be acknowledged by the courts in Britain, as part of an educational process to dispel myths about domestic violence. (The impact of Mme Justice Wilson's appointment to Canada's highest court should not go unnoticed. The Lavallee judgement illustrates that it can and does make a difference to have judges who are receptive to a female analysis of violence, who demand that legal doctrine is sensitive to its context and who render their judgements accordingly. And she is Scottish!)

The rarity of battered men is hardly surprising, given the history of heterosexual relationships, the power disparity which has existed between men and women, the socialisation of the sexes and the physical disadvantages of women. But I am frequently informed by indignant male barristers that men are battered too. Even men who would not dream of using violence against their own wives are very defensive about male violence. Dealing with the problem as isolated aberration rather than as a problem rooted in sexual imbalance is the easier route, and women are made to take their share of the blame. Blaming the victim is a constant experience for women in the courts.

One of the present difficulties facing prosecutors occurs in child killings where the only possible candidates for the abuse and death are the parents, but both deny battering the baby, or alternatively each blames the other. In the case of *R v Aston and Mason*, February 1991, both mother and father had to be released by the Court of Appeal and their convictions were quashed. The double conviction had been achieved on the basis that whichever of the two did not actually kill the baby must have known what was going on and had been complicit by failing to protect the child. Therefore, they were deemed to share responsibility. However, the Appeal Court decided on recognised authority that it is necessary in a murder case to attribute blame directly to one or other, and with reluctance set them free. The baby's mother, Christine

Mason, had maintained that the child's stepfather, Roy Aston, had inflicted the fatal injuries.

As a result, such cases are now indicted as ill treatment of a child, even where the baby dies, and the parents stand trial together. The maximum penalty is ten years. Almost invariably the woman is protecting her partner. In some of these cases greater justice would be achieved if the woman could be given the right kind of support, enabling her to disclose the truth and testify against the killer of her child.

In January 1992 Sally Emery stood trial with her boyfriend Brian Hedman charged with ill treatment of their child Chanel, who died as a result of a ruptured bowel. The baby bore the signs of terrible abuse: fractured ribs, old and fresh injuries. Sally Emery initially lied to the police, covering up for Hedman, but at her trial she gave a classic and horrifying history of being battered herself and described how this was extended to the baby within months of her birth. The fact that she had two O levels was used in comparison with Hedman's low IQ to suggest that she would be the more in control within the relationship. It is frequently assumed that only women with low intelligence are dominated. Her frozen demeanour and failure to cry in police interview, so characteristic of those who are abused, was invoked to show her hardness. Her lying to cover for her abuser, of whom she was so terrified, indicated her proficiency at deceit. With the assistance of expert testimony, it was accepted that she was not the perpetrator of the assaults on her child, but she was sentenced to four years' imprisonment for failing to protect. Battering, it seems, would have to be of the most extreme kind to absolve women from their maternal responsibility. While I accept that the protection of children must be one of the clearest priorities in society, and that parental duty must be enforced by law, I think it is crucial that we also acknowledge the full impact of extreme violence on mothers.

In June 1988, 21-year-old Susan Poole pleaded guilty to the manslaughter of her baby son Dean. The child's father, Frederick Scott, a man of 34, was convicted of manslaughter and sentenced to life imprisonment. The child who died and his older brother were severely malnourished and neglected, but reports from psychiatrists and one GP all expressed the view that Susan Poole had been unstable at the time of her child's death. She was also totally controlled by Scott. The prosecution had only one counter-report, from a psychiatrist who saw Susan Poole after she had undergone a period of treatment. In the view of Dr Pamela Taylor, an eminent consultant psychiatrist, 'the combination of her personality disorder and her depressive illness would have been sufficient to impair her responsibility for her actions in the two months leading up to Dean's death . . . and probably over a longer period of time'. Dr Taylor recommended a probation order with a condition of psychiatric treatment. Despite Susan Poole's mental condition at the time, Mr Justice Owen said, 'When one thinks of the extraordinary maternal sacrifice and care shown by lower animals one has to wonder at her apparent selfishness.' She was sentenced to seven years' imprisonment, reduced on appeal to five years, which she is serving in special conditions for her own protection.

The mothers in child abuse cases such as these spend the weeks and months after the child's death immersed in a legal process that is directed towards assessing the extent of criminal responsibility; little room is left to deal with their grief and personal guilt. Sally Emery cried out from the witness box, 'I feel guilty. I want to be punished.'

This same background of low self-esteem and battering is usually present in those cases where women are accessories to child sexual abuse, but here the sexual violation and exploitation of children produces an even rawer response. Lifting the lid off the incest taboo has sent highly charged waves of panic through the criminal justice system. Statistically, women are rarely protagonists in sexual offences, and it is important that the reasons for this are fully appreciated. Sexual offences are deeply connected with the power structure and closely related to sexual inequality and the different upbringing of men and women. Occasionally we see cases of an adult female being accused of committing sexual indecency with an adolescent boy, and there was the rare instance of the headmistress, Ruth Hartley, who was found guilty of indecently assaulting an 11-year-old girl with whom she slept naked. However, such cases have been unusual, probably reflecting society's denial of women's sexuality and a conviction that women are less prone to this type of abuse of power.

The sudden discovery that child sexual abuse is more prevalent than was ever believed has brought in its wake the revelation that 20 per cent of abused boys and 5 per cent of abused girls are assaulted by women (Dr E. Carol Sheldrick, Consultant Psychiatrist, Maudsley Hospital), though it must be emphasised that this is still overall a very small percentage. Work here and in the United States has shown that girls are more frequently abused than boys, that perpetrators are more often male than female, and that whilst male victims are likely to become perpetrators, females are more likely to continue as victims. Of those who go on to commit crimes of sexual abuse the majority have themselves been abused.

Cases are now coming before the courts where women are charged with playing supporting roles, aiding and abetting the sexual exploitation of their children by husbands, lovers and other male relatives. The children are used directly for sexual gratification or in pornographic displays. Sometimes the women themselves actively participate in the degradation of their own children, and this has particularly been a claim in the recent allegations of ritual abuse. The whole process beggars belief and throws into confusion all the shibboleths about the sacred nature of motherhood. Few of us, on the other hand, had any problem understanding the gut response of the mother who poured boiling water in the crotch of the man who had assaulted her little girl: this was 'natural', outraged, protective mothering.

However, the taboo surrounding child sexual abuse still distorts the legal process. Mothers so often are held ultimately responsible for a number of reasons: failing to provide conjugal fulfilment; failing to protect her child; condoning abusive behaviour. Furthermore, with little statistical support it is claimed that large numbers of women invent allegations of sexual abuse to get their own back on their menfolk or to inflame prejudice against them. When June Scotland was tried for the murder of her husband (March 1992), the allegation that her abusive husband had also sexually interfered with their daughter was not only dismissed by the Crown as invention but used to measure Mrs Scotland's credibility about the whole history of events. The girl's aggressive behaviour towards her father during adolescence, her suicide attempts and assaults on her own appearance, which psychiatrists saw as consistent with a history of sexual abuse, were described as rebellious teenage behaviour. Of course, there are occasional false accusations by mendacious wives. But it is the generalising of such notions which requires examination. A new myth is in the making.

In the handling of sexual abuse cases, social workers, predominantly female, are accused of hysteria, lack of professionalism and distortion of evidence.

Most people wish to see incest as very rare, occurring in families which are obviously socially maladjusted. In fact, although the sexual boundaries in such families have become confused and ill-defined, the incestuous family looks very much like any 'normal' family.

It is this very proximity to normality which discomfits people. We want our rapists, wife batterers and child abusers to have mean mouths and eyebrows that meet. If the men in the dock do not conform sufficiently to the stereotype of the deviant, or if incestuous families do not behave abnormally, they are more able to resist allegations.

While some are anxious to promote sexual abuse as aberrant behaviour, just as prevalent amongst women as men, others cannot accept the possibility that women are abusive at all. In her book *Mother, Madonna, Whore* (1988), Dr Estela Welldon explores the perversion of motherhood and provides an insight into the way women's own powerlessness can manifest itself in abuse of the one relationship where they do feel in control. She suspects that, by placing motherhood on a pedestal, we have refused to believe in the possibility of woman transgressing from the purity of her maternal role. Dr Welldon met with resistance from some feminists because her conclusions were seen as blaming women, but her work provides one route to understanding this area of crime, which until now has been conveniently labelled as the ultimate in wickedness.

As yet there is little appreciation in the criminal justice system of why women become involved, and the main response is an intensified revulsion. Like other sexual offenders, women often exacerbate their position by slipping into denial or justification. It is a familiar view of both men and women involved in these cases that if a child doesn't physically resist an adult's sexual advances then it indicates a willingness by the child to have sex. The women in these cases often maintain that having intercourse with a child is not such a bad way for the adult to teach the child about sex, or express the view that it is better to have sex with a child in the family than to have an affair. Collusion by wives in the abuse of their children is despised almost as much as the actual assaults. In fact, collusion is greatly exaggerated, and most mothers becoming aware of sexual abuse take steps to protect the child or genuinely never know, but a commonly expressed view at trial is that the wife's frigidity or rejection was the root cause of the male abuse and that she sub-contracted her sexual obligations.

The women who are convicted of sexual offences end up segregated from the general prison population for their own protection. Distributed throughout the women's prisons, they form tiny leper colonies in the institutions. The psychiatric facilities in the prison system are wholly inadequate and their problems can never be adequately addressed.

An attempt was made to break new ground in a special unit at Styal prison in 1988, where Fran Corder, a senior social worker, and Sharon Barnett, a probation officer, established a group project. All six women with whom they worked had abused children with co-defendants, such as husbands, boyfriends or neighbours. Five probably would not have abused if they had not been initiated into it by their partners. The sample is low, and any conclusions should be drawn with caution, but all the women lacked confidence and were introverted and nervous. All were heavily dependent on their partners. The idea of women's passive role in sex was entrenched in their relationships with males, as was the view that a woman's place was in the home. Unfortunately, the therapeutic scheme at Styal has been discontinued.

The method for ordering psychiatric treatment in the community is to make it a condition of probation. This means that the courts rely upon the probation officer informing on a woman who gives up on treatment. But in the eyes of the world a probation order seems like a very soft option, in no way reflecting the seriousness of offences towards children. Yet very often it would be of greater benefit to the wellbeing of a child if therapeutic work were undertaken, enabling a mother to confront her abusive behaviour. In reality, prison is the soft option for the courts.

It should be possible to mark the gravity of offences with a prison sentence which is then suspended whilst a period of psychiatric treatment is undertaken. The breach of this type of suspended sentence need not involve the commission of a further offence, as is currently the case: instead, the sentence could be activated where the offender refuses to go on with the therapy. This suggestion always alarms some psychiatrists, who insist that voluntariness is an essential feature of progress for those being treated, but the majority of those whose practices involve child sexual abuse are less inhibited and welcome any innovation which will surmount the present sentencing impasse.

There is a strange dichotomy in our criminal justice system which treats psychiatry with suspicion and at times derision whilst at the same time leaping to the conclusion that women who commit crime are mad rather than bad. However, while women whose behaviour is 'inappropriate' are subjected to a misplaced psychiatric labelling, which must be challenged, there is also no doubt that the criminal justice system is misused as a dumping ground for women who should be patients rather than prisoners. A significant majority of the women who go through the system have been subjected to more criminal behaviour than they have been responsible for. In a five-year review currently being undertaken by the Chief Medical Officer at Holloway prison, levels of childhood and marital abuse are extraordinarily high. In a review of firesetting by women in 1989, 72 per cent had been subjected to serious sexual abuse. In the preparation of court reports, it is believed by those working at Holloway that as many as 90 per cent have a history of battering or sexual abuse of some degree; 55 per cent of the women abused drugs – 70 per cent if alcohol is included – and the work indicates a strong link between opiate abuse by the women and their own experience of abuse. In 1991, research suggested that 56 per cent of the inmates serving more than six months' imprisonment might be suffering from 'a medically identifiable psychiatric disorder'. Many women in prison harm themselves, using sharp objects to hack their own flesh. Such self mutilation directly relates to the women's low self worth, exacerbated by the impossibly high expectations of society and the claustrophobia of the regime. Psychiatric disorders are often occasioned by this failure to fulfil expectations.

The idea that women can be subject to their hormones was the traditional way of explaining otherwise inexplicable behaviour in women. The special crime of infanticide is only available to women who are responsible for the death of their newly born babies, recognising that 'at the time of the act or omission she had not fully recovered from the effect of giving birth or the effect of lactation and for this reason the balance of her mind was disturbed'. The offence was introduced earlier this century because it was appreciated that a charge of murder was wholly inappropriate, but the new charge was confined to the first twelve months of a baby's life.

Historically, women had been treated with terrible harshness if they killed their child. There was an automatic inference if a baby was found dead that the mother was responsible, and undoubtedly many were executed where there had been no deliberate killing by the mother at all. Those who suffered most were poor single women, often maidservants, who tried to conceal their pregnancies because of the desperate consequences that flowed from having a bastard. Frequently the master of the household was the father. Disposal of the newborn meant the death penalty, and this was often carried out even where there was evidence that the infant was stillborn. The instances of men being indicted for killing babies or being accessories were negligible. It was not until the nineteenth century that the desperate injustice and cruelty of these decisions became accepted.

The availability of contraception and abortion, as well as a change in attitude to the whole issue of illegitimacy, has meant a reduction in the cases of infanticide. Girls and young women are less ridden with shame and fear of parental response. It makes all the more poignant the Irish case in 1984 of 15-year-old Anne Lovett, who died in a churchyard in Granard, County Longford, where she had furtively gone to give birth, or the 16-year-old girl who in 1988 was desperate to hide her pregnancy from her parents and, after giving birth in the bathroom of their home, choked the baby boy to death.

But if moral disdain has waned, the pressure of living up to the ideal is ever present. It is this pressure to be the perfect mother that is responsible for much post-natal depression. In 1989 Christine Annesley locked herself in a toilet of the maternity hospital where she had given birth to her baby son and killed him with her bare hands. She had been readmitted into hospital within weeks of giving birth because of stress, fatigue and lack of family support. In court she was described as 'not a callous mother or an uncaring mother. She set herself unattainable ideals and was concerned in case she fell short.' Pleading guilty to infanticide, she was placed on probation for two years on condition that she had psychiatric treatment.

Since the creation of the special female crime of infanticide, the law has come to a greater understanding of mental impairment. The 1957 Homicide Act created a special defence to murder, reducing it to manslaughter where the offender's criminal responsibility was diminished because of such impairment. The infanticide law involved a paternalistic and generalised approach to women's psychology and physiology, and it should now be removed from the statute books and absorbed into the Homicide Act. Childbirth and lactation do not dissolve all women's brains, but severe post-natal depression is a recognised disorder and would fulfil the criteria for diminished responsibility in appropriate cases.

Research into post-natal depression has now developed, and in the right case can reduce murder to manslaughter where the victim is other than the newborn baby, eg. another child of the family, a spouse or friend. In 1986 a young woman of 19 called Ann Reynolds killed her mother shortly after giving birth to a baby whom she had surrendered for adoption. The girl had concealed her pregnancy and taken herself off to a hospital in a nearby town to give birth secretly. In the period that followed, she clearly suffered puerperal depression, and one night, after a confrontation with her mother, she killed her as she slept. She was convicted of murder, the jury having rejected her defence of diminished responsibility, but released on appeal after a campaign by local women had led to the involvement of experts, who testified as to her hormonal imbalance, though the emphasis was placed on a chronic premenstrual condition.

Premenstrual tension (PMT) has figured a number of times in the last ten years as a defence or mitigation to crime, and in two well-publicised cases has successfully reduced a charge of murder to manslaughter. Christine English crushed her former lover against a telegraph pole with her car, and Sandra Craddock was charged with killing another barmaid at the place where she worked. Both pleas to manslaughter were accepted on the grounds of diminished responsibility due to PMT. Christine English received a conditional discharge and driving ban. At first Sandra Craddock's sentence was deferred for a period, during which she received progesterone therapy. The success of the treatment led to her eventually receiving a probation order. At a later stage, after a further conviction, her counsel sought in the Court of Appeal to establish PMT as a special defence in its own right, but the judges were having none of it – quite rightly, in my view.

The issue has created unrest amongst many men and women, the former seeing it as a 'get-out' and the latter as a reinforcement of the 'slaves to hormones' view of women. The point which has to be emphasised is that these cases of a profoundly disturbed hormonal balance, in which women's physiology affects their mental state, are extremely rare. In my own practice I have used the condition in relation to my client's mental state only once. In murder cases it can be raised only where evidence is strong that the hormonal imbalance is so extreme that the tests for diminished responsibility are fulfilled. There are probably just as many cases where exceedingly high testosterone levels in the male might account for outbursts of violence. It is just that, as usual, we are more predisposed to explore psychiatric explanations in women.

The workings of the female body and its potential for child-bearing are sometimes justifiably used in special pleading for women, but it does have the double bind of being used to shackle women to very confining roles. Biology is commonly assumed to determine women's lives, and there are times when it feels as though it does. Women are rendered much more vulnerable by virtue of their physiology, and the real evidence for this is in the extent to which they are the victims rather than the perpetrators of violence. Most of the violence women experience is in the domestic setting and not on the street. The home is by far the most dangerous place for women.

5

Asking for It

The core stereotype for women in the courts is that of victim, and blaming the victim is the classic courtroom response to crime in the private arena. A woman is eight times more likely to be killed by a husband or male friend than by a stranger. Men, by contrast, are more likely to be killed by a stranger. And the same stereotypes blight the justice system, whether the women are in the dock or in the witness box or no longer live to tell the tale.

For the defence of provocation to succeed in reducing murder to manslaughter, the victim's words or conduct have to render the defendant 'so subject to passion as to make him for the moment not master of his mind'. Inevitably the conduct of the deceased has to be called into question. In so many cases the accused's account stands on its own, unchallenged because there is no admissible evidence and no victim to counter it.

There are a million variations of how the defence has been used by people who have killed, and it would be facile and untrue to suggest that only dead women are vilified in this way. However, there is a hidden agenda for women that makes the possibilities for attack even greater.

Christabel Boyce was strangled by her husband Nicholas Boyce on 13 January 1985. They had been married for six and a half years, had two young children and lived in a run-down part of Bethnal Green. She was a social worker whose income supported the family, while he was a perennial student still working on a post-graduate doctorate long after any grant had been exhausted. Nicholas Boyce killed Christabel in their flat after she broke one of his collection of pipes. He then cut her body up into a hundred pieces while their children slept, cooking some parts of her body before disposing of them in plastic bags around the rubbish tips and wastelands of East London.

Some six days later Nicholas Boyce called with the children at the home of a friend, saying that he was going to the police because he had killed Christabel. He maintained then, and to the police later, that he couldn't remember anything about the events, or about what had happened to the body. Without the body, the police would have had to rely on Boyce's story as to how Christabel had met her death, which he maintained had been as a result of his defending himself against her. After lengthy interrogation Boyce began to impart, piece by piece, information which led to recovery of bits of the body, but the major concern of the police was to find Christabel's severed head. This was finally recovered encased in concrete and stuffed in a bag which had been thrown into the Thames.

Forensic examination of the skull showed serious injuries, and it was only then that Nicholas Boyce confessed to strangling his wife with a ligature and furiously beating her. At his trial he pleaded not guilty to murder but guilty to manslaughter on the grounds of provocation by his wife. He mounted a defence based on the character and behaviour of Christabel, maintaining that she terrified and tormented him, that he had to work day and night taking on the roles that she neglected by going out to work – like doing the laundry, shopping and feeding the baby. He claimed that she humiliated him as a man and thought his thesis worthless.

The unmanning of Nicholas Boyce by his cruel wife stunned Christabel's friends and colleagues who attended the trial: it bore no relation to the woman they knew. They had seen the efforts to function as breadwinner as well as mother and knew her as gentle, kind-hearted and generous. These were people who had observed the dynamics of this couple at close quarters and who found the descriptions by the defence untenable.

Within the privacy of marriage a very different power relationship can exist to the one presented to the world. However, the people who campaigned to clear Christabel Boyce's name were able to refute many of the suggestions made about their dead friend and were not just moved by an unreasoning commitment to her memory. After the trial they complained to the Director of Public Prosecutions that they had had no opportunity to rebut the claims made by Nicholas Boyce. To their knowledge, the defendant was a self-absorbed depressive of whom Christabel was very afraid. Shortly before her death she told friends that she had asked him for a divorce and his response had filled her with foreboding.

Nicholas Boyce was acquitted of murder. He was sentenced for manslaughter by the Recorder of London, Sir James Miskin, who retired in July 1990 amidst a furore arising from his views on justice. In a retirement interview with the BBC he took the opportunity to hold forth on his low regard for jurors and his disgust at the release of the Guildford Four, inventing a scenario to explain the discovered police interviews which involved fantastical events including the bribing of a policeman by the IRA. Sir James's views were another embarrassing exposure of what is happening under certain judicial wigs. He sentenced Nicholas Boyce to six years' imprisonment.

The trial of Peter Wood for the killing of Mary Bristow is another example of blaming the victim. At Winchester Crown Court he pleaded guilty to manslaughter and not guilty to murder, on the grounds of provocation and diminished responsibility. Mary Bristow was a single woman of 36, a graduate who had worked as a librarian for fifteen years. She had her own small house in Winchester where Peter Wood first came as a lodger to help contribute to her overheads. He became her lover, and although Mary Bristow admitted the nature of the relationship to her friends she did not acknowledge him as her boyfriend or present herself as part of a couple. For her, the relationship never had that quality, although clearly Peter Wood was emotionally involved. Because of his demands she asked him to leave, but according to friends he kept coming back, unable to accept the relationship was over.

In October 1981 Peter Wood returned once more, climbing into her house through the back and waiting for her return. According to him they talked, made love, and then he battered her with a meat tenderiser which he had previously inserted into a sock.

When she still appeared to have life in her he smothered her with a pillow and strangled her with his bare hands. At his trial Peter Wood could probably have secured a not guilty verdict by virtue of his own mental state, without the need for any attack to be made upon the character of Mary Bristow. However, attack there certainly was. According to the defence counsel, Patrick Back QC, 'she was middle class and as often happens with very clever people she was in a state of rebellion against the morality favoured by that class'. This rebellion was then presented as a rejection of marriage and a devotion to causes such as Women's Lib, pro-abortion campaigns and CND – all of which was designed to strike terror into the hearts of Winchester jurymen. For her friends, this was a crude parody of the compassionate, independent woman they knew, whose political convictions were a clear extension of her care for people. They saw Peter Wood as just another of the lame dogs who attached themselves to her, drawing on her warmth and generosity. The defence projected Mary Bristow as a manipulative woman who had played with Wood's emotions in a calculated way. To onlookers the dead Mary Bristow was on trial by inference and innuendo.

In his summing-up, the judge took up the defence line about Mary Bristow's unorthodox lifestyle, saying that highly intelligent people were not always wise. 'Playing with sex,' he said, 'is playing with fire.' His view was clear: Mary Bristow had only herself to blame, because she had conducted a sexual relationship on the kind of footing we expect only of men – uncommitted, without romance, and outside marriage.

Peter Woods was acquitted of murder, found guilty of man-slaughter and sentenced to six years' imprisonment.

Of course, lawyers are also able to undermine the credibility of male witnesses or victims, but the moral component is rarely present and seldom carries the same force. In discrediting men, it is rare that an attack goes to the foundations of their manliness, the only comparable inference being in relation to homosexuality or the sexual abuse of children. We may impugn them for their violence, neglect or greed, with varying degrees of success, but none of them would be reduced in the eyes of the court for an uncommitted sexual relationship, for choosing not to marry or for failing to fulfil domestic chores.

The essential otherness of women can also colour the decisions male lawyers make. Harold Cassell was prosecuting counsel in a case involving rape and murder. The victim was a shy 16-year-old girl who was sexually inexperienced, an only child of aging parents. Yvonne Swaffer had never had boyfriends and her limited social life revolved around the local Methodist church. She had gone rather diffidently to a local disco with some friends and never returned. Her death shocked not only her parents but everyone who knew her, and the subsequent court hearing in 1975 filled them with horror.

A man called Ronald Birchell, who was a complete stranger to Yvonne, was indicted for her killing. His lawyers claimed that he had met Yvonne as she was walking home and that she had initiated the contact by asking for a cigarette. According to him, he put his arm around her and she then took his hand and put it on her breast. They had then gone into a secluded area and she had readily made love with him. Although she had agreed to sex, she started to scream afterwards and he had stuffed her stockings into her mouth to keep her quiet. No one will ever know what a jury would have made of this account, especially with the knowledge, confirmed by a pathologist, that she was a virgin and was menstruating at the time of the offences. The prosecution agreed to offer no evidence with regard to the rape and to reduce the charge of murder to manslaughter on the grounds of provocation.

The defence then proceeded, without any challenge, to mitigate Birchell's conduct on the basis that he had been led on by a young temptress whose death was the accidental consequence of her own sexual game-playing. The hearing was over in forty minutes. Birchell got four years for manslaughter. Mr and Mrs Swaffer were left bewildered. No one ever explained to them the rationale for not proceeding with a trial where a jury could have assessed the evidence. Years later, after painful enquiries, they received a letter from Sam Silkin, the retired Attorney-General, apologising for the conduct of the case.

Men do not menstruate, so I suppose it would never occur to some of them that it would be unlikely for a teenage girl to embark on her first sexual encounter with a stranger when she was having her period.

In 1990 Harold Cassell took early retirement from the judicial post he eventually held because of his comments when he sentenced a man for unlawful sexual intercourse with his 12-year-old stepdaughter. His Honour took the view that it was understandable for a man with a healthy sexual appetite to be driven to such behaviour when his pregnant wife had lost interest in sex. He sentenced the man to probation.

The failure of understanding is nowhere more clearly visible than in the handling of rape cases.

> Women who say no do not always mean no. It is not just a question of how she says it, how she shows and makes it clear. If she doesn't want it she only has to keep her legs shut and she would not get it without force and then there would be the marks of force being used.

This was part of Judge Wild's direction to a jury in a rape trial in 1982. Similar words were used by Judge Dean at the Old Bailey in 1990, and countless other judges must be breathing sighs of relief at having escaped press attention.

The word 'no' is at the core of a rape trial. A 'no' may be taken for granted when a respectable woman is attacked by a total stranger in a dimly lit street, but since the majority of rapes are committed by men known to the victim, consent in rape trials has always been an issue which makes men very nervous. Where does seduction end and rape begin? It is the subject of the old lawyer's joke about how to tread the fine line between tax evasion, which is criminal, and tax avoidance, which is every reasonable man's goal in life. As with rape and seduction, it is all supposed to be a matter of technique. Getting a woman to submit is an acceptable part of the sexual game plan, and straying across the line a ready peril for any man with a healthy sexual appetite. The notion that women, having been pressed into submission, will melt into the experience and find pleasure in it often erases responsibility for violence, fear and humiliation. Examples abound, like this one from a trial at the Old Bailey (Sue Lees, *New Statesman*, December 1989):

Prosecuting Counsel:	'And you say she consented?'
Defendant:	'I didn't say she consented.'
Prosecuting Counsel:	'Did she agree?'
Defendant:	'She didn't agree.'
Prosecuting Counsel:	'Having said no at first, she just gave in?'
Defendant:	'She enjoyed it.'

Here the Judge intervened with some judicial assistance:

	'The enjoyment wiped out her initial resistance – is that what you are saying.'
Defendant:	'Yes.'

However, the way young women are initiated in the protocol of sex also helps keep the lines blurred. Girls are still told to be sensitive to the feelings of young men, to avoid telling them they are not fancied. Excuses are supposed to be better than rejection and confused messages can be communicated. 'I can't, I'm having my period' – 'I have to go home' – 'I have a boyfriend.' The recitation is endless: all to avoid saying the hurtful 'no'.

In English law a married woman's 'no' was meaningless, since a wife was not supposed to deny her husband his conjugal rights. There was deemed to be no such thing as rape within marriage until March 1991. Then, miraculously, the former Lord Chief Justice, Lord Lane, asserted that married women were entitled to the same protection as any other woman.

In the view of some men, any woman's 'no' is covered in ambiguity, not to be taken seriously if she is vivacious and friendly, if she dresses provocatively, if she goes out late at night or has had sex with others before. It is an exercise of male power to subject a woman to sex, and in saying 'no' to sex women challenge that power.

Despite advice from their brethren that they should watch out for mantraps containing snarling feminists, judges tend to take on the furies like demented lemmings. After every outrageous statement made by a judge in a rape trial there are calls for sackings and questions in the House. The judge in question is publicly silent but privately bewildered, asking colleagues where he went wrong.

There is surprise amongst the judiciary when they discover that (in fact) women's anger about the handling of rape cases is not confined to feminists but is more universal. Nor, of course, are the attitudes of our judges limited just to them.

Rape summons up long-learned fears whispered into the ears of boys about the fickleness and deceit of women – fears that women are vindictive and bitter, that they will stop at nothing to trap a man and stoop to anything to make him pay; fears that the line which separates rape from seduction is easily crossed, and any decent fellow is at the mercy of an unscrupulous female. Our judges are not immune.

At legal dinners, rape jokes used to be constant, although there seems to be a bit more restraint now. I am told that they are still a favourite in the male robing rooms. Did you hear the one about the woman who claimed she was raped and ran from a house clutching a doormat to cover her nakedness? Counsel for the defence asked if there was a 'Welcome' on her mat. Or the old chestnut about the woman who was describing the act of penetration by her attacker. 'He put his penis into me,' she says. 'Well, let's leave it there until after lunch,' suggests His Lordship.

The shared belief underlying the humour is that deep down women want sex but do not always know their own minds. It is not enough to say 'no'. Men hear a challenge to their masculinity in the sound. Sometimes, according to the *Boy's Own* theories about women, it is a female ploy to play hard to get in case men think they are easy or cheap. The signposts are hard to follow and the perils engage the fellow-feeling of every man who has ever pressed his attentions, as well as parts of his anatomy, on a less than enthusiastic woman.

For the most part, problems of men identifying with male accused do not arise in the trial of the stranger-rape, happening at knifepoint in the dark of night. Everyone, male and female alike, is united in their sense of outrage. However, even in these cases, distinctions drawn between worthy and unworthy women affect the strength of that outrage, as we saw in the investigation and coverage of the Yorkshire Ripper case. The whole tone of the police appeals to the public changed once it became clear that the victims were not 'only' prostitutes and that all women were at risk.

Yet even in stranger-rape cases, defences can be built upon the premise that the defendant believed the woman was consenting. The incredulity of juries is increasing slightly, the result of a growth in public awareness, and also perhaps of the greater numbers of women who sit on them. However, women on juries can be as unforgiving of unconventional female behaviour as any man. Rape still has a lower conviction rate than any other serious crime.

The complainant in a rape case is required to be the ideal victim, sexually inexperienced or at least respectable. If she is middle-aged and perhaps divorced, frustration and loneliness are presented as motives for her consenting to sex with an unlikely partner. Women are asked questions which are never put to men about why they were out alone in the street or in a pub or at a disco. They are asked about their clothing: the tightness of the fit, the absence of a bra. They are asked about their use of contraception. And this is before we even get to sexual history. There is great concern expressed about women being cross-examined about previous sexual relationships, but much of the cross-examination which does not fall under that heading is almost as objectionable. Few women escape the inquisition and possible humiliation of cross-examination by the barrister of an inventive defendant. Sometimes the questions themselves are enormously damaging. 'Is it not the case that you were smoking cannabis earlier that evening?' Juries assume the lawyer knows something they do not; the denial still leaves a lurking doubt about the kind of woman she is. In Australia and Canada judges are charged with ensuring that no questioning of the complainant is carried out in an unduly harassing or degrading manner, and in our own courts progress will be made only if judges recognise the hidden judgements secreted in these questions. I have come to the conclusion that introducing formal training sessions to raise their awareness is the only way forward – an idea which they are strenuously resisting.

Crude populist psychology is used in courtrooms to suggest subconscious desires that are not even acknowledged by the woman herself. A woman is asked whether her vagina naturally lubricated to enable penetration, thereby encouraging the jury to infer that some gratification was being found in the sexual contact. Her reliability as a witness is challenged on the basis that her true sexual nature and desire for domination is so repressed that she has now reconstructed events and believes them herself. Her credibility is thus being challenged, not on the basis of her lying, but of not even knowing that she is lying!

To explain away multiple acts of rape, a gang-bang or physical injury, defence lawyers may even suggest to the jury that many women are turned on by violence and enjoy kinky sex or a 'bit of rough'. There is no winning. Without the physical signs of resistance, such as bruising, it is (automatically) assumed that the victim consented or is subject to female rape fantasies; where she does bear the signs of attack she is challenged as a masochist.

On the one hand psychiatry is mistrusted in the courtroom as hocus pocus which distracts jurors from the main issues, but on the other it can prove very useful in undermining the value of testimony. The slightest hint of anything which might affect the mind, particularly of a female witness, can jeopardise a case.

I have heard it suggested to a woman in a rape case that she had a history of mental illness which, as it turned out, was a breakdown under the pressure of taking her university finals, from which she rapidly recovered. The suggestion was used to undermine her as someone whose mental stability was questionable and might lead to her making irrational allegations. The leaps involved in such innuendo are never examined, and the damage can be irreparable unless the woman is given time to explain at length whole areas of her life which have no relevance to the proceedings.

A woman magistrate described a foraging exercise she witnessed at a committal proceedings, where a woman was asked whether she had ever taken medication such as tranquillisers. Her truthful answer unravelled an account of depression after the death of her father. This in turn was used to suggest that she had sought solace in the arms of her assailant, over which she had later felt guilt.

Suggestions of instability cling to women much more readily than to men, and even a mention of going to psychotherapy in search of self-enlightenment is confused with mental illness. There are no dividing lines for many people. 'Psycho' means mad, and barristers know the mileage that can be made with juries at the merest hint of any problem.

Crude psychologising in courts is unforgivable, but particularly so when it is done in the name of professional expertise. In 1989 Lorraine Miles won an unprecedented legal action for rape damages in the High Court when she received £25,000. It was the first time in history that a rape victim had sued when her assailant had not previously been convicted in the criminal courts. The prosecuting authorities had taken the view that there was little chance of a successful prosecution, since there was no corroboration of Ms Miles's account. Decisions about whether or not to bring a case to court are made by evaluating the quality of the evidence; prosecution authorities claim the measure is whether there is more than a 50 per cent chance of success. Many rape cases founder on this test. Such evaluations of the evidence do not inhibit civil proceedings because the standard of proof is lower in civil law than in crime, and Lorraine Miles's law suit gave rise to what I considered to be the alarming situation of a man more or less standing trial for rape without a jury, and without the requirement that the case against him be proved beyond reasonable doubt: all because of the corroboration rule.

In civil litigation the case only has to be proved on the balance of probabilities, and Mr Justice 'fragrant' Caulfield, on balance, did believe Ms Miles's account that she was raped by Kenneth Cain, a physiotherapist, at his surgery when she had been 'prostrate, passive and a relaxed patient'. Evidence was given at the trial by Dr Gerald Silverman, a psychiatrist, who appeared for the defendant and claimed that Ms Miles might have fantasised or imagined her ordeal. He maintained that women who were raped, as alleged in this case, would recover within approximately three months, and the fact that Ms Miles was still clearly disturbed by her alleged experience so long after the event suggested that she must have suffered from some form of neurosis which would make her more likely to dream up the experience of the assault.

Psychiatrists who work with rape victims hotly dispute this generalised theory that women get over rape quickly if they are well
adjusted. The case was, however, overturned in the Court of
Appeal, primarily because the evidence was substantiated in no
independent way, and Lorraine Miles could not face taking it any
further.

The law does not require corroboration in support of a woman's
testimony, but the judge is required to warn the jury of the dangers
of convicting solely on the testimony of the woman and to tell
them to look for supporting evidence. It is an unacceptable anomaly that this has to be done, and it has the overwhelming affect
on a jury of undermining perfectly credible women. Legal grey-
suits always jump in to point out that the corroboration warning
is required in all cases of a sexual nature, that it is not just women
whose evidence needs some independent back-up. But who are
these other people whose word is questionable? Who are these
victims of sexual assault, other than children and possibly homo-
sexuals, whose accounts are always considered suspect anyway?
The word of grown heterosexual men is never automatically called
into question, because the chances of their being sexually assaulted
are pretty rare. As the Law Commissioner Brenda Hoggett and
her co-author Susan Atkins pointed out in their book *Women and
the Law*: 'Can it be coincidence that the only civil case in which
corroboration is required is where the mother of an illegitimate
child gives evidence against the father in affiliation proceedings?'

Lawyers are past masters at the art of subtle discrimination.
However, some disingenuous soul usually gives the game away,
and in the case of the corroboration rule it was Judge Sutcliffe,
who in 1976 reminded a jury that 'it is well known that women
in particular and small boys are liable to be untruthful and invent
stories'. It is interesting to speculate about when the moment of
transition takes place and lying little boys become truthful male
adults.

A ludicrous situation arises in cases where a man breaks into a
woman's house, burgles the premises and then rapes her. The
judge has the task of explaining to the jury that it could be
dangerous to convict on the uncorroborated evidence of the

woman in respect of the rape, but not dangerous so far as the burglary is concerned.

In accordance with the established case law a judge would be perfectly entitled to use the established rape case formula and explain to the jury that the burgled householder might have made a false allegation owing to 'sexual neurosis, fantasy, spite or refusal to admit consent of which she is now ashamed'. It is hard to imagine any woman who is having her stereo purloined deciding to dally with the burglar, and the Court of Appeal has now drawn up complicated guidelines as to how the judge should direct the jury in burglary cases with a rape allegation.

An overhaul of the rules on corroboration is urgently needed. It seems extraordinary that an accused person can be convicted on a confession obtained in dubious circumstances without any supporting material, while a jury is warned that a woman's charge of rape should be approached with caution unless substantiated with evidence from another source. The judge's direction should be reformulated, putting the emphasis on the jury's right to convict should they believe the woman's evidence and reminding them that all women are entitled to say 'no'. This should in no way detract from the insistence that confessions to the police be corroborated, because there is a qualitative difference between self-incriminating evidence secured by those acting for the state and the direct evidence of a witness who maintains he or she was the victim of a crime, as in robbery.

The issue at the heart of the rape case is credibility. Is the woman telling the truth about what happened? But this is precisely the decision juries make daily in our courtrooms when they assess the witnesses and the facts. Are rape cases rendered special because of the sexual component? Is rape different from other offences of violence because of the profound emotions and complicated psychological responses that men and women have to sex? Yes, it is different, but not so different as to invite a completely different set of values. In most cases juries can separate false from reliable evidence without judges or defence counsel wading in with half-baked theories about sexual neurosis and female fantasies and the need to approach a woman's evidence with special caution.

Of course, there are women who lie. There are a few misguided or malicious women who make false allegations of rape, and it is essential that the strong protections for defendants which exist within our system are jealously maintained. However, the change in social mores means few women now cover up their own indiscretions or pregnancies by laying a false allegation at the door of some innocent lover. The days of tyrannical fathers raging at the deflowering of their daughters have happily receded, and women do not feel under so much pressure to deny their willing participation in sexual acts. The premium on virginity has largely disappeared and women feel freer to include sexual activity in their lives, but they want their sexual relationships to be based on mutuality and equality. The emphasis is on choice, and women are rightly indignant that they are viewed and tested according to outmoded assumptions.

Juries gauge the truthfulness of witnesses in the way that we all do – by watching their demeanour and listening to their account, especially when it is being tested under cross-examination. Sometimes inconsistency counts against someone, sometimes it is utterly explicable given normal failure of memory or the trauma of events. Sometimes people lie about insignificant issues because of a misguided notion that the truth will count against them. There are times when this is fatal to a case, because juries then worry about what part of a witness's evidence they can believe. At other times the quality of detail and the sheer conviction with which the witness testifies on the crucial aspects of a case leaves them in no doubt as to where the truth lies. Additional evidence from an independent source makes the task easier; the privacy within which intercourse usually occurs will always mean that the jury will feel anxious about whether the allegation has been proved beyond reasonable doubt. However, there is no good reason for encouraging strong cases to fail for want of corroboration.

Discussions in courtrooms and barristers' chambers around the country expose the views still held by many lawyers and judges. Prosecution and defence lawyers frequently maintain that a rape took place because of sex starvation when the accused's wife was pregnant or ill or otherwise out of action. 'Victim to his libido' is the recurring theme in the mitigation plea for a convicted rapist.

If a woman has been in any way familiar, we are presented with the old idea of man, the overheated engine, incapable of switching off. We are to treat him as the functional equivalent of a handgun, something intrinsically dangerous.

Long sentences are not of themselves the answer to rape, and in most cases real psychiatric help would provide greater and longer term protection for women. What is needed, more than a change in sentencing, is an appropriate judicial response to rape, a change to the prevailing view that bank robbery is more deserving of condemnation. A very senior male police officer told me of a recent meeting with judges and the feeling of being catapulted back in time. The views were in keeping with those of the police ten or fifteen years ago.

Sentencing is a minefield for judges. The pressure is on to reduce the prison population, to give due credit to those who plead guilty and save victims the degradation of giving evidence about some appalling event. The youth of a defendant should reduce the length of a prison term, because of their inexperience of life and a greater optimism about their rehabilitation. Many factors count, and a cold appraisal or comparison of sentences can be a fruitless exercise. The passing of a non-custodial sentence by Mr Justice Ognall on two 16-year-old offenders who pleaded guilty to the rape of a girl in their children's home was undoubtedly the correct course, especially since it meant the boys having psychiatric treatment, but it was met with criticism by Women against Rape. Justice Ognall's use of the word 'prank' for the event, was not, however, sensible.

As we have seen, it is often in their unguarded moments when passing sentence that judges disclose their prejudices. I remember blanching early on in my practice when I heard Sir Melford Stevenson, a judge who was extravagant in doling out long sentences, being generous to a rape defendant because, he said, the girl was 'asking for it'. She had been hitch-hiking, a far more serious offence in His Lordship's view. The rape was described as 'an anaemic affair as rapes go', as though something a bit more colourful might be expected from a red-blooded rapist. The sentence was suspended.

Since then, the cases which have hit the news are legendary: the guardsman who walked free after his conviction because of his fine service record, although his victim's vagina was torn by the rings on his hand; the woman who was 'contributory negligent' because she was walking alone at night; and so on. Some of the most notorious cases have given rise to extensive criticism of the particular judges involved. In 1990, Mr Justice Jupp passed a suspended sentence on a man who twice raped his ex-wife, explaining that this was 'a rare sort of rape. It is not like someone being jumped in the street. This is within the family and does not impinge on the public.' Mr Justice Leonard, in the Vicarage rape case, passed sentences of five years and three years on the defendants because the victim had apparently made a 'remarkable recovery'. Lucky defendants! They had repeatedly raped the victim at knifepoint, forced her to have oral sex, and penetrated her anally with the handle of a knife. Any recovery was no thanks to them. Since the trial the young woman has courageously written and spoken publicly about her experience, and has been deeply critical of the judge.

In 1986 two paratroopers had their sentences of eighteen months reduced because their victim was 'dissolute and sexually depraved'. In July 1991 Mr Justice Alliot gave a rapist a three-year jail sentence, although the recommended minimum for someone found guilty of the offence is five years, because his victim was a 'common prostitute' and a 'whore'. In passing sentence he explained, 'While every woman is entitled to complain about being violated, someone who for years has flaunted their body and sold it cannot complain as loudly as someone who has not . . . '

The fact that a male judge may himself never have such an experience is not enough to explain the frequent insensitivity and apparent failure to identify with the victim. The leap of imagination required to appreciate the effect of the crime does not fail a judge when dealing with victims of terrorism or burglary or kidnapping.

According to Professor Glanville Williams in the current edition of his *Textbook of Criminal Law* (1990), the fact that some women enjoy fantasies of rape is well authenticated; he cites as his authority Helene Deutsch's *The Psychology of Women* (published forty-five years ago) and Paul H. Gebhard's *Sex Offenders: an Analysis of Types* (published twenty-five years ago). He includes no contemporary references and seems to take no account of the possibility that a woman might enjoy a private fantasy where she is in control, whilst not welcoming the reality.

A footnote in the textbook states the concerns of the lawyer MP Nicholas Fairbairn, who foresees a new peril of false complaints arising from an announcement by the Criminal Injuries Compensation Board that they value a proven rape at £2,250. Professor Williams endorses this fear: 'In view of the serious difficulties of rape charges it seems of doubtful policy to attach such a financial inducement to the obtaining of a conviction.' Nowhere is the same fear expressed about people inventing robberies or policemen inventing assaults for the purpose of reward.

These attitudes are not confined to those in the legal profession. The eminent forensic pathologist Frederick Camps, in an article in *The Practitioner* in 1962, disclosed just how much importance was then placed on medical opinion. He maintained that many allegations were untrue, reiterating the well-worn adage that rape is impossible: 'If it were not for the fact that rape can take place from fear, the problem might be fairly easy to solve, for a fully conscious woman of normal physique should not be able to have her legs separated by one man against her will.'

To ensure a fair trial for men who may be wrongly accused, it is essential that only proper admissible evidence goes before a jury, and that a jury is reminded of the high standard of proof which must exist before convicting. However, there are other important facts which juries should know and be able to place on the scales of justice. This requires direction from a judge who truly understands the offence of rape.

The very nature of rape tends to locate the crime in the privacy of a closed room, in dimly lit streets, in the shadow of darkness. There are rarely eye-witnesses. Forensic evidence may prove that intercourse took place or, with the new genetic testing of semen, confirm the identity of the assailant. But in the majority of cases the defendant is not denying that he performed the sexual act. The issue in 88 per cent of cases is whether the woman consented. Judges and juries are more convinced if they can see torn knickers and proof that the victim was beaten, but even the signs of resistance have to be more than the odd bruise, which defendants explain away as the result of vigorous sex-play and playful pinching. The paradox is that the requirement to show that they put up a fight flies in the face of everything we are told about self-protection. As one victim said when interviewed about her experience, 'Everything I did right to save my life is exactly wrong in terms of proving I was telling the truth.'

Most rape-prevention education advises women not to invite greater harm by fighting the assailant, who may have a weapon. The extensive reporting of cases where women have been raped and then killed confirms that the violence may not stop at the act of rape, and it may be better not to antagonise the attacker. The persistent cross-examination ploy of defence counsel is to deny that fear might paralyse the victim and to insist that a woman guarding her virtue would fight like a lioness. We are still haunted by powerful cultural images of what good women do in the face of ravishment. In a long literary tradition which begins with Livy and Ovid, Lucretia fights off her attacker and refuses to yield to his threats. The deed done, she takes her own life. In Lorenzo Lotto's famous painting in the National Gallery, there is a note on the table by the victim's side which declares: 'NEC ULLA IMPUDICA LUCRETIA EXEMPLO VIVET' – we would have no immoral women if Lucretia's example were followed.

What all this means is that, since there is rarely much independent evidence of the complainant's account, the jury and the judge are thrown back on the impression made by the victim in the witness box. It is as though *she* were the person on trial. Although the law has changed to protect women against being questioned unfairly about their past conduct, it still happens all too regularly. The defence has to apply for judicial leave to cross-examine, which the judge can and does allow where, in his discretion, it might directly assist the jury in their approach to an issue in the case. The evidence should not just impugn the credibility of the witness, but it is often hard to separate out those two strands.

In a recent rape trial the complainant said she would not have consented to intercourse in her bedroom because her child was sleeping there. The judge refused the defence permission to cross-examine on the statement of a former boyfriend that he had had intercourse with her in the bedroom, or to call such evidence. The Court of Appeal quashed the conviction, holding that this should have been allowed, as it did not just go to credibility but to the issue of consent (*R v Riley*, 1991).

Evidence which a judge rules admissible to assess the issue of consent almost invariably impugns the character of the woman. If there has been evidence about reddening and soreness of the victim's vagina, providing some corroboration of violent penetration, the defence may seek to introduce evidence of other recent sexual activity or practices which would account for the vaginal condition. By an alternative route an attack can, therefore, be mounted on the female witness which leaves the unspoken word 'slut' running around the courtroom. However, in some circumstances such evidence could be vital to the defence, and a blanket rule disallowing all cross-examination as to other sexual relations would be unjust. The simplification of the arguments as they are sometimes presented has not been helpful in addressing the complicated question of when such cross-examination is justified. Maintaining a proper balance between the rights of victims and those of defendants is fraught with difficulty.

Nowadays there is rarely cross-examination on a woman's past in total stranger-rape, but if the man has even a passing knowledge of the woman it is much easier to blacken her character and fabricate convincing stories about her behaviour.

There is also a strange anomaly whereby cross-examination about sex with other men requires leave from the judge, while cross-examination about previous sex with the defendant needs no permission at all. If you have a nodding acquaintance with the penis in question, the whole business is considered to be altogether less serious.

However, the issues are rarely simple. The following cases, used in a judicial training course in the United States, show the problems which arise.

In one case the victim is a trained masseuse who normally works with female clients but accepts male clients on recommendation. One such was referred to her by a doctor friend who felt the defendant was suffering severe stress in his work as an executive. She testified that the defendant came to her by appointment a week before the alleged rape and that she performed her usual massage, which did not involve touching the sexual organs. There was no conversation beyond normal pleasantries. A week later, according to her evidence, the doorbell rang at 8 p.m. and the defendant asked to come in. He appeared somewhat intoxicated and she was reluctant to admit him as she was alone, but eventually did so because he was so insistent that he just wanted to talk to someone. He said he was feeling low and wanted a massage. She said it was too late, whereupon he became belligerent and loud in his tone. She asked him to leave and he calmed down, saying how depressed he was over work problems and all he needed was a massage. She reluctantly agreed.

After the defendant had undressed and covered himself with a towel the complainant began the massage. Within a short time the defendant started making inappropriate comments about her looks, and when he turned on to his back he grabbed her hands and forced them on to his penis. When she resisted he became violent, struck her to the floor, removed her pants and raped her. He then dressed, threw some money on the massage table and left.

Medical evidence showed a bruise on the side of the woman's head where she said it had struck the table in the struggle, and there was flesh under her nails which she said was a result of her scratching her assailant. A neighbour testified that she appeared at her door at 8.20 p.m., said she had been raped and asked that the police be called. The victim appeared in control and was not hysterical, but asked to wait at the neighbour's flat as she was afraid to go back to her own.

The defence applied to cross-examine the witness as to her sexual past, claiming that they had evidence that on a previous occasion a client had asked her to massage his penis until he ejaculated and that she had agreed to do so for an extra fee. They also wanted to produce evidence from the police files that some neighbours had complained to the police about her activities, alleging she was operating as a prostitute.

Should a judge allow such cross-examination and subsequently let such evidence be given? Few judges would allow the evidence of unsubstantiated complaint by neighbours to the police, but many would allow the initial questions about her conduct with a past client and whether the woman had ever masturbated clients in the course of her work. She may deny this quite truthfully or may lie in her denial, but in either case the focus of the trial moves to the morality of the woman. There is no doubt such allegations would add to a jury's general suspicion that massage provides a cover for prostitution. But even if a woman had been prepared to masturbate a man on a previous occasion, does that make her more likely to have consented to full intercourse on this occasion? What prostitute fails to get her money in advance, and why the evidence of struggle?

In another case the victim was a young married woman whose husband frequently worked away from home. She testified that when he was away she sometimes went for a drink to a local pub on her way home from the office. This pub was frequented by old schoolfriends who still lived in the neighbourhood.

On the day in question she called in for a drink and met an old boyfriend whom she had known as a teenager. They had several drinks together and the defendant suggested he walk her home. She agreed, and when they got to her door he asked if he could use her telephone. She testified that she went to the bathroom whilst she believed he was making the phone-call. As she came out he pulled her down on to the couch and told her he wanted her. When she resisted and told him to leave he ripped off her blouse and punched her in the jaw. He then pushed her on to the floor, pulled off her pants and had intercourse with her. At this moment, as in some Feydeau farce, her husband came through the door. The husband testified that he saw the two having intercourse on the floor and that the lights were on. The defendant immediately got up, said, 'Your wife isn't worth shit,' and walked out before the husband could do anything. He gave evidence that his wife's blouse was torn and that her jaw was red and beginning to swell. She was crying and hysterical. The husband called the police immediately and the police doctor confirmed the swelling to the jaw and testified to reddening of the vulva. No sperm were present, as no doubt the spouse's timely arrival deflated enthusiasm, but ejaculation is not necessary to prove rape.

The defendant's counsel applied to cross-examine the complainant on her previous sexual conduct. The defence had statements from the barman in the pub who had seen the complainant drinking in the bar, often getting drunk. He had also seen her leave several times in the company of men. Another witness would testify that he had met the complainant in the bar some months earlier and had drunk with her a number of times. On one occasion he had invited her back to his flat, where they had had intercourse. A third would say that he, too, had known the complainant at school and that in recent months she had made a pass at him, telling him her husband was out of town and inviting him in.

Judges vary in their approach to this kind of material and its admissibility. There is insufficient opportunity for scrutiny of judges' rulings because when such evidence is allowed the result is invariably an acquittal. The woman has no right of appeal, and therefore no appeal or law-reporting ensue. Some valuable research was conducted in 1982 by Zsuzsanna Adler at the Old Bailey, which showed that judges then frequently allowed cross-examination as to sexual history. A new monitoring project would be very instructive on the present approach to these decisions, particularly outside London, and would undoubtedly affect judicial awareness. However, the real way forward requires proper judicial training to address these and similar issues.

This raises another problem in rape cases: that not enough account is taken of the traumatic effect of the experience. Women who have been raped use different coping devices just to live with themselves after the assault, and some are able to draw upon reserves of composure and poise which can work against them with the judge and jury. Others manifest signs of rape trauma syndrome, including a strange distancing from the event, which makes them seem cool and unemotional. The very resources a woman may use to assuage the horror of the experience can be held against her by police officers, lawyers and judges at her trial. Dr Philip Sealy, a British psychologist, conducted research ten years ago which showed that the law is more likely to protect the woman who makes a favourable impression. There is no reason to think that anything has changed.

The American celebrity trials of William Kennedy-Smith, nephew of the former President, and of Mike Tyson, the boxing champion, highlighted the problems. When a woman has gone voluntarily with a man to the beach or his room and has willingly participated in some level of intimacy, her consent to those stages of the contact is imported into the sexual act, unless like Desiree Washington, the beauty queen who was raped by Tyson, she is the perfect witness, radiating truthfulness and tangible distress. By contrast, the victim in the Kennedy-Smith case, Patricia Bowman, was considered unimpressive, and the suggestion of drink and drugs hung over the trial.

In *The Fact of Rape*, Barbara Toner quotes a police officer and a barrister on the importance of a woman's performance. The police officer remarked, 'A good witness relives the experience in court. She doesn't hold back her emotions. If she wants to cry, she bloody well cries. If she wants a drink of water, she asks. She re-experiences the feelings she has at the time. A bad witness will frustrate the court.' The barrister said:

> When I say she was a good witness, I mean she was clearly telling the truth. There was a marvellous moment when she looked towards the dock and caught his eye. She totally broke down. The defence counsel and I both agreed it was one of the most harrowing moments we had been through, because she was obviously reliving one of the worst moments of her life. A bad witness is one who will be dogmatic about something that she couldn't possibly be dogmatic about or doesn't answer the questions, or has a detached sort of manner.

Yet often the one thing a victim cannot bring herself to do is to relive the event before a courtroom of strangers. The reason for a rape victim's inability to 'emote' may be nothing to do with her credibility but a direct result of the rape itself. This is something the judiciary should learn about and be able to explain to a jury.

Women frequently describe their trauma in the courtroom as a further abuse. This may sound hysterical and exaggerated, but part of the problem is that a woman's powerlessness in the trial evokes all the feelings of powerlessness that were experienced in the original rape. She has no lawyer and is no more than a witness being called by the Crown, subject to the same constraints. American films like *The Accused* mislead British women into thinking they will have their own barrister who will talk them through the issues. In reality, counsel for the prosecution is constrained from talking to a victim at all under the Bar's professional rules. The process, therefore, seems remote and unconcerned with her feelings.

A central problem about 'consent' is that the real issue for the jury is not whether the woman did in fact consent but whether the male defendant thought she consented. In a recent case in Nottingham an elderly woman was so paralysed by fear that she responded like an automaton when she was attacked by an acquaintance in her own home. The defendant maintained that she gave him no indication that his advances were unwelcome and put up no resistance whatsoever. The woman described with terrible poignancy getting into the bath after the assault and how, whilst lying in the water, she wanted to slip below the surface and die. Those in court felt it was the sheer power of her description that secured a conviction. However, not all women have that facility. If a man can satisfy the jury that he might well have thought a woman was consenting, he is acquitted. In proving this scenario he is usually allowed to introduce evidence of the woman's sexual history to support his state of mind at the time: that she was a woman indiscriminate in her choice of sexual partners. Unlike the woman, the defendant, if never convicted before, can call character witnesses to say what a decent, gentle fellow he is. A woman can say 'no' repeatedly, but if the defendant says he understood it was a cry of ecstasy he may well be acquitted.

In criminal law it is quite usual to apply a subjective test in deciding whether an accused intended to commit a crime. The *mens rea* or mental element of a crime is usually based on the intention of the accused at the time. However, there are significant areas of crime where the law imposes an external gauge as to what is permissible. In self-defence, for example, the level of the force used to protect yourself has to be reasonable. To succeed as a defence to murder, provocation must be words or deeds which would make a 'reasonable man' lose control. The issue therefore arises as to whether there should be a similar rule for sexual offences, with an objective rather than a subjective test. The jury would then be asked whether a reasonable person would have known that the woman was not consenting. The criteria should be absence of consent, not presence of dissent. Making such a change should not be leapt upon in the mistaken belief that it would remedy all the problems, but if a judge had to emphasise to a jury that the man's belief must be reasonable it would undermine the theory that women say 'no' meaning yes.

Sir Matthew Hale, an eighteenth-century legal commentator, is held responsible for much of the jurisprudence about rape. It was he who devised the jury direction about treating the evidence of women with caution. He was also the authority for the non-existence of marital rape.

'It is clear and well settled ancient law that a man cannot be guilty of rape upon his wife.' That was the statement of the law, until 1991, in Archbold, *Criminal Law Practice and Proceedings*, which is the criminal lawyer's bible. It was in March of that year that the Court of Appeal overturned 250 years of immunity for husbands, an historic decision upheld by the House of Lords on 23 October 1991. Husbands can now be charged with rape, and it is likely that the change will be incorporated in a new statute.

Hale was not stating a principle of criminal law founded on any judicial decision. It was no more than his personal view as a product of his times and was an extrapolation of contractual principles. Marriage was a contract between husband and wife, one of the terms of which was that the wife would consent to sexual intercourse at any time. If this was true then, it certainly does not reflect the views of modern women, who feel quite clearly that as equal partners in a marriage they have every right to say no to intimacy. And not only women, but many men in recent years have also found it unacceptable that husbands should be held in law to have dominion over the will of their wives. Yet it was only after protracted argument and pressure, largely from women, that the climate made it impossible for the judiciary to do anything but adapt the law.

The law must be responsive to the mores of the times. Despite recommendations in 1981 by the Law Commission that the husband's immunity to prosecution for rape be abandoned, it took a decade and another recommendation before the courts responded, and this has highlighted the footdragging so familiar in the legal system, illustrating the contortions which lawyers will go through rather than admit the law has got it wrong. In the House of Lords' judgement of 1991 Lord Keith said that the ruling showed that the 'common law was capable of evolving in the light of changing social, economic and cultural developments'. This pace of evolution is not acceptable to most sensible people.

It has always been possible to prosecute a husband for aiding and abetting rape when he lets other men assault his wife, and one of the anomalies of recent times was that, where a couple cohabited without the benefit of clergy, there was no legal problem in mounting a prosecution for rape against a live-in partner. A woman who chose to live with someone rather than marry him had more protection than her married neighbour. Similarly, since 1949, women who had, by a process of law, obtained a separation order, or a judicial separation, or *decree nisi*, or a non-molestation order, were all deemed to have withdrawn their consent to intercourse; there was no bar to prosecution for rape in their cases. However, a woman who had not yet put the legal wheels in motion, or who for religious reasons had not sought a separation or divorce, could remain at the mercy of an abusive husband.

In 1984, in a case tried at Wakefield Crown Court, a man was charged with a number of offences allegedly committed against his estranged wife. On the prosecution's own case, he had followed her to a park where he attacked her, kicking her in the face and ribs. It was alleged that he then pulled her to a nearby public lavatory, ordered her to remove her pants, held her by the hair whilst forcing her to perform oral sex, and then made her have sexual intercourse. Finally, he made her go into a cubicle and repeat the procedures. It was said, not surprisingly, that the woman was deeply traumatised by the events, having been profoundly degraded and violated.

The husband was not charged with rape because the law considered sex to be a husband's right while a marriage still subsisted. He was charged with assault and indecent assault, but the judge felt unhappy about the apparent inconsistency. His concern was not, however, that a husband could get away with rape. It was that, if the law maintained that by the marriage contract a woman consented to all acts of sexual intercourse with her husband, then it would be ridiculous to say she did not consent to physical acts of a sexual nature done prior to intercourse. The 'implied consent' of the wife extended to the indecent assault as well. In the spirit of logical purity, absurdity was added to absurdity and the indecent assault charge was dismissed.

There then ensued the sort of Alice in Wonderland process which gets the legal system a bad name. Despite the fact that the woman did not consent to any of the sexual acts, and repeatedly made that clear, because she was a 'wife' everyone pretended that she did consent. The sexual elements of a brutal attack were peeled away. The court, left with a bit of kicking and hair-pulling, sentenced on that basis. To add to this nonsense, the Court of Appeal decided in another case, soon after, that while marriage implied consent to intercourse and other sexual activity, this did not extend to fellatio.

The move away from the need to have a separation order or decree to charge a husband with rape developed in the late 1980s, when a number of judges set limits on the immunity. A Leicester case before Mr Justice Owen in 1990 was greeted in the press as a revolutionary breakthrough. The husband had broken into the home of his wife's parents, pursued the woman screaming through the house, torn off her nightgown and beaten her whilst attempting rape. Her throat bore the marks of throttling. He was sentenced to three years' imprisonment but his defence barrister indicated that he intended taking it to appeal and was quoted as saying, 'It is a very important case. It means that any woman, without having the benefit of any sort of court order, can now *unilaterally* withdraw consent to intercourse and still have the protection of the law.' The logical inference is that the woman has to secure the agreement of her spouse before she can say 'no'.

The resistance to change was based on exaggerated fantasies that police stations were going to be full of malicious wives. Yet if there were any substance in this we would surely have seen many more unwedded couples locked in combat over unwelcome sex.

It has also been suggested that if a woman could easily make such an allegation it would undermine the institution of marriage because reconciliation would become impossible once a criminal investigation and trial took place. Children would suffer, and might well resent what had been done to their father. Yet another argument against change was that proof would be difficult. A case would depend solely on the testimony of the wife, and the police would have the time-wasting and distasteful task of investigating the complaint of a possibly vindictive spouse.

When married women involve the police the rape has usually taken place against a background of domestic violence. Forced brutal intercourse is often the culmination of beatings and other indignities. Often the women feel unable to start legal proceedings for separation or divorce because they have nowhere to go, no emotional resources left after years of abuse. Recourse to the police after a rape can be the end of a very long, dark road.

Undoubtedly, women who experience rape within marriage face difficult evidential hurdles as well as cynicism when they come to court. All the problems in ordinary rape cases will be even greater for wives, and they will have to be carefully counselled about their chances of bringing a successful prosecution. Sentences will be at the bottom end of the scale, as was shown in the passing of a two-year suspended sentence at Manchester Crown Court in October 1991, in one of the first prosecutions for rape of a man still living with his wife. The court heard that the defendant had dragged his wife upstairs, threatened to kill her and then raped her – all in a bizarre attempt, so he said, to save their crumbling marriage.

Professor Glanville Williams, an academic authority on clinical law, has become quite exercised about the extension of the rape law to husbands. In two articles in the *New Law Journal* (10 January and 22 February, 1992), he has scolded feminists for this reform. Not only does he advocate the return of the immunity for husbands, but he believes live-in lovers should also be exempt. In his view, husbands who enforce intercourse should at most be charged with common assault and tried in the Magistrates Court. Alternatively, a new, less serious, offence should be created, called 'marital abuse', which would not carry the threat of imprisonment:

Occasionally some husband continues to exercise what he regards as his right when his wife refuses him, the refusal most probably resulting from the fact that the pair have had a tiff. What is wrong with his demand is not so much the act requested but its timing, or the manner of the demand. The fearsome stigma of rape is too great a punishment for husbands who use their strength in these circumstances. Of course, the husband who uses force against his wife is a cad, an uncivilised bounder.

Suggestions that 'real rape' should be distinguished from 'date rape' are often floated. A sub-category of the offence should be created with a less odious name, to encompass forced intercourse between acquaintances – as though it were inherently different. There are degrees of seriousness in rape, but that does not alter the elements of the offence. Differentiating the degree of seriousness should continue to happen at the point of sentencing, and it should be done by assessing each case individually, within a sensible sentencing framework which recognises that rape psychologically damages its victims. However, the attempt to rename the offence reflects not only a distrust of women but a misappreciation of the crime. 'Is it wise,' posits Professor Williams, 'to arm her with such a powerful weapon as a charge of rape, when its use may greatly impair the happiness of both parties?'

The rape campaigns have tried to shift the perception of rape as being a crime about sex towards an understanding of it as an offence of violence. However, for many men violence equals force, a male threat which they understand. They fail to appreciate that there are many other, less explicit, ways in which men can cause women to fear them. It is the absence of actual force which often persuades people that something less than 'real rape' has taken place.

Every year candidates are interviewed for permanent places in sets of chambers. It is a painful process, with many aspiring advocates competing for the few tenancies, and disappointment is inevitable for the majority of applicants. The great breakthrough in recent years has been the number of young women lawyers coming to the Bar. Most of them are clever, ambitious and with a clear sense of themselves as women entering a male world. Repeatedly the subject of rape creeps into the interviews, together with an enquiry as to whether our Portias have strong views on the subject.

The question is loaded, because the professional code of conduct of the Bar requires that you accept any brief that comes your way. This is the already mentioned 'cab-rank' principle, based on the fiction that no taxi-driver ever turns out his light when you ask to be taken to Brixton. Yet many women declare an instinctive ambivalence about rape cases. The men immediately argue for the civil liberties of defendants who may be innocent of charges and deserve a rigorous defence. It is never our function as defence counsel to judge the guilt or innocence of our clients, and as women at the Bar we adhere to that principle just as men do. It is indeed essential that no defendant should go unrepresented because of an abhorrence felt about the charges laid against him. Otherwise there would be a large body of abandoned accused. In practice, some women rely upon the good will of the solicitors who brief them, and hope that rape cases will go somewhere else. Otherwise they grit their teeth and get on with the job, trying to conduct the case without the use of sexist innuendo. Others have no problem, because they will not entertain considerations of sexual politics. As in any other case, they see it as their duty to use every legitimate tactic to undermine the case for the other side, and if that means reducing the witness's moral value in the eyes of the jury, that is the course to be taken.

It is not difficult for most women at the Bar to understand why rape is so controversial: it invokes women's innermost fears, while for male colleagues it is just another of the outrages perpetrated by human beings upon each other. In the gamut of bombing, killing, stabbings and abuse, what is so special about rape, other than it usually happens to women? The apparent contradiction is hard to explain. Rape involves an invasion of the parts of a woman's body preserved for chosen intimacy, for communication of their deepest feelings, for pleasure of a deep and exquisite kind, for the creation of life. It is a violation which rages against women. Psychiatrists tell us it is perpetrated by woman-haters, men with low self-esteem. Far from being an offence of overwhelming sexual passion and excess of ardour, as it has so often been presented, it is, as the campaigns have tried to show, indeed a crime of violence, intended to humiliate, debase, overpower, control. And so rape is a metaphor for the worst kind of oppression. I am sure many of the new generation of women lawyers feel that the aggressive maleness of the crime combines with the essentially male nature of the legal process to make the defence of a man charged with rape an undertaking that they would rather avoid. However, the pressure to do the job as well as men means that some women lawyers are still unwilling to admit a moment's hesitation.

The debate has engaged me as a woman and as a lawyer for many years. I have defended men charged with rape and secured their acquittal. I have felt ashamed as women I am cross-examining flash angry eyes at me for betraying them. Rape separates the girls from the boys. The fundamental difference in the way that men and women perceive rape has affected the conduct of cases, the nature of admissible evidence, and the pattern of sentencing by judges. If the criminal justice system were more even-handed in the way that rape is investigated and tried, women lawyers would feel less compromised by the role they are expected to play.

The forecast is not completely bleak. The Australian Chief Justice Bray has said we have to dispel 'the absurd propositions that a willingness to have sex outside marriage with *someone* is equivalent to a willingness to have sexual intercourse with *anyone*; that the unchaste are also liable to be untruthful and that a woman who has sexual intercourse outside a stable relationship deserves any sexual fate that comes her way'. New members of our own High Court bench are also expressing enlightened views. In March of 1990 Mr Justice Rougier said in sentencing, 'Women are entitled to dress attractively, even provocatively if you like, be friendly with casual acquaintances and still say no at the end of the evening without being brutally assaulted.' That right to say 'no' is the more potent with the onset of AIDS.

Since writing on this subject, I have been involved in endless discussions with colleagues at the Bar who regale me with stories of women who have indeed lied. Often it is the same story. In my view, Mr Justice Fennell very properly imprisoned a woman in 1990 for making a deliberate and calculated false allegation of rape. If women campaign for rape to be taken seriously, then on those rare occasions when a woman does make a false complaint she must bear the consequences.

In the rape debate it is very easy for the arguments to become so polarised that eyes are closed to the problems on both sides. I remember in the early days of campaigning for fairer procedures offering myself as a volunteer adviser to a group involved with the issue. My services were turned down because it was known that I defended men on rape charges and would not accept a rule against defending in such cases. As a lawyer concerned with civil liberties, you have only to be familiar with the travesties which took place in the American South, where black men were and still are regularly framed for the rape of white women, to appreciate the problems in a society filled with competing prejudices. Class also plays its role in rape: a middle-class woman making an allegation against a working-class man is more likely to be believed, and for a middle-class male accused the tables are turned if the woman is less socially acceptable.

Demands for justice are not necessarily the same as demands for Law and Order. So often discussions on rape descend into demands for punitive sentencing and fewer protections for the defendant, as though greater justice for victims required a price to be paid by all accused. As with the campaigns on pornography, which bring together feminists and the moral majority, the making of a clear distinction between the different approaches to these issues is crucial. I want the inherent prejudices against women to be recognised in the courtroom and all steps taken to eliminate them without putting in jeopardy the person who stands trial.

After speaking at a conference recently, a senior police officer sympathetically pointed out that there was anxiety about publishing a racial breakdown of conviction statistics in rape cases, because so many offenders were black. Such figures, however, reflect more upon the underlying attitudes which prevail in courtrooms, than upon any particular tendency of black males to rape. On racial grounds, black men probably lose much of the male solidarity which surrounds rape, particularly if the complainant is white. Black men too have to deal with the weight of mythology about their sexual appetites, their lack of control, the size of their equipment and their desire to punish white men by taking their women, all of which tells against them in the courtroom. In the morass of prejudice, black women have the hardest time being heard and securing the protection of the courts. Black victims face both the rape myths that confront all women, and stereotypes of black women as more likely to consent to sex, more sexually experienced and less likely to be psychologically damaged.

When I ask women magistrates and lawyers who know the system what they would do if they were raped by an acquaintance, many say that they would think twice before exposing themselves to the legal process. Men in the law express the same reservations for their wives and daughters, though often more vigorously.

Rape is still seen from a male perspective, which historically linked the crime to property rights and protecting the vagina from intruders. Ask a woman, and she would say that penetration by a bottle or a broom handle or a fist are all as violating as penile rape, yet the definition still insists on the marauding penis. Rape with an implement is usually charged as indecent assault, unless there is serious physical damage, and the maximum penalty is two years. Women who are buggered against their will are not necessarily protected by anonymity. A young female transsexual who was raped withdrew her complaint when she realised she could not be a victim of rape because she was still regarded as male and her attacker could only be charged with indecent assault. She too would not be afforded any protection against attendant publicity. The whole area of sexual offences is ripe for reform, with women being heard in a rational way and making a real contribution to the change. There should be a sensible reappraisal of the corroboration advice to jurors. Judges should not be mentioning the need for any more special caution than that which jurors should have in all criminal cases. Rape should be redefined to include penetration with instruments and non-consensual anal penetration. We should explore the possible role of a victim representative in the court, whose function would be to explain the process to the witness and familiarise her or him with the procedure without treading in the realm of evidence, so that coaching is avoided. The victim counsel, or '*amicus*', would act only in sensitive cases and would not participate in the adversarial process in front of the jury. However, they could participate in arguments to the judge about admissibility of evidence concerning the victim's history. Alternatively, the Crown Prosecution Service should have their own staff lawyers who are specially trained and charged with much of this task. Child witnesses would particularly benefit from better support in the courts.

Discussions about rape unearth profound feelings once you move beyond the trite condemnations. The subject of rape is complex because of the confusion with genuine intimacy which invades the emotions of everyone in the courtroom. It is never going to be simple, and women are often just as confused as men are. The singularity of the law of rape stems mainly from a deep distrust of the female accuser and from a view of sexual relations seen from a male perspective. Judges to this day advise juries in the language of our old misogynist friend, Sir Matthew Hale, that the accusation of rape is one that is easily made and, once made, difficult to defend, even if the accused is innocent. In my experience the reverse is true: the charge is hard to bring, but easy to defend.

6

Naughty but Nice

The double standard in relation to sex is still invoked all the time in our courts. It is simmering beneath the surface in divorce, child custody and in every arena that women enter. Barristers have a strange shorthand for discussing cases back in their chambers. My first exposure to this was when I came upon a member of chambers confiding to my pupil-master that he lived in a block of flats and that his wife was having an affair with the man on the floor below. I coughed to indicate my presence, and then began to sidle towards the door to provide some privacy for these disclosures, until it dawned on me that he was talking about a divorce case in which he was acting.

The formula of talking about your client in the first person is accepted practice. 'I am a golden-hearted whore,' bellowed our head of chambers, a venerable and aged gentleman, seeking our views as to what sentence his client was likely to get for running a brothel.

Golden-hearted whores feature prominently in anecdotes, and Cynthia Payne, who was tried for supplying sex for luncheon vouchers in her Streatham house, provided more than her fair share. Warm, welcoming women providing favours for men who succumb to the weakness of the flesh are a beloved subject in any predominantly male environment, and court cases that hinge on the subject are a wonderful source of titillation. In the heart of the serious business there is all this sex, and the chaps love it. Juries love it too, and you can always rely on them retiring for hours in a sex case, because everyone has a legitimate excuse for telling their most salacious stories.

A woman barrister tells of being junior counsel in a pornography trial. At the outset of the case the judge called counsel to his room backstage, but the clerk of the court whispered to her, the one woman in the line-up of lawyers, that the invitation was not extended to her: the judge wanted to speak privately with the men. She felt irritated, but duly waited outside, intrigued to hear what could be too delicate for her ears after she had ploughed through mountains of filth in preparation for the trial. According to the lawyers who emerged, the judge had said words to the effect, 'Come on, chaps, we're all men. The acid test for this stuff is our own reaction – did any of you get a rise out of it?' Apparently, if the material was so sordid that decent healthy men of law were revolted instead of being turned on, it had to be obscene.

It is very easy to call down judicial wrath by daring to suggest that our judges are guilty of anything more than the odd unguarded utterance or occasional lapse of judgement. Yet what we are talking about here is something much more pervasive, a cultural aura that excludes women and is so familiar to such men that they are oblivious of it. It is the oxygen of their mutuality. When you try to take it away panic sets in. They are in terror that they will never breathe again.

A showpiece of this exclusive male atmosphere was the libel action in which Andrew Neil, editor of the *Sunday Times*, sued Peregrine Worsthorne, then editor of the *Sunday Telegraph*, for defamation because of an article which suggested he consorted with a call-girl. The court case was like an up-market stag party, with a great many *doubles entendres* and boy talk amongst the all-male participants; the women in court felt as though they were eavesdropping on a chaps' night out. Despite the class divide and the war of values between the old Conservatism in the form of Peregrine Worsthorne and the new Toryism as represented by Andrew Neil, they none the less shared a common language in their attitudes to women. What fun those lawyers and witnesses had, exploring sex within the panelled walls of Court Number Thirteen! The issue was whether the woman in question was indeed a call-girl. A search for precise meaning justified long discussions of bimbos, bimbettes, nightclubs and fornication. Mr Justice Davies, presiding with enormous enjoyment, asked what Mr Worsthorne had meant by calling Ms Bordes a bimbo. 'By bimbo I meant an attractive girl who has a very attractive frontal . . . ' The normally loquacious Mr Worsthorne affected a loss for words and enthusiastically illustrated his definition with his hands, measuring out generous breasts, a word everyone was at pains to avoid. 'Whatever the word is, she looks in your eyes as if you're Einstein but doesn't really think that at all. The kind of girl we all know when we meet her.' A lot of nods were exchanged. If any of the legal chaps were so inexperienced as to be unfamiliar with such sirens, they certainly were not going to admit it in the High Court. This consensus is pretty much the same whether at the Garrick Club, a working men's club, or behind the bicycle sheds. Talking lewdly about women is fun, and the presence of a woman spoils it unless she is the defendant, in which case she is treated as part of the furniture and largely ignored.

Tessa Sanderson, the Olympic gold medallist, suffered the consequences of the pervasive double standard in her libel action against Mirror Group Newspapers. She sued successfully over the published allegation that she had stolen the husband of Jewel Evans, by establishing that the marriage had already broken down before she embarked on a sexual relationship. But her damages were significantly reduced as a result of her being presented to the jury as someone whose reputation was not worth much because she was an adulteress. (There must be a few judges and cabinet ministers who would not pass the adultery test.) George Carman QC told the libel jury that Tessa Sanderson had fallen from her 'high moral pedestal'. She had tasted 'forbidden fruit' and her reputation was in 'shreds and tatters':

> If a young lady chooses to get into bed with a married man she can't expect to be treated with the reverence of a mother superior of a convent. It is the first time I know in an English court that an adulteress wants a jury to order newspapers to pay her compensation for disclosing her adultery and their view as to the consequence of that adultery.

In cross-examination Mr Carman entertained the court by asking Ms Sanderson whether, on her visit to Buckingham Palace, she had mentioned her adultery to the Queen.

In 1975 Patrick Back QC gave a jury his views about sexuality in a pornography trial:

Sex in itself has lost what I call the element of naughtiness. It has lost a lot of its excitement. It has lost a lot of its mystery, and it has lost – saddest of all – its romance. There was a time when for a young man there was a mystery about a girl. There was a little distance which she kept and her mystery in itself was tantalising. Perhaps in those days sex had its own appealing titillation. (*Daily Mail*, 12 November 1975)

But in the criminal courts yet another double standard exists. Prostitutes are divided into those who can be indulged as naughty but nice, like Madame Sin, as Cynthia Payne described herself; and those who are depraved and corrupting, like Janie Jones.

Janie Jones ran a prostitutes' outfit for rich gentlemen; and during the late 1960s and early 1970s she was very much in demand at high society parties. She catered for curious tastes, and one of her clients was an hereditary peer, a wealthy landowner related to the royal family. He asked to be supplied with young girls and Janie Jones supplied him with 19- and 20-year-olds who pretended to be 12. Another client was a London property developer.

The police had a particular down on Janie Jones, a cheeky, mischievous woman who would not co-operate with the protection rackets that operated around prostitution. Janie was adamant that her troubles largely flowed from refusing to pay off police officers, who would guarantee non-interference in her activities if she made contributions to their private benevolent funds.

In 1973 Janie Jones's house was raided and her little black book of clients removed. It made interesting reading, and the police interviewed a number of the prominent persons whose names were in it. Terror struck the hearts of strong men at the thought of the public exposure that might follow should they give evidence against the wicked Janie. The luckless lord and the property developer then claimed that she had been blackmailing them, threatening to tell all if they did not pay up. This allegation had the happy consequence that they were guaranteed anonymity, since the law had recently been changed, to protect victims of blackmail and encourage them to go to the police without fear that their identity would be disclosed. When Janie's case came for trial the two men escaped attention, apart from a little rebellion against hypocrisy by the *Socialist Worker*, which revealed their names. The evidence about blackmail was totally rejected by the jury, but when Janie Jones was convicted of controlling a ring of prostitutes she was sentenced to seven years' imprisonment, a punishment which many felt disregarded that fact.

Janie Jones had accepted that she ran an escort agency and that when the stars of stage, screen and the Upper House came to town she would find them a woman. Her claim that what happened thereafter was beyond her ken persuaded nobody. On her own account she was a great party-giver, and evidence of two-way mirrors and sex orgies brought queues of people to the public gallery and many bewigged observers into the well of the court. Her parties were no naughtier than Cynthia Payne's and she was adamant that she was never paid for the sex her girlfriends supplied. But she was perceived as a bad girl, dubbed by the press a 'Vice Queen' and referred to by a judge as one of the 'wickedest women' he had ever tried. She feels bitter now that 'respectable' people went scot-free, their reputations intact.

Cynthia Payne, in contrast, made it quite clear at her trial in 1986 that she was one of the old school who never kiss and tell. She claimed to have amongst her clientele a number of prominent men – but even if her teeth were pulled she would not reveal their identities. She also struck the right tone in the courtroom: ribald, sexy, lovable and nice. It was a delicious cocktail, and even with the prosecution in the hands of Anthony Longdon, one of the Bar's most charming advocates, there was no hope of securing a conviction.

What was she doing, she implied, other than providing men of a certain age with a bit of fun? Here was a defendant who did not need to be told to turn up in her Marks and Spencer's best. She looked mumsy and comfortable and called everyone 'dear'. People who live off immoral earnings are supposed to be Maltese and have gold in their teeth, or black and wearing a lot of jewellery. This was the acceptable face of prostitution.

'Angela', a woman in her late 60s, was not as lucky as Cynthia Payne. She was charged in 1987 with running a disorderly house where, behind closed doors, she entertained men to indulge whatever fantasy took their fancy. She carried on her work without disturbing her neighbours until the day she was telephoned by Special Branch with a request to change her telephone number. It was explained that her number was very similar to that of someone related to a person in the government, and that that 'someone' was receiving phone-calls from Ms Angela's clientele. A change of telephone is not very convenient for someone whose business depends on the phone, so Angela made the not unreasonable suggestion that the important person's relative might be asked to make the change instead. Before she knew it, she found herself the subject of police interest and was eventually arrested. There were no witnesses apart from police, who maintained they saw men leave the address rubbing their behinds, presumably as a result of being chastised, and red in the face from the activities within. Whips, bondage implements, a ragbag of costumes and pornographic literature were amongst the evidence. Angela was convicted, her sentence of imprisonment suspended only because of her age.

There is something ridiculous about bringing the formality of the court to bear on the daily grind that is prostitution. Some of the funniest moments I have witnessed in court have been when female clients have been able to subvert the court's authority by poking fun at the well-rehearsed notion that men are victims of their sexual drive. This usually involves a scenario where the prostitute is in the witness box explaining an indecorous attempt to satisfy a customer's needs, and winks continuously at the judge, assuming that he will know what she means.

The declared aims of laws against prostitution are the 'preservation of public decency', curbing the nuisance of soliciting on the streets and protecting the prostitute herself from violence and exploitation. Contracting to provide sex for money is not in itself unlawful. The law is invoked only to criminalise concomitant activity. This has helped sustain the fiction that the law is not concerned with morality. However, moral opprobrium is always present.

Selling sex as a commodity is perceived as depraved, but it is the seller, not the buyer, who bears the responsibility. The purchaser is seen as the victim of his own sexual needs; again the law promotes the myth that men are ruled by their libido. Prostitution is tolerated because of an acceptance of male promiscuity which is not afforded women.

This used to be very evident in the cases where a woman was convicted of soliciting while her customer was guilty of no offence. Legislation was introduced to make the male behaviour of kerb-crawling a crime, but only because 'respectable women' had to be protected from persistent propositioning by a stranger. The full force of the law is rarely put behind the new offence and it is still used infrequently. When it was introduced, lawyers and politicians expressed concern about innocent men being set up by the police, or innocent activity being misinterpreted, and it is for this reason that very strict evidential rules are applied. The police have to see two overt acts before they can make an arrest, which is frustrating to officers who watch a man driving around a red-light area for lengthy periods selecting his woman but making only one approach.

Prostitutes are not so fortunate; they can be charged for loitering simply because they are known to police and have been seen waiting around in a particular area. 'Loitering' is the charge selected by the police because it does not require repeated acts once a woman is on record. The very term 'common prostitute' enrages the women, who feel that the language demeans them as much as the activity.

Because of the evidential difficulties in securing convictions, the police policy on kerb-crawling now is to move men on, reminding them that they could receive a rather embarrassing letter in the post if they continue their activity – 'Could create problems with the wife, sir.' The resulting problem for the prostitutes is that they have to choose their 'john' at speed, getting into cars quickly before having the chance to get a good look at him. Many of the women say they have antennae for identifying the real oddball, but the new policing methods reduce the chance to assess the customer. The English Collective of Prostitutes, a campaigning group, has been reluctant to see the law used because it makes life harder for the women.

Who are these men who have to pay for it? According to police officers it really is the fellow next door who turns up on the car registration computer when they do a check on a vehicle number plate. There is no shortage of custom, and in the entrepreneurial 1990s many women are taking to the streets, selling the one commodity they have which they know is in demand. Between January and July of 1990 in the King's Cross area of London alone there were 338 arrests for soliciting and 132 cautions. The research of Dr Susan Edwards, an eminent feminist academic, has shown the alarming increase in the number of women forced into prostitution by poverty in Britain today.

Changes in the law now mean that prostitutes are not imprisoned for loitering or soliciting, but since non-payment of fines leads to custody too many women in our prisons are still there for prostitution.

Men who use prostitutes may raise sniggers in court, but they are not despised in the same way. When a member of the aristocracy appeared at the Old Bailey to give evidence in a cheque-fraud case it came to light that he had been using the services of a call-girl and paying with cheques. Everyone smiled benignly and just thought how daft he was. There was no question of his not being able to show his face in the club.

When Alan Green, the Director of Public Prosecutions, resigned in 1991 having been seen at the back of King's Cross, allegedly looking for a prostitute, the sympathy for him was shared by most of us in the profession. He had been the fairest of prosecutors in his days at the Bar and was an exceptional Director, of unquestioned integrity and courage, who had the unenviable task of dealing with the Irish miscarriages of justice. It was suggested by prostitutes in the red-light area that he was subjected to special police attention. Some lawyers and journalists believe this might not be unrelated to his sanctioning the prosecutions of police for malpractice; he was apparently detested in sections of the force. Whatever the truth, his judgement that it was impossible for him to remain at the head of a prosecution service which makes decisions about whether kerb-crawlers should be prosecuted was right; but in well-meaning but misconceived allegiance, a number of senior members of the Bar publicly advocated that he remain in the job.

When I was first in practice I appeared in court for a Glasgow woman who was facing prison because she had a suspended sentence for soliciting. Much to our delight, the magistrate, a deputy stipendiary (a professional magistrate) gave her another chance. A short time later he met a mutual friend and told him that he had succumbed to my plea because his own first sexual experience had been with a Scots prostitute. He is now a judge, his youthful peccadillos no source of shame or handicap.

The legal treatment of prostitution reveals another prejudice – that of class. The British are famous for institutionalising social and moral hypocrisies. The well-bred unemployed are referred to as socialites; the poor on the dole are spongers. The upper-class divorcee is rarely included in the term single parent. The prostitute who can afford the title call-girl and who has a flat in the expensive part of town does not face the indignities of the courts and runs few of the risks faced by her poorer sister, who works on the street. The laws against brothel-keeping prevent two or three women sharing a flat for their work, which would reduce the risks of assault and provide companionship.

The harassment of women on the street is legendary and takes new forms. Putting 'Sexy Sadie' stickers with a telephone number on telephone boxes brought the self-promoters before the court for causing criminal damage. Ever inventive, the ladies shifted to calling cards, which involved no glue and, therefore, no damage. British Telecom, morally indignant, responded by cutting off the phones connected to the numbers (although they have maintained sex chat-lines, from which the company makes a lot of money). What has a girl to do but sue – only to find that litigants must come to the court 'with clean hands', a legal fiction used somewhat selectively.

Prostitutes are regularly beaten up or raped by clients, but are inhibited from taking legal action because they know the problems they face once they go to court. Any excuse turns into a credible defence when the complainant is a 'tom', as prostitutes are called by police. The general yarn spun by defendants is that the prostitute tried to rob him and when accused became physically violent. The likelihood of a woman taking on a man in this way is forgotten when she is a whore.

In her book *Misogynies* (1989), Joan Smith highlights the contrasting attitudes to the murder of prostitutes as against that of 'innocent' women by the police investigating the Yorkshire Ripper killings. She recalls the words of a senior police officer at a press conference:

> He has made it clear that he hates prostitutes. Many people do. We, as a police force, will continue to arrest prostitutes. But the Ripper is now killing innocent girls. That indicates your mental state and that you are in urgent need of medical attention. Give yourself up before another innocent woman dies.

This distinction, between respectable women and the others, whose lives seem to have a different value, is made repeatedly in the press, by the police and in court. One of the most prevalent kinds of serial murder is indeed that of the prostitute; she especially represents the myth of Eve, of woman as responsible for male concupiscence and carnality.

So entrenched is the idea that prostitutes have it coming to them that, in order to allay speculations and emphasise the seriousness of the risk to real women, the police often feel obliged to stipulate that female victims are not prostitutes. Police statements in July 1990 in connection with the killing of two young women whose bodies were found in a car described them as 'very respectable, they both came from very respectable families'.

The risk of violence does not only come from the client. In June 1990, in a rare case, a notorious pimp called Colin Gayle stood trial at the Old Bailey on eighteen counts of rape, threats to kill, actual bodily harm and living off immoral earnings. The victims of his appalling assaults were the young women prostitutes who became involved with him and who supplied him with money to pay for his cocaine habit. The evidence of brutal beatings with a metal rod and hammer sat uncomfortably with the love letters the women had written to him. Why would beaten, bruised and disfigured women return to their tormentor?

Love poems were written to Gayle by one young woman who had received terrible injuries at his hands, resulting in damage to her kidneys as well as extensive cuts and bruising, because he did not think she showed enough respect.

Amongst the prosecution evidence were letters written by Gayle promising that he would stop the relentless beatings: it was probably those careless pieces of self-incrimination which secured his conviction. Even so, he was acquitted of the charges in relation to one of the prostitutes because her evidence was confused. In the view of police she 'lost' the jury by swearing and being foul-mouthed.

The prosecution have a terrible problem in these cases because the women themselves are terrified of the consequences of giving evidence. The fear of reprisals from the accused or his friends is enormous and the women also know that they will be cross-examined in detail about their lifestyles in a way that will reinforce hostile views towards them. After a similar trial in 1984, the prostitutes who had given evidence for the Crown were enraged at the short sentences which were passed because the pimps would be back on the streets seeking revenge within months of the case. Gayle, however, was given fourteen years, an unusual response to assaults on prostitutes and one which he is taking to the Court of Appeal.

By contrast, the courts are punitive to prostitutes who 'roll' or rob their clients. Sometimes a woman appears in the dock charged with complicity in a robbery in which she has acted as a foil, enticing a male into an hotel room or secluded place where he has subsequently been robbed. A 16-year-old girl was recently convicted and imprisoned for assuming this role and the judge made great play of her wickedness, which seemed to him to go beyond that of the older youths who committed the robbery and had put her up to it. More recently, women have been arrested for operating a 'sting' by persuading men to part with money for an hotel room and then disappearing into the blue. These sorts of offences are seen as taking advantage of men at their most vulnerable, because reporting the events to the police could have humiliating ramifications.

Prostitutes have come to expect poor treatment in the criminal courts, but they have problems in the civil courts too, particularly concerning the welfare of their children. Many prostitutes who appear before the courts say they do this work because it fits in well with their child-care arrangements: they can work during school hours or in the evenings, when they have a babysitter. Many are women living alone with children, with little prospect of any other kind of employment.

Charges of living off immoral earnings were introduced to reach the pimps who exploited women and forced them into sexual misery. However, many women complain that the law is too frequently used against boyfriends and husbands who exercise no control over them at all but whom the courts think ought to be breadwinning and functioning in a conventional way. If the men have no obvious source of income they are readily convicted and are usually imprisoned.

The evidence offered to prove that the man knowingly lives wholly or in part on the earnings of prostitution is usually that the woman pays the rent or buys the food or gives the man money or buys him drinks. The defendant has to prove that he did not know the money came from prostitution or that he did not receive anything at all. The men who suffer most are black, because of the way the police choose to prosecute, assuming that predatory black men are more inclined to put women on the streets. The effect is to prevent these women having any semblance of a home life.

In 1987 the High Court upheld a refusal to include a former prostitute on an *in vitro* fertilisation programme because of her past history. She had also been rejected by an adoption agency, because like any man with a previous conviction she could be eliminated as unsuitable. Although she and her husband were desperate to have a baby and even braved the exposure of her previous convictions to challenge the decision, her past 'immorality' disqualified her. Men are luckier: their use of prostitutes is rarely recorded and their promiscuity is never an issue.

There is so much discrimination in the area that it makes one doubt the whole ethos of the criminalisation of prostitution. A number of reasons are given to justify the criminalising of soliciting. One is that it reduces the public nuisance to ordinary, decent people. Although it is in fact rare for women to operate in areas that have not developed a red-light reputation, people living in and around the area are often offended by the attendant problems of discarded condoms and approaches at night. Other countries are experimenting with the idea of strictly designated areas for the purpose of prostitution, licensing of brothels and the use of planning law to control their location. Local residents can make objections at planning hearings if nuisance is a serious problem – all of which shifts some of the problems associated with prostitution away from the criminal courts. Where any passerby is seriously affronted, public order charges of insulting words and behaviour can still be laid.

It is also contended that women need to be protected for their own good, since some women are forced on the game by men. This, however, could be covered by existing laws to protect children from exploitation and female adults from coercion and extortion, as well as by legislation concerning assaults.

Lindy St Clair, a prostitute who lost her High Court challenge to the Inland Revenue's taxation of her earnings from prostitution, wittily accused the government of living off immoral earnings. The outlawing of prostitution and then the application of fiscal regulations as if it were any old job is an indication of the double-think involved in the whole issue. The income from prostitution would probably write off the national debt if properly audited, but, as it stands, only women on the low end of the scale are 'taxed', in the form of regular fining. Women appearing in the central London courts describe the fine as their licence fee and get straight back on the job to pay it.

It is odd that, while many people persist in the view that prostitutes are abnormal, flawed, and to be contrasted with wholesome, decent women, discussion about decriminalising the oldest profession immediately raises an outcry about the respectable wives and mothers who will flood its ranks. The contradiction for the law is that, while it wishes to control the activities of women who sell sex, it sees the need for a class of women who will do just that in order to service men. Prostitution also challenges traditional order, and raises fears that if the taboo were lifted even more women might see it as a means of securing financial independence. The established female role would be further eroded.

'Saving' women from prostitution could be more properly addressed by removing sexual and economic inequalities, providing job opportunities, training and equal pay – in other words, by recognising the economic realities which drive most women to the streets. Unfortunately, economic realities do escape some members of the bench.

The chasm of class misunderstanding still exists, and was especially apparent in the Thatcher years when the judicial equivalent of 'get on your bike' was often repeated in the courts. Men and women in the dock would be informed that the vacancy columns in newspapers were full of jobs. While everywhere else the economic hardship of unemployment was being recognised, some judges and magistrates still insisted on confronting the workshy. Women who resorted to prostitution were equally misunderstood.

Recently, organisations such as the Mothers' Union have suggested looking again at whether criminal sanctions against prostitutes are necessary. The increasing risk of AIDS has highlighted the health dangers for men and women of unprotected sex. Unfortunately, many prostitutes' clients refuse to wear a condom during intercourse and will pay extra for its absence, and that pressure will continue whether there are brothels or not.

There are compelling arguments for and against the decriminalisation of street offences and the legalisation of brothels. Although the arguments are mainly articulated on the grounds of keeping neighbourhoods decent and avoiding offence to citizens, the core argument is about the symbolic importance of punishing deviant sexuality. It would be quite possible to divert the police vice squads on to more pressing crime problems by abolishing the soliciting laws and using in their place, where it is occasionally necessary, offensive behaviour legislation. At the same time, provisions protecting children from sexual exploitation and adults from coercion and fraud could be strengthened. It would be interesting to look closely at the reforms in the Australian state of Victoria and in Holland to see whether legalisation has seen an improvement. The creation of legalised brothels there has not removed all street soliciting but has greatly reduced the numbers. Brothels are not run by the state but have to maintain health standards for permits to be obtained, and their location is controlled by town-planning laws. Failure to have a permit or planning permission means they are closed down. Inevitably, advertising has to be permitted for a legalised brothel system to work, and strict codes are established regulating where such information can appear.

Police claim that 'respectable clients' who use street prostitutes would never risk entering a brothel for fear of being seen, and that likewise some women with children who work on a casual basis would not want to chance being discovered. However, risk is half the excitement for many of the men, and since danger of criminal prosecution has not dampened enthusiasm it is unlikely that entering a brothel would. The majority of women on the street would welcome decriminalisation and might feel differently if they realised a brothel scheme would not be run by the government. It is my fear that AIDS will have to reach epidemic proportions amongst heterosexuals in Britain before we ever consider this alternative.

In the meantime, the courts should be challenging the sexual double standard which is fuelled by a sensation-loving press: it is not only prostitutes who suffer the consequences, but many other heterosexual and especially homosexual women.

In 1975, Elizabeth Thompson was convicted with a man called Kenneth Fromant of the murder of her friend's husband. She was described in the press as 'fun-loving' and a 'goer', which in the demotic of the media has only one meaning. In court her sexual activities and the number of men she had slept with became a sideshow which almost overshadowed the main event.

The background to the case was the arrival in Plymouth of the gasmen who introduced more than North Sea gas into the lives of local housewives. One of Lizzie's friends had a serious affair with a gas-fitter, Ken Fromant, and talked incessantly of getting away from her husband if only he would let her. The husband ended up dead, and the allegation was made that the fatal knifing was done by Lizzie Thompson acting in misplaced loyalty to her friend, in conjunction with Fromant, the lover.

She fought the case hard, denying that she had been involved and claiming that she was having the blame put on to her by the victim's wife, who had in fact carried out the murder with Fromant. By the end of the trial the jury had a palsied view of the Plymouth wives and Lizzie Thompson was convicted. She feels very strongly, as does her counsel, that in the trial so much play was made of her sex-life that she was held in despise by the jury. She served eleven years of a life sentence, forfeiting parole because she insisted on her innocence.

One of the effects of the change in women's status in society has been the greater confidence it has given them to express their sexuality freely, a factor which has highlighted so many of the dichotomies in the law. The new confidence has enabled gay women openly to declare their sexuality. The fact of lesbianism has never even been acknowledged in the criminal law, which is an extreme expression of the way the law denies the existence of active female sexuality.

In a divorce case reported on 21 May 1954 in *The Times*, the judge was so wedded to Queen Victoria's disbelief in the very existence of lesbianism that he refused to grant the divorce. In his judgement he said:

> At the highest the wife and Miss Purdon were seen hand in hand, used to call each other darling, kissed on the lips, spent a good number of holidays together, were constantly alone in the wife's bedroom at the vicarage and on two or three occasions occupied the same bedroom at night ... It was a very odd business, two grown women spending all this time together often in the same room and often in bed together, but the court is quite satisfied that that is perfectly innocent.

Although in theory there are laws which can be used against lesbians such as 'Behaviour likely to cause a Breach of the Peace' or 'Indecent Assault on a Woman', in practice lesbians are rarely charged under these laws because there is little male interest in the punishment of female homosexuality. The law puts much more emphasis on protecting women from vaginal penetration by an unsanctioned male and on protecting men from homosexuality.

However, when a woman's lesbianism is before the court as part of the general evidence, another agenda operates, as in the case of the prostitute or the promiscuous woman. Women who have rejected heterosexuality and their prescribed role are perceived as threatening; some lesbians challenge the idea of passivity so strongly that the law is used symbolically for public condemnation.

In 1975 the Women's Report contained coverage of a trial where a husband bludgeoned his wife to death because she told him she was a lesbian and wished to leave him for her lover. He was convicted of manslaughter on the grounds of gross provocation and sentenced to thirty months, thereafter reduced to less than a year. Yet the wounding of her lesbian lover led to one woman being imprisoned for seven years in circumstances where corresponding heterosexual domestic violence would have had a much less severe result.

Another scandal of the penal and justice systems is the inappropriate detention of people in prisons and special hospitals. This is partly because of the devastation of psychiatric facilities in ordinary hospitals through lack of funding. However, many women are made the subject of Mental Health Act sections who should not be sectioned at all. They are left to spend indeterminate periods in the prison asylums that are euphemistically called Special Hospitals, places like Broadmoor and Rampton, largely because they have been aggressive and angry or generally acted inappropriately for their sex. Lesbian women are particularly susceptible to being labelled as 'inappropriate'.

To get into these places, patients have to be diagnosed as mentally ill and deemed to be a danger to society or themselves. For women it is very often the latter, because their desperation is so often turned inwards. Many of the female patients in Broadmoor are there for comparatively minor crimes, whereas the detained men have committed sex offences or sexually motivated murders. A young woman interviewed in the *Independent on Sunday*

(4 November 1990) believes she would not have been sent to Broadmoor had she been a man. She had been convicted of criminal damage of windows:

> It's not right for women to smash windows. But then half the women I met in Broadmoor had behaved in ways that were not acceptable for women. They didn't need to be there. The only way to get out is to conform. That means behaving in a ladylike way. What I needed was help and care. Broadmoor didn't give me any of that.

The woman was 18 at the time of the offences, homeless and without family support.

Prue Stevenson of the Women in Secure Hospitals (WISH) campaign has been attempting to effect some change for this forgotten and neglected group of women who, once saddled with the Broadmoor label, become pariahs. In an article for *Openmind* in 1989 she describes the attack on identity and sense of self that women, especially lesbians, experience in places like Broadmoor, where they are put under pressure to wear make-up and feminine clothing, grow their hair and have tattoos removed. Most women comply, since to refuse could go against them in assessing their readiness for discharge. However, the process of making women conform starts much earlier in the criminal justice process, and young lesbian women feel they are partially punished for non-compliance.

Lesbian women experience the criminal justice system, from policing onwards, as hostile, treating them as social outcasts and sometimes as freaks. As the victims of crime they are at a profound disadvantage, and have difficulty persuading the police to pursue complaints of sexual harassment, verbal abuse and assault by men. It is a particularly courageous gay woman who will brave the attack upon her character she knows will attend any trial such as rape. Some attacks are not confined to cases where gay women have been sexually assaulted. In almost any case the fact of her sexuality will be used against her. A gay policewoman told me that she has always had to be prepared for an attack in the witness box on the basis that her arrest of a male accused was based on hostility to men.

In itself, lesbianism is at the bottom of the hierarchy of priorities in the criminal law. As we have seen, the historical legal preoccupation with vaginal penetration had its roots in male concerns about virginity, pregnancy and paternity, with sex used as a means of social control. In the past century the traditional male view, which has directed the law, has displayed greater concern about protecting young men from homosexual sex than it has women from unwanted heterosexual sex, except where the heterosexual sex involves a marauder having violent intercourse with a respectable woman. The difference in the ages of consent is indicative of the preoccupation with protecting young men for as long as possible from these 'corrupting forces'. Compared with men who have consenting sex with girls under 16, men who commit consensual offences with male partners over 16 are five times more likely to be prosecuted, and three times less likely to be let off with a caution (research by Peter Tatchell for Liberty, NCCL 1992). Men who commit consenting homosexual offences are four times more likely to be convicted than men who commit heterosexual and violent sex offences. Prison sentences for consenting homosexual relations with men aged 16–21 are sometimes as long as for rape, and often twice as long as the jail terms for unlawful sexual intercourse with a girl aged 13–16. This speaks loudly as to whose fears are given priority. The law and the courts treat male homosexual approaches and behaviour in public lavatories as far more grave than the sexual harassment women experience daily. Indeed, attempts to have sexual harassment treated with any seriousness at all are met with derision.

Hardly a woman exists who has not had to deal with unwelcome sexual attention. Yet the subject is met with collective denial by many men. The spectacle of the American Supreme Court Judge, Clarence Thomas, being questioned about such allegations is a case in point. The observing senators probably knew to a man that somewhere in the corridors of power lurked a female political lobbyist or researcher who could make similar claims about their own behaviour.

A lot of men think sexual harassment has nothing to do with

them, that it is an invention of militant feminism put forward in
a spirit of prudery and puritanism by women 'who should be so
lucky'. For these reasons, women who like men and enjoy sex
often don't want to involve themselves in the issue.

Of course, sexual attraction is a component in many of the
relationships which compose our daily round. The gentle flirtation
of our social commerce is a harmless and pleasant aspect of life.
Many of us know from experience that the positive exchange of
sexual energy can be as creative at work as elsewhere, but sexual
harassment is of a different order and both men and women
know the difference. One involves a mutuality and the other is
unwelcome. It is not the product of the fevered feminist imagination. Most women can give plentiful accounts of dealing with
groping and risqué remarks, and some women with a quick wit
or a strong arm can handle anything. However, many women feel
humiliated and demeaned by the experience. There is a sense in
which women who complain are considered by confident women
to be whingers, who have let it happen – what has been described
as an extension of the 'good girls do not get raped' theory.

The public discussions about the Thomas débâcle involved the
usual victim-blaming, with Professor Anita Hill being asked why
she had not complained at the time: 'Why did you not leave?'
The questions addressed to women, be they battered or raped or
harassed, are always the same. 'Why did you go there?' they asked
Patricia Bowman, the unsuccessful complainant in the Kennedy-
Smith trial.

The male verdict on the complaint of Anita Hill was that soon
a chap would not be able to enter the office and say 'That's a nice
dress, Doris,' without letting loose the furies. No man can be that
disingenuous.

The combination of sex and power is a particularly destructive
one. All things are not equal when someone in a superior position
within an organisation presses attentions or constantly comments
in a very suggestive way about the appearance or clothing of a
more junior member of staff, or insists on talking about sex, or
engineers intimate interludes. As women become more successful
and powerful themselves they experience less harassment.

A complaint by the woman is rarely taken seriously and can

be career suicide, alienating the boss and every other male and sometimes female in sight. The complainant is hardly likely to secure the patronage of the spurned office romancer in any bid for promotion. The perpetrator, for his part, usually feels confused and defensive, often unaware of the misery he has caused the woman. Alternatively, his ego is so bruised that he can no longer find a way of working effectively with the victim.

From time to time I have adjudicated in internal hearings within organisations on allegations of sexual harassment. Dispute resolution is a sensitive business and both parties have to feel the justice of the outcome. In each case the male party has accepted that he perhaps 'went too far' but has only with hindsight recognised the issue of power imbalance. In these cases the most important lesson for the man is an understanding of the responsibilities that go with power, and the recognition that it is an abuse of his position to leave a woman uncertain about her right to say 'no' to his familiarities without a career comeback.

There is no good reason for the law on sexual offences to differentiate between the sexes: sex-neutral laws would penalise behaviour which is violent or antisocial or involves exploitation of the vulnerable, whether they be men or women, rich or poor, white or black. Relationships within society are being renegotiated as a result of women's changing status. The new terrain is sometimes a hard place for men to travel when they are still using an outdated map. The challenge now is to create a climate of mutual respect in which we can locate our human relationships.

7

And She was Black

The issue of race is highly contentious in legal circles. Judges will not have it that the colour of a person's skin in any way affects their judgements, even if it is suggested that attitudes may be unconscious or that discrimination can be indirect. Many see racial disadvantage as rooted in society, requiring a political resolution, outside the province of the courts. They describe their function in a mechanistic way, involving the application of 'the law' as an impartial set of rules to be applied without fear or favour regardless of sex, colour or creed.

Yet something does go wrong. Although black people constitute less than 5 per cent of the population Home Office statistics for 1992 show that they make up 22 per cent of the prison population. Indeed, 29 per cent of the female prison population is now black. Since social deprivation is linked to criminal behaviour it is not surprising that black people, who have experienced discrimination and disadvantage, might be over-represented. However, it is hard to accept that this alone accounts for the discrepancy. There are, of course, those who choose to interpret the statistics as proof of black criminality; such crude views defy contradiction or rational debate. However, it is always maintained by the preservers of the status quo that the research so far conducted into any sentencing disparity is still inconclusive.

The research work of Baldwin and McConville ('The Influence of Race and Sentencing in England', *Criminal Law Review*, 1982) and of Crowe and Cove ('Ethnic Minorities and the Courts', *Criminal Law Review*, 1984) came ultimately to the conclusion that black defendants were treated no more harshly than white defendants, a view supported by Home Office research. More recent research, on the other hand, by the West Midland probation service, showed that black defendants were more likely to get immediate custodial sentences (35 per cent compared with 21.4 per cent) or a suspended sentence (13 per cent compared with 8.9 per cent). They were less likely to get community service, a fine, or a supervision or probation order. Judges and magistrates were also less likely to obtain psychiatric and social reports on a black accused, where they had the discretion, and if reports were available they took less notice of the recommendations by probation officers. When the details of the cases were examined to see whether any special characteristic explained the higher sentencing, it was found that on balance the white offenders had committed the more serious offences.

Subsequent studies by Middlesex and West Yorkshire probation services have reached similar conclusions. According to *Hansard* (11 November 1991) the average sentence length for West Indian male adults is almost eight months longer than the average for a white male adult. For West Indian female adults the average sentence is over thirteen months longer than for their white counterparts. The Prison Reform Trust report, *Indentikit Prisoner*, showed that adult male prisoners of African or Afro-Caribbean origin were serving sentences 44 per cent longer than those of white adult males, while black women were serving sentences on average twice as long as white women.

The current, very comprehensive, study by Roger Hood of the Cambridge Institute of Criminology for the Commission of Racial Equality is also likely to knock squarely on the head the idea that there is no sentencing differential based on race.

In 1991 Eric Smellie, the Race Policy Officer at the National Association for the Care and Resettlement of Offenders (NACRO), conducted a piece of research amongst a cross-section of people who had just gone through the system. The perception of those who appear in court, black and white, is that the system is discriminatory against ethnic minorities and that prejudice does exist. This was echoed in the National Census for 1991, in which over 40 per cent of the population expressed the view that the rich had a better chance of securing justice and that black people did not fare well within the criminal justice system.

There is an unwillingness to admit that the problem exists because those involved in the administration of justice know the courts must be above reproach – the one area of society which should be beyond doubt. The legal establishment can accept that people may be discriminated against in education or employment because of their colour, but insist that as far as the courts are concerned the problem is in the minds of defendants (which they consider unsurprising since recipients are rarely satisfied with the justice of their deserts). If something cannot be measured in empirical terms it does not exist. If there is no proof beyond reasonable doubt of discrimination, it has to follow that the courts are colour-blind.

The problem with conducting research is that different responses may be obtained in different regions and before different courts. Equally, the outcome may vary if the researcher asking the questions is white or black. It has also been shown that surface examination of the offence and the sentence may show no discernible difference in approach, because in such an assessment no account is given to the complicated process which has gone before.

Black people are more likely to be stopped and searched by the police, more likely to be arrested. Their sense of injustice often leads to greater confrontation with police and consequent accusations by the police that they have been disorderly or violent. Black people, in their understandable distrust of the frequently all-white bench of magistrates, will elect trial by jury in the Crown Court more often than their white counterpart, and this leads to longer sentences on conviction because higher courts have greater sentencing powers. It is also noteworthy that a significantly greater number of black defendants are ultimately acquitted at trial, suggesting that the original arrests may well have been unwarranted. The whole process confirms a sense of unfairness.

The contact of black communities with the police is so often negative that it inevitably spills over into the courtroom. However, when some judges see part of their role as validating a pressurised police force, they are faced with an unpalatable choice and either side with the police or avoid criticising them in the way that an aggrieved defendant feels an impartial judge should. The judge's attitude may not actually affect sentencing, but it will affect the way the court process is experienced by the black defendant.

Black defendants face all the usual problems; fear, worry, confusion and concern for their families – but they also have especially low expectations of how they will be treated, expecting hostility from court staff and the bench. Authority is white, and the courtroom reinforces that message. Not only are the great majority of lawyers and almost all judges white (only two of the 440 circuit judges are black, and there are no black judges at a higher level), but so too are the clerks, the probation officers, the press reporters, the ushers, the policemen, the dock officers. The Society of Black Lawyers states that 'the poor image which black people have of the courts leads to the sense that if one is black in court one has to prove one's innocence rather than the court prove one's guilt' (NACRO Report, 1992).

Members of the Society also comment that 'the sense of having to prove one's credibility is also felt by black lawyers. They feel they often have to spend the first five or ten minutes demonstrating their credibility to the court . . . before they can genuinely get on with the job of defending the client.' (An experience echoed by some white female practitioners.)

At a meeting of the Bar Council on the subject of ethnic minorities at the Bar, a leader of one of the circuits (a geographic division of the practising Bar) regaled the assembly with a tale of one of his black members who appeared in court to prosecute. The barrister bore a conventional English-sounding name whereas his white adversary enjoyed something more unusual. The judge, presented with the list of counsel, was rather surprised to hear the black man embark on an address to him. Assuming the stereotypical position whereby black lawyers are not seen in court representing the Crown, he patronisingly explained that in his neck of the woods it was traditional for the prosecutor to open the case.

Real men do not cry, and black men do not prosecute. This is largely because prosecution work tends to go to particular chambers where black lawyers are hardly to be found.

The experiences of African, Afro-Caribbean and Asian defendants within the criminal justice system are in some ways different, and while a sense of alienation is shared by all the groups, they face different forms of racial stereotyping. Asians, unlike other ethnic minorities, are considered industrious and family-minded, which means, for example, that they are more likely to obtain bail than West Indian or African defendants. However, like Africans they are seen as more dishonest and lacking in credibility than West Indians. The special burden carried by West Indians is that they are often assumed to be more violent. The ultimate albatross for all black men, of whatever race, is that they are sexually insatiable.

The experience of black women is the corollary of that of black men. On a recent visit to Holloway to talk to women about separation from their children I was surprised at the numbers of black women and questioned the probation staff on the size of the ethnic population. That week the number of black women in Holloway had passed the 50 per cent mark (counting both unconvicted prisoners awaiting trial on remand and those already sentenced). This is ten times the ratio of black to white in the population at large. I know that Holloway presents a very different picture from other prisons because of its wider catchment area and because it covers the metropolis and the major ports of entry. But the visual impact of so many black women kept incarcerated by so many white women (few of the officers are from ethnic minorities) was shocking.

Why should black women be deserving of prison sentences or refusal of bail? A reasonable percentage can be accounted for by the high incidence of black women from abroad being convicted of importing drugs, but this does not provide a full explanation. In addition to the factors affecting the treatment of black men, many are penalised for failing to conform to 'appropriate' notions of womanhood. To some judges and policemen the lifestyles of many black women in Britain today, particularly Afro-Caribbeans, seem unorthodox. The set-up is often matriarchal, lacking the 'restraining male influence', for which judges tend to look. Fewer black women have a tidy domestic picture to present to the court. The fact that the family unit of four is no longer an accurate reflection of social organisation amongst the white population, and that the percentage of single-parent families is high regardless of race, does not help black women, because we are now also seeing a moral and political crusade against the 'lone parent'.

A recurring theme for young black men refused bail is that they have insufficient roots in the community to guarantee their staying around to stand trial. Often they will have children but live separately from the children's mother rather than under the same roof. The men are often just as deeply involved with their children as any white father, and the likelihood of their absconding is no greater than that of most, but their family attachment is minimised by the difference in lifestyle. The historical background to the different cultural attitudes to the family is rarely acknowledged by the courts. To ignore the role of slavery and the consequent separation of black families, with women bearing children and raising them separately, denies the experience of many black people. The old taboo on illegitimacy was hardly a concern to those who were denied any legal status whatsoever.

The courts see single motherhood as a signal of an unstable background, regardless of the different family structures. Afro-Caribbean girls are often given independence at an earlier age than white girls and are allowed to be responsible for their own lives. They are assertive in a way that is not accepted in the dominant culture. The writer Ann Oakley has pointed out that the dividing line between what is masculine and what is criminal is at times a thin one; assertiveness and independence are seen as exclusively male characteristics, and when displayed by young black women are seen as indicative of 'trouble'.

Black women are far more frequently refused bail, because they are more often seen as homeless, their domestic arrangements not conforming to name-on-the-rentbook requirements. There are also very few bail hostels for women, and there is a general assumption that ethnic women will disappear into a subculture which will be difficult for the police to penetrate. In addition, poverty within the black community often means that it is difficult to obtain financial sureties. Black women who should be on bail can thus have it refused, only to be acquitted at their trial several months later. The shocking revelation was made in March 1992 by the Howard League for Penal Reform that 59 per cent of people on remand are not in the end sent to prison, yet the conditions in which they await trial are often worse than those experienced by the convicted.

Another objection to bail frequently raised by the police is that they consider it likely that the accused will commit further offences. This last objection, usually based on the existence of previous convictions, communicates the view that the woman is so undisciplined that appearing in court operates as no constraint on her behaviour. If the court sees a young woman who is affecting lack of concern they read her demeanour as supporting the police view, and off she goes into custody.

Black working-class women are often less submissive in the face of the legal system than their white counterparts. This is not to say they are unafraid of courts – they are as much in terror of them as any woman – but they see no reason for colluding in a system which discriminates against them. They arrive at court angry. Their anger is rarely understood: it is taken for aggression, and an unwillingness to show deference. Even if they themselves have not gone through criminal proceedings before, they have often learnt from the experience of male family members and friends not to have high expectations. The collective experience goes into court with them.

Young black women in particular are seen as 'lippy', often expressing their feelings with dagger-looks and with 'tchuking'. Nothing is more irritating to policemen, prison officers, judges and magistrates than this extraordinary sound of teeth-sucking, a hiss of insolence when it resounds in a courtroom. Even those who are unfamiliar with its use can tell that it combines the criticism of a 'tut' with the despair of a snort. There is always a danger that judges, threatened perhaps subconsciously by a woman's anger, will seek to quell it with incarceration.

One of the views firmly held by white defendants, which leapt from the NACRO report on the courts in 1991, was that black people did not know how to play the system, not realising that passive, remorseful behaviour served you best. But for many black people the court appearance is their last stand. The whole process has been humiliating. Often until the moment before entering the court they have been addressed in terms of abuse. The women talk of feeling dirty, like scum; the relative calm of the courtroom is their last chance to say: I am not going to be crushed.

A classic story of a black woman's road to crime is told by a young woman who was first convicted at the age of 14. The family was celebrating her brother's marriage, and the wedding party was in full swing when the police raided the house, suspecting that drugs were being consumed. The festive spirit was immediately spoiled and the house was turned upside down in the presence of all the guests. No drugs were found, but the girl became involved in a struggle with the police and was arrested. Despite all the claims that girls are treated lightly and are cautioned for first offences, she was brought to court and given a two-year conditional discharge as well as a fine and compensation to the officer for a torn epaulette amounting to £82.

It took the schoolgirl a long time to pay off the money, and her deep sense of the unfairness of what happened lives on. The conviction counted against her when she left school and tried to get a job, and offences of dishonesty started to accumulate. In interview, this woman made the important point that even as a girl she had the physical appearance of a mature woman, and she was dealt with as such. She felt that this assumption was often made about black girls if they were physically well developed.

Another handicap for black women is that police consider their colour before their gender, and in situations of arrest they are often dealt with quite aggressively. The police assume, as they do with black men, that black women will be violent, and that perception informs the way they handle a situation. In turn, any altercation with the police is dealt with seriously by the courts; defendants on charges of assaulting police are invariably sent to prison.

Assumptions about the sexuality of black women are insidious. They are deemed to be inherently promiscuous, not only happy to have sex with anyone but to do so with rampant regularity and abandon. This belief, which excites both fascination and disgust, is often subtly present in courtroom exchanges and socal enquiry reports, and affects the way they are sentenced. A black woman barrister told me of a recent attempt to have a violent husband imprisoned for recurrent breaches of an injunction not to molest his wife:

> The judge questioned why the battered wife, who was my client, had allowed her husband back into the house. He asked me to take instructions as to why my client was a tease. My client took offence and, to add insult to injury, the judge explained that, although he had heard it said that black women were highly sexual, he was not making that assumption about her. In fact, he allowed the husband to return to live in the house for a few weeks and ordered my client to stay at a relative's so that the husband could look after his tropical fish.

His Honour's compassion for God's little creatures did not endear him to the battered wife, nor to her barrister.

Another young black woman lawyer told me recently about the experiences of a client of hers who had been criticised by the police for lying to them by using the designation 'Mrs' when she was not married:

> The acceptance which is now generally shown towards people living together does not extend to black women. It is assumed that there is less commitment in relationships entered into by black women. The image conjured up when a black woman says she lives with a man is not one of the young couple testing the ground of their relationship but that of something much more sleazy and devalued. It was to avoid those inferences that my client described herself as married, but it was used against her.

In rape cases, particularly, the black experience seems to represent an amplified version of the handicaps facing women generally, whether in the juvenile or the higher courts. When black women are raped they have problems having their allegations heard, because all the usual assumptions merge with those about black sexuality and aggression. Black Afro-Caribbean women are not readily seen as fragile creatures in need of protection, but as well able to look after themselves. It is also assumed that they are much more open to casual sexual contact and that less commitment to formal marriage means promiscuity.

The double disadvantage for black women was clear in the case of PC Anderson.

The woman was young and black, a single parent. She had been out for the evening with some friends and was on her way home when a car pulled up alongside her. She quickened her pace and the driver called after her. The car crept in pursuit and stopped. The occupant was a policeman, which would normally reassure a woman alone, but this was not a woman who trusted the police.

What happened thereafter is a matter of dispute. The woman told a court that the police officer forced her into the car and threatened to charge her with soliciting for the purposes of prostitution if she did not engage in sexual activity. He verbally abused her and threatened her before making her perform oral sex and raping her.

The officer agreed that whilst on duty he had stopped her, and that indeed he had indulged in sex with her, but that she had offered herself to him voluntarily. He told the court that it was 'the best sex he had ever had'. The trial judge, Mr Justice Jowett, stepped in twice to prevent the woman defence counsel from questioning the victim about her sexual history and to stop PC Anderson referring to the victim by her surname, as though she were the person on trial and not him. The jury convicted, and PC Anderson was sentenced to seven years' imprisonment.

One of the interesting features of the case was that the young woman had, in great distress, confided the events to a friend, and that it was the friend who made an anonymous call to the police. The victim had not wanted to go to the police because she says she was convinced that they would not investigate one of their own and she did not believe that her word would be accepted against that of a policeman. She had no confidence she would get justice, and now maintains she was right. PC Anderson appealed, and his conviction was quashed on the grounds that the judge had not directed the jury as to his good character, a matter which the Court of Appeal seemed to think might have made all the difference in the world to the jury when judging the contradictory accounts.

Most people would take it for granted that policemen have good characters. 'Good character' in the language of the court means only that you have no previous convictions. You could be a drunken bully, who is bigoted, racist and misogynist, and still claim to be of 'good character'. Immediately after the result of the appeal I canvassed the views of every lawyer I met at a legal gathering. The judgement was greeted with cynical hoots of laughter and sometimes anger. As criminal lawyers we all welcomed the precedent that judges should remind juries that a defendant has never committed an offence before, but as juries know, that is not really how truth is judged.

Interestingly, the lawyers varied in their reasons as to why, in their view, the conviction was quashed rather than the 'proviso' being exercised, which means there is acceptance that the judge erred but that the Court of Appeal feels the omission did not affect the outcome. Some believed it was because the defendant was a policeman; others that the determining factor was that this was a rape trial; for others, the fatal combination included the fact that the complainant was black. No one thought they would have got a quashed conviction in a robbery or an IRA case where the only evidence was an oral confession denied by the defendant and where similarly the issue for the jury would be whom to believe.

The judges in the Appeal Court emphasised that their concern was that the case turned on which of the two parties, the man or the woman, was to be believed, and that the reminder that the policeman had no convictions (no policemen could remain in the job with a criminal conviction) may have produced a different outcome.

Black people are twice as likely to be apprehended on the street as white people; they feel that there is an accepted belief that they are dishonest. It is only in cases like that of the 'respectable' black trainee solicitor who is arrested wrongfully that the scandal of their experience is exposed. For women, that assumption of inherent dishonesty means that the usual mitigation for crime, like depression or menopausal pressures, is not even considered.

On 31 July 1985 the *Sun* ran a front-page story alleging that busloads of black women had gone on a seaside shoplifting spree, swooping on to shops for wholesale theft. This sounded like organised crime gone mad, but the story concluded, rather tamely, by adding that two women were arrested.

A colleague of mine represented a hospital sister who was arrested at the Chelsea Flower Show. Not many black faces are to be seen at the Flower Show, a quintessentially English, middle-class affair, but the woman in question was in fact both English and middle-class, and also a lover of gardens and horticulture. To her amazement, she was pulled out of a group of women who were queueing to use the ladies' lavatory by two young police officers who maintained that they had seen her put her hand twice towards the handbags of other women. She was aghast. No stolen article was found on her and no person in the queue had complained, but she was charged with attempted theft and trailed through the nightmare of a Crown Court trial before being acquitted.

Black mothers often feel that their bond with their children is perceived as less significant and that their views on a child's welfare are less valuable. One mother, sentenced to two months in prison for refusing access to her daughter's father, felt that she was viewed as bloody-minded and obstructive, when in fact she was trying to express deep concern for her child's well-being. Her ex-boyfriend was a drug user and the little girl returned from visits describing in detail his use of drugs and drug involvement with others. The mother feared that the influence of drugs would affect his ability to care for the child when she was with him, and wanted any access to be supervised. In court, her concerns were ignored. She explained:

> The judge thought I was a stubborn, determined person who was going out of my way to break a court order. I think had I not had two children by different fathers they would have viewed me as a different type of person. I think the judge was trying to say, 'You can't have your children and do what you like with them.' I think the colour factor comes into it, but it's something that can never be proved.

The heroism of 'mother figures' who bring up families in the face of hardship and poverty is part of the received wisdom.

While young black women are often underestimated as committed mothers, older black women are almost invariably seen as over-committed matriarchs, who indulge their sons. The assumption is that black women protect their wild boys from the forces of law and order. The Brixton riots in 1985 were fired by the shooting of Mrs Cherry Groce when the police were looking for her son, Michael. The race riots which took place in Tottenham later that year were sparked off by the death of a black mother, Mrs Jarrett, who suffered a heart attack while her home was being raided by police.

Many of the older black women who live in Britain today are first-generation immigrants who came to this country with high expectations. The experience of their children going through the courts is shameful to them, and there is a shocking sense of betrayal when they find that the authorities are not even-handed. In his book *What Next in the Law?*, published in 1982, Lord Denning seemed to be maintaining that black jurors could not be trusted in cases involving black defendants. He cited as his example the Bristol Riots Trial of 1983, when a number of black defendants charged with riot were acquitted. His argument was of the same specious quality as Norman Tebbit's query as to which side 'our immigrant population' would support in the cricket season. The jurors who were most affronted by this attack were the church-going older women, who had approached the evidence with scru-pulous care. That older group of women are often particularly tough on black criminality. The threatened action of two of them took Lord Denning's book off the shelves and forced some careful editing, and a subsequent leading article about the anger of the black community (*The Times*, 24 May 1982) forced him into retirement.

In the early 1980s a campaign developed around the case of the Mozart Seven – not a chamber orchestra but a group of black women from the Mozart Estate in West London who had been arrested on assault charges arising out of an appalling example of overzealous policing. A young black man was seen on the estate by the police, who decided to stop him for questioning. The officers gave chase, pursuing him in and out of gardens and over fences. An elderly West Indian woman who had been cleaning up outside her door was going back inside, weighed down with cloths and a bucket of water, when the running boy barged past her into her house. They fell over each other in the entrance and the boy slammed the door shut to stop the police catching him. The woman then told the police through her front window that the boy had run through the house and leapt out of a back window. The police, however, immediately assumed that the boy must be connected with her and that she was harbouring him. They made no attempt to run to the rear but started pushing the door down. The woman's daughters and female neighbours arrived on the scene and remonstrated with the police, insisting that there was no need to force an entry: she lived alone with a handicapped son and was probably too frightened to open the door. A dreadful fight broke out, in which one police officer was bitten and all the women were arrested.

It came to light that the boy was not in fact wanted for any wrongdoing and had no connections whatsoever with the family. The women were seen as violent troublemakers and went through a long period of anxiety and a very noisy trial, where some of them were able to voice their profound anger. The jury was racially mixed, and perhaps the knowledge and understanding of those from the ethnic minorities contributed to their discussions. All were acquitted, bar one who was given a suspended sentence, and a white juror, insisting that his anonymity was maintained, sent a cheque so that the elderly mother could enjoy some sort of treat with her handicapped son, as compensation for her ordeal.

Although the outcome was good, the trial was a perfect example of alienation, in that it turned on the word of police officers against the word of the women. The women saw the court all too willingly siding with the officers, while counsel for the defence were prevailed upon to restrain their clients' anger and to ensure that they behaved 'properly'. The coercive régime of the court was a source of extreme frustration to them.

Asian women's experience of the courts is different from that of other racial minority women so long as they are very traditional. An interesting paradox was presented to the courts during the Grunwick dispute, when very assertive, politically organised Asian women picketed their place of work and were arrested for offences arising out of the dispute. Mrs Desai, the union leader, was charged a number of times and defended the cases successfully, and with great dignity, discarding the stereotype and earning herself an individualised hearing.

If black Afro-Caribbean women suffer from a female version of the myths about black male sexuality and violence, Asian women suffer from feminised versions of the 'untrustworthy oriental'. They are often given an even lower rating on the credibility scale than other black women, and there is a suspicion that behind the demure exterior lurks deceit and dishonesty. A recurring lapse is the misreading of Asian peoples' failure to make eye contact, which is a mark of respect and culturally inculcated from the earliest age but is seen in the courts as shiftiness.

Asian women on trial often have language difficulties and an interpreter has to be used. Conducting a defence through the medium of a translator is never satisfactory because the usual methods of measuring truthfulness are greatly reduced: questions and answers become mechanical and bland, and the emotion and subtlety in a person's intonation are lost. The delay before the answer is treated with suspicion: jurors imagine the witness understands more than she is letting on, and that she is using the time to consider her response. It is true that if you try to conduct cross-examinations in poor English, the risk of misunderstanding is considerable, but the accused is not as 'real' when she is distanced by language from those who try her and she suffers the consequences. The ultimate linguistic failure happened in the case of Mrs Begum, a battered wife who pleaded guilty to the murder of her husband in Birmingham Crown Court in April 1985 without understanding the language spoken to her by her lawyers or the court clerk.

As with white working-class women, it is assumed that violence is an acceptable part of black women's lives. Black women's organisations campaign vociferously about the neglect of black women who are subjected to battering. The police and courts tend to make cultural assumptions about women who enter into arranged marriages, imagining that any woman who is prepared to engage in such a bizarre custom is subjugated anyway. There is also a reluctance to interfere, because it is assumed that such violence is customary in immigrant communities. 'They're not like us and we have to tread with care or we will be accused of racism by their community leaders,' was one of the explanations I was given by a prosecutor. If police do arrive on the scene, and the wife has poor English, the police tend to rely on the story being told by the men around. Repeatedly, Asian women report that by the time police turn up they are too distressed to be very coherent, and little effort is made to discover what they have suffered.

It is true that the pressures on women in some of the Asian communities are great, because it is considered an insult to the honour of the man's family if his wife should leave. A number of Asian women have been killed in recent years by their husbands or a member of their husband's family because they have attempted to leave or seek help from the criminal justice system and been fobbed off.

Southall Black Sisters, a group which campaigns vigorously for women, raises the important issue that many immigrant women, who originally acquired entry to Britain through their marital status, feel obliged to stay in violent marriages because to leave may jeopardise their right to remain in this country. Such fears make women diffident about calling in the police or, if they do, about answering all their questions, which in turn is perceived as slyness.

The problems are not confined to the Asian communities. In the trial of a Ugandan woman for grievous bodily harm to her husband by pouring hot cooking fat over him, it came to light that, although she had called the police repeatedly, her violent husband had never been arrested. Indeed, it was suggested to her that she was not telling the truth when she said in interview to the CID that she had made many previous complaints: there was no record of such complaints and the claim that she was exaggerating her husband's brutality was put to her again at her trial by prosecuting counsel. It was a prosecution witness, a neighbour, who inadvertently came to her aid. He complained in the witness box about the number of times he had been awakened, first by her screams and then by police mistakenly ringing his doorbell when they came in answer to her calls.

*

As we have seen, black women are given probation less often than others, and a review of social enquiry reports showed that recommendations as to sentence are less often made. The inevitable consequence is that prison is a likelier option: two to three times more likely, according to the statistics. They are also assumed to be involved in drugs, and that cultural inference is hard to shift when they appear in the dock. However much they might deny involvement in drugs offences, there is a particular burden on the black defendant in challenging such charges.

Social enquiry reports are not scientific documents and are bound to be subjective. They are also, inevitably, directed at the middle-class magistrates and judges. In an increasingly punitive climate there is a temptation to pander to the expectations and prejudices of the bench in ways which will secure a favourable outcome. (It is an approach to which we have all succumbed, lawyers and probation officers alike. We have all experienced the fear that our client will turn up with a mohican haircut, or with her tattoos showing, or with a ring in her nose or a jumper shot with lurex, especially when the judge really is a conformist and is likely to draw adverse inferences.)

However, the probation service is now actively addressing the issue of racism and sexism in reports, and their studies have identified stereotyping as a particular problem. The accepted image is an easy shorthand to fall back on when there is little time. When I was making a television programme on a similar subject I interviewed the BBC's head of comedy, who told me that reliance upon stereotypes in sitcoms was partly due to the need to impart information quickly and to create shared laughter in shared values. The problem is that these values can become reinforced, allowing prejudice to creep in. In the courtroom their use prevents important distinctions being made between each case and each person. Basic information is provided, responses are triggered, and the individual who is encased in this envelope of assumptions is never allowed to surface. For black women, emerging as special and different is especially tough.

Black women lawyers have well-tuned antennae and empathise with the problems faced by women clients of their race. As the barrister Tanoo Mylavagnum says, 'You cannot be a woman lawyer, experiencing discriminatory practice yourself as a professional, without being alerted to the way that the same attitudes affect women who do not even have our class advantage.' Black women lawyers complain that the problems of being taken seriously are exacerbated for them and that the difficulty of securing authority within the courtroom is all the greater if you are female and black. Those who are successful are constantly told by white colleagues that they do not 'seem' black, as though there were some special stamp of blackness which they had shrugged off. Such comments are proffered as compliments; it is often not understood why they are offensive.

Another woman barrister, a rising criminal practitioner, describes defending a black client who was one of several defendants; the other lawyers were all white. She had the strong feeling that the trial judge, who is renowned for his rudeness, was particularly dismissive of her legal arguments. At one stage, when she sat down, he sent her a note asking her whether her accent was English, and if so where she had been to school. She ignored the note, uncertain what it meant, but felt very undermined, as though her fluency and education were being questioned. After making her final speech to the jury, the judge summed up to the all-white jury with this remark: 'Members of the jury, we are British and this is a British court and British standards of behaviour are being protected.' She felt that the comment diminished her own address to the jury, as coming from someone with a different and less valid value system.

Elizabeth James, a British barrister of Nigerian descent, was defending a Nigerian woman charged with a credit-card fraud when the judge opined that 'this type of crime is far too prevalent amongst the Nigerian community'. There is absolutely no support for his view, and she had the courage to challenge him in court and to say that she took personal exception to the remark.

It is not just the ethnic minority communities who suffer racial prejudice. Those who do not hold British passports have similar experiences. To be foreign is a handicap for anyone in British courts. Thirteen per cent of the women imprisoned in England and Wales are women from overseas imprisoned for drug offences, usually importation, mainly from Nigeria, Ghana and Jamaica but also from India and Pakistan or Latin America. In Holloway prison, the ratio is higher (26 per cent), because of its London location and because it includes women awaiting trial. In Cookham Wood, a female prison which is used to incarcerate women with longer sentences, there are times when the proportion of foreign inmates (usually black) is around 60 per cent. The conviction rate is high, because even where the women claim they have been duped or pressured into carrying drugs, judges and juries are sceptical. The worlds they are hearing about are so alien to British people that the accounts often seem fantastic. A woman from Colombia, currently serving nine years, said that her trial judge suggested to her that she had read too many books about the Mafia or watched too many films. Yet the more we hear about the Latin-American drug cartels the more real seems her terror at what could be done to her family.

To people coming from impoverished lives in Third World countries, the financial rewards for importing and distributing drugs, though often not very substantial by Western standards, are considerable. The sums range between hundreds to a few thousand pounds, and for many these incentives outweigh the risks of arrest. The use of women as couriers or 'mules' is frequent and intentional. The belief that women travellers attract less attention from Customs and Excise officials was initially well founded, particularly if they appeared respectable or had children with them, although nowadays the policing of our ports is sensitive to the ploys of drug importers and women can expect as much scrutiny as men.

The inventiveness of the importers knows no bounds, with drugs secreted inside toothpaste tubes and cosmetics, the heels of shoes, in dominoes, draught sets, artefacts and false-bottomed boxes of every variety. A ploy used for a while in some importations was for the courier to arrive at an Asian or African airport and check in perfectly ordinary luggage with no drug contents, and for the drugs organisers to pay off airline employees to put exact duplicate luggage directly into the hold. When the luggage arrived in London the courier would pick the cases containing the contraband off the carousel and take it through the green light. If stopped, they would be able to produce the luggage label attached to their tickets, showing that there was some mistake, point to the luggage still circling the carousel, and identify it as theirs. There is no end to criminal ingenuity.

The press has recently pounced on the swallowing of condoms full of heroin and cocaine, but this method had been used for years, sometimes to ill effect when the contents have begun to leak into the intestines of the courier.

In the streets of African, Colombian or Indian cities, an endless supply of poor women can be persuaded to earn cash which will see their children through school, pay for medical bills or just secure their family's existence for the foreseeable future. Few are aware of the sentences they are likely to face, or of British sentencing policy, so that its rationale of long sentences to discourage others is a nonsense; little publicity is given to the experience of these women in their communities.

The courts are anxious to show that no leniency will be extended, however heart-rending the personal circumstances of those caught bringing drugs into the country. They are obliged to follow the guidelines established by Lord Chief Justice Lane in the case of Aramah, a drugs appeal which presented the opportunity to set down the tariffs for drug-related crime. A strict equality principle operates, which has led to a large increase in women of all nationalities going through the criminal justice system and ending up with very long prison sentences. For these defendants there is no slow induction into the vagaries of the courts. The experience is usually new to them, and the implications of their foray into criminal activity comes as the most profound shock. Many cannot speak a word of English, and court interpretation can often be inadequate. Spanish-speaking Latin Americans explain that having a Spaniard to translate often distorts what they mean because of linguistic differences and nuances. They rarely have friends or family in this country to provide emotional support, and their lawyers become their only contact with the outside world. They often have an innocent belief that their legal representatives might have some special influence with the authorities.

I remember especially an elderly Indian woman who had been used by her son-in-law to bring in quantities of cannabis when she travelled to this country with her grandchildren, who had been to stay with her for the holidays. It was her first journey abroad apart from a pilgrimage to Mecca, and she had been so terrified of the moving escalator on her arrival at Heathrow that she had been unable to stand upright on it, but simply crouched on one of its steps in a state of panic. She was sentenced to three years' imprisonment, with little account taken of what a nightmare prison would be for someone who spoke not a word of the language, who had never undressed even in front of her daughters, let alone strangers, and who was in purdah because of the recent death of her husband. In the cells she clung to me in abject terror, pleading like a little girl. The interpreter who was with us explained that she was saying that she did not want to die away from her home. As they peeled her away from me and took her to the prison van, a little trail of betel-nuts that she had been chewing fell and lay scattered on the ground. I wept for her as I made the miserable journey back into London.

An analysis undertaken by the Probation Service in 1989 showed that the average sentence passed by the courts is 6.25 years for couriers of cocaine and 8.5 for heroin. A significant number are therefore serving in excess of ten years, and many of those feel they are sentenced more harshly than British women for the same offences. Cannabis is a class B drug and the sentences are usually shorter: two to four years.

The number of couriers receiving sentences of more than four years has increased sixfold between 1984 and 1989. These women are often ruthlessly exploited by drug barons, but when they are caught they are too afraid to name names because they know that the consequences could be terrible for their families back home. On the rare occasions when Mr Big is caught he faces a sentence of fifteen to twenty years, whilst the tariff for others in the chain moves down from that. The rhetoric in the courtroom is that drugs would not enter the country without the courier. The role is central to all the problems involved in drug abuse, and in my experience juries, ever sensitive to the effects of drugs, are understandably resistant to the arguments about whether the transporter actually knew herself to be in possession.

Juries are also unable to accept the gullibility of some women who unquestioningly carry items for friends and acquaintances. Maria Gonzales was convicted of bringing four kilos of cocaine into this country from Colombia and was sentenced to fourteen years' imprisonment. The substance was pressed inside long-playing records and would in no way be detectable to the untrained eye. However, she was a vivacious woman who had worked as an air hostess when she was younger. Clearly the jury had difficulty believing that she would not suspect the motives of a man friend asking her to bring some personal belongings to one of his friends in Europe.

Because the sentence on conviction for drugs couriers will automatically be imprisonment, the courts sometimes feel that there is no point in obtaining social enquiry reports. Most of the information would inevitably have to come from the woman herself because there would be little access to information from abroad: the assumption is that the woman will have told anything significant to her lawyers. In any event, this is one of the areas of crime where a respectable past and family responsibilities cut no ice. There is also a cynical belief that the couriers will invent handicapped children and dying mothers just for the day in court. These women, who are referred to inside prison as 'deportees', feel aggrieved that they do not have this opportunity of presenting their background fully to the tribunal. Some of their circumstances could then be substantiated and allowances should, in their view, be made for the pressures on their lives.

Martha, whose daughter in Columbia is seriously ill with leukaemia, is currently serving nine years. The girl, along with Martha's other children, is being looked after by her elderly mother. She had lengthy letters showing the truth of her history, but the court showed little interest in them. It was clear, listening to her, that she was uncertain who was who in the courtroom or what function each person played in her trial. This is an experience shared by many people, white and black, but it is exacerbated when language is an additional problem:

> I explained my situation to the judge, explained it to the solicitor [prosecutor] the reason I was involved in this case and they didn't believe me. They didn't believe me so the result . . . nine

years. I couldn't take it in my mind. It took me quite a few days to think: nine years away from home! I was just thinking of being in there. It was horrible, I wished to die.

Another courier is Stephanie, who is of Jamaican origin but whose home was New York:

You are prejudged for the idea that you are from Colombia or Jamaica. Jamaica is a drug country, drug-orientated. Or you are from New York. It is a bad place. That is where the guns and the drugs are. All the bad things that happen, you are just a part of it. You should know what is happening and you have been doing it all your life. That's your lifestyle.

Basically I think the judge looks at the stereotype. If you're a woman, you shouldn't even think of committing a crime in the first place. You should be home with your children. But then in most cases the reason they've done it is because of the children, which sounds horrible. But it is to send them to school, to feed them, to clothe them. Depending on which country they are from, there are probably no social services nor any help from the government. So it's looked on as, well, you shouldn't be in court in the first place. You expect some kind of punishment, but six, eight, ten, twelve years! It is a bit much, especially for women. We know that even though we scream equality, in the home the woman she's the backbone. In most cases she is both mother and father in the home.

Many of the women feel that they are dealt with as if by rote by both judges and lawyers. Stephanie saw her solicitor on only a few brief visits, and her barrister, whom she had never met before, arrived fifteen minutes before the start of the case. The solicitor was away on holiday so there was no familiar face at court. Defendants in these cases have little power, and at times feel forced to accept a poor service from the legal profession.

At the time of her trial Martha's English was negligible and she too felt that she was never able to get her case across. She describes the experience as deeply traumatic. Like Stephanie, she felt dissatisfied with her representation because, although she had had a conference with a barrister at the prison, someone different turned up on the day. She could not believe that it was sufficient for someone to read the papers in the case and to talk with her for as little as half an hour. It is not unreasonable for clients to want the opportunity to talk to their lawyers at length if they are facing imprisonment of maybe ten years. But there is pressure in the court to get a move on, and the lawyer fears the judge's wrath. Since the solicitor Martha was familiar with was not present either, the trial was like a bad dream in which she felt like a powerless observer rather than a participant.

The problem of last-minute changes in counsel is an old chestnut for the courts. Complaints are myriad and resolution is difficult for those who are trying to administer the courts speedily. It can only be reduced as a problem if more and more cases are given fixed dates in advance and if the real seriousness of importation cases is recognised. Needless to say, foreign prisoners are not a vociferous or influential group of complainants.

For the women from outside Europe who are convicted of drugs charges there is no parole, no home visits, and few visitors, because everyone they know is elsewhere. Prisoners can now buy phone-cards, but a call to Nigeria or Latin America is expensive, and few can afford to buy more than the occasional card out of their prison earnings. They are given one free five-minute phone-call to their families every three months.

Some of the women arrive in this country pregnant, and because they will not be released by the time the child is eighteen months the baby is taken away soon after birth to be cared for in a British foster home, ultimately to be reunited in the years to come. A recent deportee faced the excruciating problem of her child not wanting to go to live in Africa when she herself was released and deported. The grief of most of these women is too terrible to describe, the damage caused out of all proportion to the crime, and their cries of pain reverberate throughout the prisons. Yet few can be returned home to serve sentences there, either because of the absence of reciprocal arrangements or because their own countries often do not recognise the criminality of what they have done. Some countries, such as Nigeria, are now introducing laws to charge them on their return with exporting the same drugs, so that they face a double punishment.

Until our sentencing policy is revised and real distinctions between defendants are made based on the circumstances which drove them to offend, we are denying justice to these women. But when judges try to use their discretion, they are criticised for leniency. The Court of Appeal's response has been to set tariffs to even out any disparity, and there is now new government pressure to have a consistent sentencing policy on drugs offences, with the result that even less account is taken of the very different personal factors involved. Some are ruthless exploiters of drug dependency, but many are themselves the exploited.

Those who go through the criminal justice system rarely have much voice, but immigrants are one of the most silent groups. There are few votes in prisoners, and none in foreign men and women charged with crime. They are the most vulnerable of all the adults who appear in our courts. In the 1990 Administrative Law Reports a shocking case of sexual blackmail of a female immigrant unravelled some of the abuse to which immigrants are exposed but to which our courts rarely give credence.

Adebola Makanjuola came to Britain as a visitor from Nigeria, but once here applied to upgrade her status to that of a student and sought permission to stay for the duration of her studies. Whilst her application was being processed she began her academic course, a perfectly lawful thing to do. However, a police officer who called at the house where she was staying, looking for another occupant, proceeded to quiz her in the presence of her boyfriend about her immigration status. When she told him of her application the officer became very officious, telling her she was acting unlawfully and that he would have to make a report. Ms Makanjuola and her boyfriend became very distressed and the officer changed his attitude, turning more solicitous and eventually suggesting that if the young woman were sufficiently obliging he might forget he had ever seen her. He shifted from cajoling to threatening and back again until it was agreed that Ms Makanjuola would have sex with him if he would not proceed against her. In an adjoining room she was subjected to anal intercourse. As a post-coital bonus the officer gave Ms Makanjuola the advice that she should obtain a letter from someone who would sponsor her in this country, even suggesting that the letter need not be real but could be written by her boyfriend. It would, according to him, reassure the authorities.

The young woman sent the forged letter to the Home Office and was arrested by the police for fraud. She appeared at the Magistrates Court at Old Street and her counsel recounted the whole sordid business to the magistrate, who clearly did not believe a word. Adebola Makanjuola was fined and recommended for deportation. Fortunately, she was represented by a lawyer who was troubled by her story. She could not name her blackmailer but was able to describe him as having red hair and was very clear that she had seen him at Stoke Newington police station when she was being charged. The lawyer partly specialised in immigration cases and had noticed in various statements to solicitors that there seemed to be a rogue police officer who used his power to obtain sexual services. On occasion he would force couples to prove that they had a 'genuine marriage' rather than one conveniently arranged for immigration purposes by making them perform sexual intercourse in his presence.

The officer was identified by his victim on an identification parade as Sean McCarthy, and Adebola Makanjuola then courageously brought an action against him for sexual assault. The Commissioner of Police was named as a party in the action because he was the policeman's employer at the time and therefore responsible for his actions. The trial at the High Court was a humiliating process, with Sean McCarthy making a complete denial and insisting he spent that particular evening watching *Pot Black* on television. The thrust of the cross-examination of Adebola was that she had made no mention of Mr McCarthy's appalling bad breath, which she could not have failed to notice even when being penetrated from behind.

The judge, however, believed Ms Makanjuola and affirmed the fundamental principle that minorities and disadvantaged people must be protected by the courts. He found that she had been assaulted by this halitosis-ridden snooker fan and awarded her £8,000, with £2,000 exemplary damages. But he decided that the officer was acting outside his duties and therefore made no award against the Commissioner of Police. Adebola Makanjuola was not deported. She stayed to complete her course, but it was a long and hard fight. The case highlighted the failure of the criminal law to protect those who are most vulnerable. There was no way that this woman could have complained and been believed. At the criminal court her account was seen as an example of the machinations of an alien woman. Had her lawyer not made the connections and championed her struggle through the system she would have been ejected from Britain and have forfeited her chance of receiving an education.

Of course, the courts cannot be held responsible for the aberrant conduct of the odd policeman, or for racism in the police and prisons, but they must not compound that injustice when it does take place.

Black defendants particularly suffer from one of the great losses to the legal system: the removal of the right of the defence to challenge jurors without cause. When I first came to the Bar it was possible to challenge up to seven jurors on behalf of each individual client. This right was reduced under a Labour administration to three challenges per defendant, and was finally removed altogether in 1988 because it was claimed that anyone who carried the *Daily Telegraph* or who looked as though he or she had half a brain was being dismissed by manipulative defence lawyers.

There was no doubt that efforts were made to second-guess the type of juror from all sorts of aspects of their appearance, a lot of the time to little avail. (I myself, for example, had a sneaking aversion to men who had badges on brass-buttoned blazers and women who looked like my old headmistress.) But there were occasions when the challenge had a valid and important use. In cases involving aspects of child-rearing, such as cases of baby-battering, it is helpful to have people who have not forgotten the demands of a newborn. Equally, age can be important in cases involving youths, where their lifestyles may be incomprehensible to jurors of an exclusively older generation. However, it is particularly worrying that in cases of a racial nature we can have all-white juries trying black defendants.

After the abolition of the defence right to challenge, it was thought that at least the judge had a residual right to affect the racial make-up of the jury in the interests of justice. However, Lord Justice Lane scuppered that in the case of Ford in 1989 by ruling that this was not an appropriate use of the judge's power, and that 'fairness' was achieved by random selection.

A mechanism to secure a racially balanced jury has to be available if a trial is to be fair. If the courts do not take appropriate steps to remedy the present inadequacy the results could be as horrifying as the riots that erupted in the United States last spring after a non-black jury acquitted four white policemen, in the face of incontrovertible evidence, of beating up a black motorist. That tinderbox should not be ignored.

In my view, judges should be persuaded, in cases where cultural differences may affect a jury's interpretation, to allow the admission of evidence about the workings and experience of particular sections of society. In one Irish case I found it very valuable to call someone to explain the way in which open-house is a special feature of Irish life, although it may seem unorthodox to others, and to confirm that Republican politics do not automatically mean support for the IRA.

I have also been allowed to call a woman Asian anthropologist to testify on the role of the wife in a very traditional home of a particular sect, so that the jury could assess the possible impact on her behaviour in the police station when interrogated by male police officers.

Some developments are taking place. Judges are consciously endeavouring to remove the spectre of cultural indifference from the courts. It is rare now for courts to insist, as they did until recently, that Rastafarians remove their hats, which their religion requires them to wear to cover their dreadlocks. But before reaching the position where racism is completely ousted there has to be recognition that people do not start equal – that the old British playing field is not level. The baggage which comes with the defendant or complainant to the courtroom has to be thrown into the scales. All the experiences of black people at the hands of the law have been absorbed into the collective consciousness of their communities: the black taxi-driver badly beaten for no reason by off-duty policemen; the middle-aged woman who suffered a dislocated shoulder when her £20 note was automatically suspect and she was wrongfully arrested with force by a detective; the young man whose head was stamped on in a police station; the unprotected Asian families burned out of their homes.

When the subject of racial and sexual awareness training is raised amongst lawyers it is usually greeted with sneers. Yet the work which has been going on in the United States for some years now has been highly successful, and judges themselves speak of the benefits of understanding racism in securing confidence in the system.

One of our High Court judges, Sir Henry Brooke, who successfully chaired the Bar's Race Relations Committee and skilfully steered through the policy of setting a target of 5 per cent for chambers' recruitment of black barristers, is now heading a group which will be advising the Judicial Studies Board on race issues. New assistant recorders are given a lecture on respecting racial difference in the courts. But a friend, recently inducted, told me how, within hours of the talk, a prospective judge in one of the case studies was regaling the crowd with his Peter Sellers imitation of an Indian witness, while others were running down the Irish. The judicial lunch table at one of our courts was the subject of another complaint about derogatory Irish remarks.

The extent of the problem is still denied, and the willingness of the judiciary to embrace the idea of training is still remote. At a recent meeting on racism in the courts, the invited audience of senior members of the profession, as well as judges, needed to be convinced that they had any role in resolving the problem. A complaint was made from the floor that black lawyers expressed no interest in becoming prosecutors and that the fault lay with them. The reluctance to prosecute is an expression of concern about being directly involved in the process of criminalising black people in a society. Rudy Narayan, the black lawyer, explained to a jury in a race trial that he addressed them with one foot in the dock.

Until there is a clear appreciation of racism and the social factors which bring black people before the courts, and an understanding of the subtle dynamics which work in the courts to discriminate against them, they will continue to be amongst the sections of the community least well served by the law. Any failure to do justice will come back to haunt us.

8

Man – Slaughter

The trial of Ruth Ellis, the last woman to be hanged in Britain, was over in one and a half days, a feat which would no doubt win the acclaim of many judges today, who bemoan the long duration of trials. In some cases the issues are so narrow that they can proceed at quite a lick, but these are rare. A murder trial, which involves exploring the psychological state of a defendant against a complicated background of emotion, violence, insecurity and abandonment, inevitably takes a good deal of time and is built upon a very full knowledge of the person represented.

In the years since Ruth Ellis stood trial psychiatry has come to play a much greater role in murder trials, and we as lawyers have become better versed in its language. There is also, as we have seen earlier, a growing understanding of domestic violence and the reasons why it is endured.

Ruth Ellis's case would have been conducted differently today and would very likely have led to her acquittal of murder. This is largely because of the changes in the law in 1957, which introduced a number of fresh concepts to homicide trials. Parliament established two statutory defences to murder, reducing the offence to manslaughter (a) where the accused was suffering from a mental disorder which diminished his or her criminal responsibility, or (b) where the killing was a response to provocation.

Provocation was available as a defence prior to the enactment, but because of concern that vengeful behaviour would escape just punishment, which for murder meant the death penalty at that time, it was narrowly interpreted in the case law. Provocation was interpreted for juries by the judges as conduct immediately preceding the killing. The archetypal case was that of the betrayed husband finding his faithless wife and her lover *in flagrante* and killing one or the other, or both. Words, for example, could not amount to provocation prior to the 1957 Homicide Act.

As for diminished responsibility, until the Act, the only debate about mental states was whether a defendant was sane or insane according to the 'M'Naghton rules'. There it had to be clearly proved that at the time of committing the alleged offence the party accused was labouring under such a defect of reason or disease of the mind that he did not know the nature and quality of the act he was doing, or that he did not know it was wrong. The defendant had to think he was squeezing an orange when he was throttling his victim. By the 1950s the test had become seriously discredited as a method of determining the mental state of an accused. The verdict of not guilty to murder by reason of diminished responsibility, reducing an unlawful killing to manslaughter, does not require that someone is certifiably insane, just that he or she has a definable degree of mental disorder. The defence can include a difficulty in controlling one's actions, provided this arises from an abnormality of mind.

Even today, the issue of whether someone suffers from some abnormality of mind which diminished their responsibility for a killing is one which taxes juries. It used to be said that juries were reluctant to convict people of murder when they faced the death penalty, but even without the ultimate sanction there seems to be an unwillingness in jurors to declare someone guilty of wilful murder when they were in the grip of overwhelming emotional turmoil. Equally, juries are reluctant to let a person who takes a life escape all sanction, which is why self-defence is rarely successful in murder. However, the willingness to accept manslaughter as the appropriate plea often depends on the sympathies evoked by the defendant. In mercy killings, where family members bring to an end the misery or pain of a terminally ill relative, judges and juries alike are usually prepared to stretch the definition of diminished responsibility.

There seems little doubt that the outcome of Ruth Ellis's trial in 1955 was affected by a moral evaluation of her way of life – as a sexually active divorcee, a mother of an illegitimate child and a club hostess. The tabloid press would still have a field day at her expense, but today's jury, furnished with as much information as has subsequently come to light, might take a more generous view.

Ruth Ellis's own leading counsel, Mr Melford Stevenson, later became a High Court judge and the scourge of the Old Bailey. When I started practising, in 1972, he had just conducted the trial of the students who had taken part in the Cambridge riot case, involving a demonstration against the Greek colonels, and sentenced them all to imprisonment and borstal. He was held in very low esteem by many of my generation as a judge of the old school, dogmatic and misogynist. Many senior members of the legal profession speak of his charm off the bench, but that is hardly the essential test of a judge's ability.

My one particular memory of Sir Melford, as he had then become, was his sentencing in 1974 of the young woman prison warden who became emotionally involved with Myra Hindley at Holloway prison. She pleaded guilty at the Old Bailey to conspiring to effect Myra Hindley's escape. Their conspiracy was based on grandiose plans to flee together to South America, where they would work together as missionaries. The woman had been a nun and had never lived outside the confines of rigid female institutions. Any careful examination of the evidence showed that the plot was fundamentally flawed, that it was essentially the fantasy of two people whose relationship was blighted from the start. For a wardress to become a prisoner carries a special burden of resentment from both staff and prisoners, but Sir Melford passed a sentence of six years.

When Melford Stevenson represented Ruth Ellis he was relatively inexperienced in the criminal courts: he was mainly a divorce practitioner, and had done few major criminal trials. He had none of the instinctive feel which the good jury advocate needs to overcome the unspoken prejudices which lie beneath the surface in any criminal case. Nor did he have the empathy which might have helped Ruth Ellis tell her story in a more compelling way. So many witnesses, particularly women who have gone through an emotional battering, disengage from events and give their evidence in a cool, remote way. Her own counsel has to break through that, or at least enable her to explain that detachment; otherwise a jury is left unpersuaded of the defence. At the time, the view was openly expressed that either of his two junior counsel, Peter Rawlinson or Sebag Shaw, would have had more appeal to a jury. Just reading the trial accounts, it was clearly a case which any criminal advocate would have longed to get their hands on.

Mr Christmas Humphreys, who must be the only Buddhist to sit on the bench, opened the case for the Crown on 21 June 1955. Ruth Ellis stood alone in the dock charged with the murder of David Blakely. Humphreys laid emphasis on the fact that Mrs Ellis was conducting simultaneous love affairs with two men: with David Blakely, whom she killed, and with Desmond Cussen. What was never explored was the true nature of her relationship with Cussen, whom she leaned on for emotional support but never considered seriously as a lover: it later transpired that their sexual liaison lasted only a matter of weeks, in June 1954. Mr Humphreys told the jury that Blakely was trying to break off the association and that Ellis was angry about this, even though she had another lover at the time. He described how she took a gun, found David, and shot him dead by emptying that revolver at him, four bullets going into his body, one hitting a bystander in the thumb and the sixth disappearing completely. After the shooting outside a public house in Southhill Park, Hampstead, Ellis was questioned by a police officer who told her that he had seen the body of David Blakely and understood she knew something about it. Her reply was 'I am guilty, I am rather confused.' She then made a written statement to the police describing how, after putting her child to bed, she had picked up a revolver that had been given to her by a man as security for a loan three years ago, and had put it in her handbag. She had gone out, she said, with the intention of finding Blakely and shooting him.

Christmas Humphreys called only a few witnesses to provide evidence in support of this stark history of the relationship between Ruth Ellis and David Blakely and the events surrounding the killing. After each person completed their testimony, Melford Stevenson rose briefly to his feet to announce that he had no questions. The case for the Crown was over within the morning.

In his opening speech to the jury, Melford Stevenson made great play of the fact that the defence did not challenge any part of the prosecution's version of what had taken place:

> It can't happen often in this court that in a case of this import-
> ance, fraught with such deep significance for the accused, the
> whole of the prosecution's story passes without any challenge
> from those concerned to advance the defence. There is no ques-
> tion here that this woman shot this man. We are not seeking to
> raise any further doubt in your mind about that. She is charged
> with murder and one of the ingredients in that offence is what
> lawyers call malice. The law of England provides that if a woman
> had been subject to such emotional disturbance as to unseat her
> judgement, then it is up to you to say that the offence of which
> she is guilty is not murder but manslaughter.

Melford Stevenson went on to express his opinion of the victim: invidious as he found it to speak ill of the dead, the story could leave no doubt in the minds of the jury that Blakely had been a most unpleasant person:

> The fact stands out like a beacon that this young man became
> an absolute necessity to this young woman. However brutally
> he behaved and however much he spent of her money on various
> entertainments of his own and however much he consorted with
> other people he ultimately came back to her and always she
> forgave him. She found herself in an emotional prison guarded
> by this young man from which there seemed to be no escape.
> It was in these circumstances, driven to a frenzy, which for the
> time being unseated her understanding, that she committed the
> crime of which you have heard so many details.

The jury was informed that the defence would call an eminent psychiatrist who would tell them that 'the effect of jealousy upon the feminine mind, upon all feminine minds, can so work as to unseat the reason and can operate to a degree in which in a male mind it is quite incapable of operating'. The two feminine minds on the jury must have loved this description of their frailty.

The defence tactic of keeping clear of the prosecution case may

well have been based on the idea that the less said about Ruth
Ellis's lifestyle the better, and that what was said should come
from her, carefully circumscribed by her own counsel. But juries
have a sixth sense when they are not hearing the full story, and
their conjectures about what they are not hearing can sometimes
be more damaging than the real thing. Sometimes it is better to
reveal the defence hand completely. It is as much in those subtle
displays of judgement as in fine advocacy that you find great
lawyering.

The defence must have realised that Ruth Ellis could appear
rather hard-faced because of the way she described the events.
Even when there is no challenge to the evidence of prosecution
witnesses, they can be the source of crucial material which sheds
light on a case and provides corroboration for the defence. Melford
Stevenson was unlikely to secure anything very useful from the
evidence of personal friends of Blakely, who gave evidence for the
prosecution. But amongst the witnesses for the Crown was someone who knew intimately the suffering experienced by Ruth Ellis.
Desmond Cussen, her 'alternative lover', was the only real friend
Ruth Ellis had, and his love for her was unquestioned. He
undoubtedly hoped that in time she would get Blakely out of her
system and look upon him with more favour. Cussen knew that
Blakely was happy to exploit Ruth Ellis sexually and financially.

Unlike Ruth, a daughter of the lower classes, David Blakely
came from a well-to-do family. His father was a doctor of sufficient means to provide his son with a small private income. At
25, Blakely had no steady job but hung around the edges of the
motor-racing world, fancying himself as a driver and as the creator
of a prototype car. He seems to have been intoxicated with the
fast life as well as with hard liquor. When he first met Ruth, who
was managing hostess of a run-down nightclub in Belgravia, he
was engaged to a 'suitable' young woman from his own background. No doubt Ruth provided an earthy sexual diversion, but
the relationship developed into a compulsive affair in which she
was regularly beaten and humiliated. She obviously had hopes that
this was the relationship which would provide her with social
acceptability and a real partner, a delusion which was somehow
never dispelled even when Blakely had affairs with other women,

refused to involve her in some parts of his life and made it clear to her that she was despised by some of his own circle.

Ruth Ellis gave evidence on her own behalf. Whenever a defendant walks from the dock to the witness box to give their own account there is always a strong sense of anticipation; you can almost feel it, especially in a murder trial. For the defending counsel this is the moment to turn the case round and view it from a different perspective. Taking a defendant through the evidence may seem like a straightforward process to the onlooker, but there is a special skill involved in choreographing a witness's account so that, while coherent, it also gives the jury a sense of the misery and turmoil that can lead to behaviour that would normally never even be contemplated. The counsel's task is to enable the client to communicate their sense of desperation, or whatever other aspects of their emotional state figured in the offence. It should be like watching a *pas de deux*, and the parties must be in step. Defendants themselves often have very little insight into what is needed. They don't say, 'I was suffering from depression,' or, 'I was provoked beyond endurance.' They have to be drawn out so that they describe exactly how they were feeling at the time, the things that were running through their heads, their emotional state in the weeks and days before the crime was committed. Expressing such emotion in a court of law, particularly Court 1 at the Old Bailey, is a daunting prospect and is usually only possible if the person on trial has established a degree of trust and understanding with their counsel.

Any reading of Ruth Ellis's testimony makes it clear that Melford Stevenson had little point of contact with the woman he was representing. At best she was an enigma to him; more likely he saw her as a woman of little virtue. The defence lawyer's theory of the case is inevitably informed by their own attitudes.

She responded to his questions methodically and briefly: expansion was rarely sought. Even when she was dealing with the violence and rejection which would form the basis of any defence of provocation, weak answers to Stevenson's own questions were left unpursued. She was never asked to explain when she said Blakely 'only hit me with his fists and hands', even though she was clearly subjected to regular beating causing bruising, black eyes and treatment at the Middlesex Hospital, and even though Cussen could have confirmed this. Like many battered women before and since, her reduction of his violence was probably a coping mechanism, and it also displayed the complicated emotions that go with loving someone who treats you like a dog. Her feelings when Blakely finally dumped her, aided and abetted by his circle of friends, were never fully explored, nor was there any probing of the intensity of emotion that she must have experienced during her long vigil outside the building, in which she could hear him laughing and socialising. Every sense of herself as an outsider, beyond the pale of his social class, must have been reinforced, and her head must have been buzzing with visions of Blakely with another woman. None of this reached across the courtroom to the jury. Her irrationality was explained as jealousy, the fury of the woman scorned, rather than as the response of someone who had been systematically abused, exploited and humiliated.

Counsel for the prosecution asked only one question in cross-examination: 'When you fired that revolver at close range into the body of David Blakely, what did you intend to do?'

It was not even a leading question. Ruth Ellis replied: 'It is obvious. When I shot him I intended to kill him.'

I can almost hear the silence in the courtroom when she gave that answer, and the gloom it must have invoked in her lawyers. Yet no attempt was made to recoup in re-examination. No doubt she did intend to kill him at that moment, but the real issue was whether she had been provoked beyond endurance, whether her action was that of someone out of control, a product of desperation in intolerable circumstances. When he came out of the public house, did he see her and ignore her, and did that final act of rejection cause her to snap? It was a case which had to engage the sympathies of the judge and jury in order to surmount the obstacles presented by the law as it then stood.

Where her lawyers had their hardest task was in dealing with Ruth Ellis's decision to take a gun with her when she went to the address in Hampstead where she suspected her lover would be. From such a deliberate action the jury would reasonably assume, in the first instance, that this was a premeditated act of revenge, and that the hours of waiting could have provided a cooling-off time. The immediacy or 'heat of the moment' principle is an important aspect of provocation, and it was bound to fail in this case unless Ruth Ellis had some explanation of how her intentions varied at different times, and how the unexpected sight of him led to a sudden temporary loss of self-control. The questions put to her did not seem designed to elicit such an account, if one existed or had ever been explored with Ruth Ellis in the preparation of her case.

What I read between the lines is a half-hearted attempt to introduce a defence of *crime passionnelle* into the English law that was doomed from the start; certainly it gained no credence from the psychiatrist who was called. His proposition was that a woman was more prone to hysterical reaction than a man in the case of infidelity, and that in such circumstances she was likely to lose her critical faculties and try to solve the problem on a more primitive level. Most of the male-dominated court probably agreed with this, but the implications of introducing it into our jurisprudence probably struck terror into the heart of every philandering husband.

The evidence was completed and the rest of the day was spent (in the absence of the jury) presenting the legal arguments to Mr Justice Havers, father of the recent Lord Chancellor. The judge seemed anxious for Melford Stevenson to convince him that he understood the law in relation to provocation, and his questions indicated that he had taken the view that Blakely's behaviour fell short: 'What do you say is the evidence of conduct on the part of this deceased man of a nature which has hitherto been considered by the court to amount to provocation?'

There were then muddled exchanges about the effect of infidelity, jealousy and 'new law'. Finally the judge gave Melford Stevenson the opportunity to clarify the defence position. 'Does your proposition come to this?' he asked. 'If a man associates with a woman and he then leaves her suddenly and does not communicate with her and she is a jealous woman, emotionally disturbed, and goes out and shoots him, that is sufficient ground for the jury to reduce the crime of murder to manslaughter?' No mention whatsoever was made of Blakely's violence nor of his psychological abuse. Apparently Melford Stevenson was unable to answer Mr Justice Havers's question.

The following morning the trial judge addressed the court before the jury returned. He ruled that there was not sufficient material to support a verdict of manslaughter on the grounds of provocation and that as a matter of law he would so direct the jury. The death sentence was more or less passed at this point. Melford Stevenson made no comment, and indicated that in the circumstances he accepted that he could not make a closing speech to the jury. The judge then summed up, telling the jury that it was not possible to bring in a verdict of manslaughter. The jury retired for fourteen minutes before returning with their verdict of guilty. The ritual of the black cap and the grisly formula that she would be taken to a place where she would be hanged by the neck was pronounced. Ruth Ellis was led away.

Despite the uproar at a woman going to the gallows, and many efforts to obtain a reprieve, the execution took place three weeks after the trial, with the traditional crowd gathered outside the prison awaiting the publication of the death notice on the gate.

Given the state of the law of homicide at the time, the same result might well have followed whoever the judge and counsel. What ensued, however, was a public debate over whether a distinction should be made between a killing of this kind and a cold-blooded murder. The important postscripts to the Ellis case are that it lent fuel to the powerful campaign to abolish the death penalty, affected the development of a psychiatric defence to murder which fell short of insanity, and helped to codify the provocation law. That these adjustments to the law have continued to prove inadequate in dealing with the experience of women is powerfully shown by more recent cases.

Provocation is a defence to murder and only to murder. In any other case, such as assault, it can only provide mitigation. If a defence of provocation is successful and reduces the charge to one of manslaughter, the court still has to pass an appropriate sentence. Women invoke self-defence or provocation defences infrequently, and the reason is that the legal standards were constructed from a male perspective and with men in mind, and women have a problem fulfilling the criteria. The question for the jury in a case where provocation is raised is whether a reasonable man might have suffered temporary and sudden loss of self-control so that he was no longer 'master of his own mind' in circumstances similar to those described in the evidence. The issue is one of opinion, not law, but the judge has considerable power in the way in which he presents provocation to the jury.

Little account is taken of the cultural differences between men and women and the way that our socialisation affects our responses. Women are much less likely to respond to provocation immediately, for obvious physical and psychological reasons, and therefore self-defence and provocation are less available to them. But the legal standards are built upon ideas of instant ignition and a hotheaded rush to action. The spark has to be immediate, an assault which requires self-protection or a blow, a curse, an insult that goes to the core of a man's being. Judges try to create a parallel analogy, the trigger to violent reaction being terrible insults against a woman's chastity or her way of life, both of which are male ideas of what might make a woman run amok.

The majority of women convicted of homicide kill a member of their own family or someone with whom they are intimate or whom they look after. It is rare for a woman to kill a stranger. In 1987, 36 per cent of those convicted of murder had killed their husbands (a crime which in former times was indicted as treason). In the majority of these killings there was a history of cumulative violence towards the woman, yet a significant number would fail the test for provocation. Fortunately for most of the women – or unfortunately from another perspective – the toll of violence usually means they are able to invoke a defence of diminished responsibility, suffering as they almost invariably are from depressive illness or post traumatic stress disorder as a result of the abuse. By and large this reliance on their psychiatric state takes the sting out of the weakness of the other defences, because the women are then sentenced with appropriate compassion, but there will always be women who slip through that net. There is also the principled concern that women should not so readily be pushed towards a pathological explanation for their behaviour, an argument which seldom troubles women looking at prison bars, who understandably value their liberty and the companionship of their children above all else.

It is well established that retaliation and revenge have no place in our legal code, and if a woman is seen to bide her time and to strike when her attacker's defences are low, she is seen as playing dirty and loses the protection of the law, unless she can invoke mental disturbance. It matters not that she may have been subjected to years of beating and may feel that no other avenue is available to her. If she makes a deliberate decision to kill she is guilty of murder, even if at the time she is no longer mistress of her own mind. Temperature seems to be all important. If the crime is to be reduced to manslaughter the act has to be in the 'heat of the moment' with no time to 'cool off'.

The immediacy principle makes no sense when the provocation takes the form of long-term abuse. When a person lives with persistent violence and alcoholism she often becomes overwhelmed. Her whole life is out of control. She would not be thinking rationally for some time, and her feelings often would not manifest themselves as 'snapping', in the form of the crazed outburst, but may seem more controlled: a snapping in slow motion, the final surrender of frayed elastic.

Sara Thornton stood trial in February 1990 charged with murdering her husband, Malcolm, having attacked him with a knife as he lay drunk on a couch. The Crown accepted that her husband was deeply alcoholic and violent towards her but maintained that she had attacked him in a calculated way, having deliberately gone into the kitchen and sharpened the knife. Because she had had periods of mental breakdown in the past and because of the delay between her husband's last threat and her strike, Sara's trial lawyers saw this as a case of diminished responsibility, but her plea to that effect was not accepted by the Crown, and she was convicted.

The psychiatric evidence of the defence was that Sara Thornton was in a state technically described as a 'fugue' at the time she killed her husband. This term would seem to describe an interval where the person is not in control. In answer to questions by the prosecutor the psychiatrist agreed that this was not a treatable condition. What Sara Thornton was undoubtedly suffering from was the cumulative effect of domestic violence and the psychological demands of dealing with a chronically alcoholic partner. She had only been married to Malcolm Thornton for ten months, but those months had taken their toll. She was, in the language of provocation, no longer mistress of her own mind at the time of the killing, hence the 'fugue' state, but she was not fulfilling the definition of diminished responsibility: an abnormality of mind. She was functioning in conformance with the classical provocation scenario, except that there was no word or deed triggering her action. It was an accumulation of abuse, evoked as her husband lay on the couch, which drove her to violence.

Unlike English law, which views the elements of suddenness restrictively, Australian law would have no problem with the delay which preceded Sara's action. Judges there recognise the concept of cumulative provocation, acknowledging that a series of provocative incidents, which may in themselves be trivial, could constitute serious provocation if viewed cumulatively. It is recognised that deliberate preparations for killing may be made while in the heat of passion and that such deliberations are distinguishable from cases of pre-planned killings.

The common law in Australia has developed in a way that is attuned to women's lives, and the judges' decisions have now been consolidated in legislation which specifically stipulates that the provocative conduct of the deceased is relevant, 'whether it occurred immediately before the act or omission causing death or at any previous time'. The statute states unequivocally that provocation is not negated as a matter of law where 'the act or omission causing death was not an act or omission done suddenly'.

However, counsel for the Crown in Sara Thornton's case maintained to the jury that an acquittal would provide Sara Thornton, and I suppose any like-minded women, with 'a licence to kill'.

At her appeal in July 1991, Sara's new counsel, Lord Gifford, argued that 'the slow burning emotion of a woman driven to the end of her tether . . . may be a loss of self-control in just the same way as a sudden rage'. However, the court remained influenced by the fact that Sara had equipped herself with a sharpened knife and had in the week before his death threatened to kill Malcolm

Thornton. Her conviction was upheld. She is now applying for Executive Clemency.

Other women have fallen foul of this same problem: their behaviour is seen as premeditated because, evidentially, delay before action is interpreted that way. However, in the context of the abuse, and because of the genuine snooker in the omnipotence of the abuser, the killing seems to the woman like a rational and coherent response.

On 9 May 1989 Deepak Ahluwalia had yet again beaten his wife and threatened her with a hot iron. There was a well-documented history of domestic violence. He had beaten her, tried to strangle her, threatened her with knives, pushed her downstairs, sexually abused her and raped her. The attacks often took place in the presence of their children, who cowered in fear of him. His wife, Kiranjit Ahluwalia, had obtained court injunctions against him twice but had failed to get them enforced after threats from his family. He was constantly threatening to kill her and she lived in terror of him. Like so many battered wives, she could sense his mood swings and could read the signals which meant the onset of an attack, but she usually felt powerless. That night she could take no more and, when he fell asleep on the bed, she poured petrol over his feet and set it alight.

Deepak's death led to a charge of murder against his wife, who was not the conventional broken victim but a woman who had accepted long-term violence because of cultural constraints:

> This is the essence of my culture, society and religion, where a woman is a toy, a plaything. She can be stuck together at will, broken at will. Everybody did what they wanted with me, no one ever bothered to find out what kind of life I was leading after I married – one of physical and mental torture.
>
> The culture into which I was born and where I grew up sees the woman as the honour of the house . . . In order to uphold this false 'honour' and glory she is taught to endure many kinds of oppression and pain in silence. Religion also teaches her that her husband is her god and fulfilling his every desire is her religious duty. For ten years I tried wholeheartedly to fulfil the

duties endorsed by religion. For ten years I lived a life of beatings and degradation and no one noticed; now the law has decreed that I should serve a sentence for life. Today I have come out of my husband's jail and entered the jail of the law.

For Kiranjit Ahluwalia, diminished responsibility was not argued as there were varied opinions on the nature of her depression after suffering the effects of years of abuse. She explained her failure to leave or disown her husband in the context of her culture and religion, where community expectations mean enduring domestic violence in silence because of the shame which disclosure will bring upon the family.

The problem for Kiranjit's lawyers was that she had waited for him to fall asleep, and it was this aspect of the evidence that was emphasised by Mr Justice Leonard. Judith did the same before cutting off the head of Holofernes. M. J. Willoughby, an American academic lawyer, expressed the view in her work on battered women who kill their sleeping partners that 'society gains nothing, except perhaps the additional risk that the battered woman will herself be killed, because she must wait until her abusive husband instigates another battering episode before she can justifiably act'.

The requirement that a battered wife must wait until assault is underway before her apprehensions can be validated in law is an acceptance of murder by instalment. If a person being held hostage killed a terrorist captor, the fact that he was sleeping would be of no consequence. The prison of the violent marriage is hard to contemplate for those on the outside, and the question 'why didn't she leave' is based on incomprehension.

In 1984, after years of torture, Pauline Wyatt shot her husband as he slept. In her interview with the police she articulated in a way that defeats most women the emotions which ran through her head at the point of killing him:

I was frightened to death of him, but I couldn't get away . . . I couldn't see any way out . . . My mind snapped and I just got the shotgun. I couldn't take any more . . . The end of the gun was very close to him . . . I thought of my kids then fired it . . .

He drove me to it by the life he was giving me . . . it was living hell.

She was acquitted of murder by a jury and convicted of manslaughter. In his summing up the judge made very little of the absence of a word or action operating as the immediate trigger for loss of control. Much depends on the attitude of the judge and indeed the prosecutor. In some cases, because of the background, the prosecution and the judge accept a plea to manslaughter even where there has been some premeditation, as in the Maw sisters case, where their violent father was lying unconscious on the mattress upstairs when agreement was reached that he must be killed (Court of Appeal, December 1980). Similarly, a plea to manslaughter on the grounds of provocation was accepted by *R v Ratcliffe*, May 1980, where the accused borrowed a knife from her neighbour, intending to kill her husband, and did so six days later.

It is wrong to characterise the courts as unsympathetic to the plight of women in violent relationships. In the majority of cases, women who break under the pressure of domestic violence are treated with mercy. However, the vocabulary of the discourse is limited, and the criteria are inflexible, because of a fear that juries will apply provocation too freely.

In the same week that Sara Thornton's appeal failed, a trial judge accepted Joseph McGrail's plea to manslaughter of his wife on the grounds of provocation and passed a suspended sentence. Mr McGrail had lived with Marion Kennedy for more than twenty years. They had two sons, both handicapped and both in care. Ten years previously Marion began to drink and eventually became addicted to sleeping pills. When she had been drinking she used to insult her husband and swear at him. She was a scold, a nag.

One day in February 1991, when Joseph returned from work to find her drunk again, he could stand no more. He kicked her hard enough to cause her to die of internal bleeding. The judge commented that living with Marion 'would have tried the patience of a saint'.

In March 1992 Rajinder Bisla, having strangled his 'nagging' wife in front of his three children, was also given a suspended sentence. No doubt, like Joseph McGrail, he snapped, and we should welcome the humanity which was shown to him. Justice for women does not have to be secured by denying it to men. However, the willingness to recognise the male experience is a reflection of the male nature of our courts. Nagging is seen as the female equivalent to violence. Yet men married to intolerable women usually have many more alternatives available to them and find it easier to leave.

In July 1992 Kiranjit's case, mentioned above, came before the Court of Appeal. Attempts were made by my colleague in chambers, Geoffrey Robertson QC, to contextualise his client's behaviour against the background of prolonged violence. He tried to press the argument that immediacy has been an evidential development and that no such requirement exists in law. On 31 July the Court quashed Kiranjit's conviction. The three judges, headed by the Lord Chief Justice, Lord Taylor, ordered a retrial, on the grounds that new medical evidence, which might have proved a defence of diminished responsibility, had not been brought forward, and should be tested in court. Lord Taylor went to great lengths in his judgment to say that any alteration in the existing legal definition of 'provocation' as 'temporary and sudden loss of control', must be a matter for Parliament, not for the courts, since it involved changing 'a particular principle of law [which] has been confirmed so many times and applied so generally over such a long period'.

It is clear that there must be a change in the application of the law so that cumulative provocation is a defence: delay in responding to years of violence and then suddenly acting when a persecutor's defences are down may be about sheer survival. The judgments in the cases of Sara Thornton and Kiranjit Ahluwalia mean that statutory change is now necessary, along the Australian lines. Already the MP Jack Ashley has proposed legislation removing the requirement that loss of self-control be sudden.

Often in cases where a woman is offered the opportunity of pleading guilty to manslaughter she could be pleading self-defence but feels that she cannot endure a contested trial, and prefers to accept the offer, in the expectation that with the prosecution on her side she will secure a favourable outcome. This happened in the case of Joan Calladine (reported on *Dispatches*, Channel 4, May 1990) who stabbed her former husband. Evidence showed that she had been subjected to twenty years of violence at his hand. She came home one night to find him slumped in a chair asleep. When he woke he started punching her in the face. She went to the kitchen and took hold of a knife. He followed her, continuing the beating, and she stabbed him. Many cases follow these lines, and the women take a course of least resistance in the proceedings which follow.

Over the years it has become clear to me that women in all gradations of case are much more prepared to settle for a plea to a lesser offence than to fight all the way. Who can blame them, when it avoids the horrors of a full trial, with the attendant scrutiny of your life and possibly a less favourable outcome? For similar reasons, women are less inclined to choose trial by jury, in cases where there is a choice, because the delay and terror of a trial is even more intimidating and disruptive of their lives than it is for men. They often do not have the same will to take on the system.

There are also trials where the defendant is not so compliant and suffers the consequences.

Karen Tyler maintained from the outset to the police that she had killed her father with a kitchen-knife in self-defence, and at no time was diminished responsibility countenanced. The Crown charged manslaughter, accepting that her violent, abusive father must have provoked her beyond endurance, but said that she was looking for some pretext to injure her father because of the way he had treated her and her mother. In the words of the prosecutor: 'He gave her that pretext by slapping her and causing her minor injuries. It was an unlawful killing.' The Crown made great play of the fact that the teenager was the same height as her father and that, although he was heavier than she, he was under the influence of alcohol. Karen Tyler was convicted of manslaughter at Chelmsford Crown Court; despite the monstrous record of her father's brutality, and the fact that she had given birth to a baby daughter whilst awaiting trial, she was sentenced to four years' imprisonment. This was halved on appeal. Karen Tyler was released after eight months after a campaign by her family and neighbours.

Amelia Rossiter ran a mixture of self-defence and accident at her trial. She had killed her husband after a row, and she too was convicted. The jury probably took the view that she had used excessive force because of the number of stab wounds on her husband's body and because of the inconsistent accounts she gave at different times. In evidence, Mrs Rossiter never suggested that she had lost control, despite the injuries having all the signs of a frenzied attack. She also made little of her miserable life with her husband and his abusive and violent behaviour that evening out of a resigned sense of loyalty to him and to their children.

Her conviction was quashed in April 1992 by the Court of Appeal because, in their judgement, the trial judge should have directed the jury on provocation, even when that was not the defence she was placing before the court.

Sometimes women who kill their husband or partner cannot live with the idea that it was anything other than a terrible accident. Jean Harris, the American headmistress who shot her lover, the Scarsdale diet doctor Herman Tarnhauser, also avoided a middle course, pleading her case on the basis of accident/self-defence, the gun having gone off in a struggle. She too was convicted. Whatever the sex of a defendant, juries often feel that the taking of a life requires acknowledgement of wrong doing, even when set against a background of abuse. Campaigners, rightly concerned with these issues, sometimes fail to recognise the risks involved in criminal trials. Any counsel advising a client who faces a possible term of life imprisonment is going to be very mindful of her liberty.

Usually a criminal lawyer in a murder trial obtains a psychiatric opinion as to the accused's state of mind at the time of the offence. There are sound reasons for doing this which have nothing to do with sticking a psychiatric label on a woman. Even if psychiatrists do not agree upon diminished responsibility, if provocation is successful the reports may be helpful for the purposes of mitigation and sentencing. Psychiatric counselling can eventually be invaluable, because women who kill their husbands, however monstrous they may have been, feel personal guilt and grief, which they have little opportunity of handling in the prelude to their trial. If the reports support the view that the woman was suffering from a mental disorder, it is then necessary to raise the defence with the Crown to enable them to secure a psychiatric opinion as well. If the experts on both sides agree that the woman was suffering from mental illness at the time of the offence, the Crown almost invariably accepts a plea to manslaughter.

What happens most often in domestic homicide cases is that the woman has available to her a number of different defences, but if one of the avenues affords a manslaughter plea which is acceptable to the Crown, whatever the basis, she is likely to enter that plea rather than fight for a total acquittal and risk conviction.

Pamela Sainsbury was subjected to years of the most extreme violence and degradation imaginable before she killed her husband. He had treated her like an animal, leashing her with a belt around her neck, forcing her to eat from a dog-bowl, subjecting her to humiliating perversions. She was socially isolated by him and constantly accused of infidelity, so that she never raised her head in the street for fear of his accusations. If she used a word of more than two syllables she was beaten for trying to be smart.

On the night of the killing she had been suspected again of looking at another man. She was beaten savagely. She could take no more and knew that when he woke the violence would start again and this time he could kill her. She could barely walk because of the damage he had caused her leg, and their children were asleep in the house. She could see no escape, and as he lay asleep she tied a rope to the leg of the bed, looped it around his neck and, going to the far corner of the room, out of his reach, pulled the cord with what strength she could muster. The rope garrotted him.

Pamela dragged his body into a wardrobe, where it remained for several days before she dismembered it and disposed of the pieces in a nearby field. She could not face going to the police because she knew it would involve immediate separation from her children, and instead told everyone her husband had left her. Some months later she confided in a friend, who informed the police.

Cases involving the disposal or dismemberment of a body can pose additional difficulties for a defendant because of the risk that the jury will transfer the deliberateness of the behaviour after the event and the cover-up to the actual killing. However, the full story of Pamela's life was so terrible that it is unlikely that any jury would have felt anything but overwhelming sympathy for her position.

Pamela Sainsbury's case was prepared on the basis that all the background would go to the jury and they would be invited to consider not just diminished responsibility but self-defence and provocation, despite the inherent difficulties which each presents when the killing is not in the face of the abuse. No contested trial took place, because a plea to manslaughter was acceptable to the Crown and to the court, and she was happy to enter that plea.

The development which went unnoticed in the Sainsbury case was that four psychiatrists, instructed by the Crown and the defence, had all agreed that Pamela was at the time of the killing suffering 'acute stress reaction', which involves no pre-existing mental illness but is a recognised classification of mental disorder, dependent upon the subject experiencing trauma. Not all psychiatrists or courts accept that acute stress reaction falls within the definition of diminished responsibility. Her action was in direct response to her husband's provocative behaviour and there was no suggestion that she required treatment after her trial. Mr Justice Auld commented at the time, 'You killed him in a sudden and impulsive act driven as much by fear and hopelessness as anger.' Undoubtedly, had the provocation law clearly embraced the situation of cumulative violence and a contextual interpretation of 'sudden', the Crown and defence would have had to look no further. The likelihood that Sara Thornton was also experiencing acute stress reaction or another stress disorder is very high.

Lawyers in the United States have been establishing new precedent by creating a battered woman's defence. In cases involving relentless domestic violence, rather than attempting to secure conviction on the lesser charge of manslaughter by virtue of provocation or diminished responsibility, they are mounting a case of self-defence even where the killing has all the appearances of a deliberate act. The lawyers involved in these American cases feel very strongly the injustice in sending a woman to prison for killing her persecutor, but one of the strongest motivating forces in developing the defence has been the inflexibility of sentencing in the United States. Sentences are generally even longer there than here, and since some form of custodial sentence almost inevitably follows convictions for homicide whatever the degree, they try to go for broke. There have been some extraordinary acquittals, including exoneration for a woman who shot her policeman husband with his own gun whilst he lay asleep. Before going to bed, he had told his wife that when he woke he expected her to be available for sex and that she had to 'come across' or he'd beat hell out of the kids. Her account of her husband's continuing abuse deeply affected the jury. In another case, a wife hired hitmen to kill her husband, who had terrorised her and would not let her live a life free of him. Again the jury acquitted.

Self-defence is a complete defence to murder and means a defendant walks free from the court if it succeeds. It is permissible in law for someone to act in self-defence if placed in immediate peril and if some instant reaction is necessary to avert the danger. If the attack is over, or is not imminent, then the employment of force may be seen as revenge, or punishment, or the settling of an old score. The force must also be reasonable. The use of a knife, a heavy weight or a gun is often a crucial handicap for a woman, since the use of a weapon may be regarded as involving excessive force and the act of securing it can allow for the argument that her behaviour was calculated or not in immediate response to an attack. Yet many women are incapable of defending themselves without having a weapon to hand.

When men determined what is acceptable conduct in response to attack and what might constitute self-defence, they were thinking of other men, of similar stature and strength, locked in even combat, where the introduction of a weapon would be bad form, stacking the odds on one side. The law takes insufficient account of the disadvantages women feel in the face of male strength. It is illustrative that the most common murder weapon used by wives is the knife, and the scene of her crime is most often the kitchen, while men kill their wives with their bare hands in the bedroom.

The legal perception of self-defence is the meeting of force with roughly equal force; it is based on what seems fair in the eyes of men. The test is objective, but an element of subjectivity has been introduced to account for the race, sex, or special characteristic of the person in the dock. This is the narrow opening into which arguments about the history of domestic violence could be crammed, but women are still hamstrung by the spectre of the vengeful wife. It is in the ancient legal authority of Blackstone's *Commentaries* that we find the clear statement that revenge is no defence. The classic pronouncement in modern times, which is used daily to guide us in the courts, comes from Lord Morris of Borth y Gest, and in the ordinary case it is a perfect statement of the present law:

> It is both good law and good sense that a man who is attacked may defend himself. It is both good law and common sense that he may do, and may only do, what is reasonably necessary. But everything will depend upon the particular facts and circumstances. Of these a jury can decide. It may in some cases be only sensible and clearly possible to take some simple avoiding action. Some attacks may be serious and dangerous. Others may not be. If there is some relatively minor attack, it would not be common sense to permit some act of retaliation which was wholly out of proportion to the necessities of the situation. If an attack is so serious that it puts someone in immediate peril, then immediate defensive action may be necessary. If the moment is one of crisis for someone in immediate danger, he may have to avert the danger by some instant reaction. If the attack is over and no sort of peril remains, then the employment of force may be by way of revenge or punishment or by way of paying off an old score or may be pure aggression. There may be no longer any link with a necessity of defence.

The problem with that statement is that battered women feel incapable of leaving, incapable of taking the commonsensical steps which may be possible between equally matched men. They are no match for their husbands, not just pound for pound in the weighing scales but in their feelings of powerlessness, in the weakness of their low self-esteem. Seeing one event of violence in terms of immediate peril or as a moment of crisis which passes is contextual distortion: when the abuse is constant it is inappropriate to pull out one single fragment of that history. This is a perfect example of the law, which by its letter seems fair but in application is anything but. Treating as equal those who are unequal only creates further inequality. Battered women should not be expected to play by the Marquis of Queensberry rules, and it should be recognised that the peril has not passed for a woman and her children when a wifebeater is merely resting before the next round.

Cases of women who kill are now being handled with a gradually increasing comprehension of domestic violence, which is invariably the backdrop to domestic homicide, whether it is husband or wife who is in the dock. Judges and juries can be greatly assisted by hearing from experts like the psychologist Sandra Horley, who as Director of Chiswick Family Rescue has worked for years with battered women, counselling over two thousand.

June Scotland, who killed her husband and buried his body in the garden, was questioned by police about her failure to leave him despite adequate opportunities. The level of her husband's violence was disputed. She had been physically battered, but the real violence was psychological – his abuse of the children, his constant criticism, his despotic rule of their lives so that the whole family was in terror of his moods.

The Crown persisted in a charge of murder against her because of the deliberate steps she took to kill her husband, poisoning his food before hitting him with a rolling pin. However, all the psychiatrists in her case agreed that she was suffering from an acute depressive state by the time she started planning his death and was already mentally ill. In her case, the psychiatric evidence and that of the expert on domestic violence combined to provide the jury with an insight into her powerlessness and fear which they could then apply for themselves as they saw fit. She was acquitted of murder and convicted of manslaughter on the grounds of diminished responsibility. Her sentence was one of probation.

Men who kill their wives are rarely raising their hands for the first time. In appropriate cases the self-defence law will be invoked for women who kill and, if the courts fail to leave the issue to the jury, legislative change will be necessary. Had the psychiatrists in Pamela Sainsbury's case not spoken with one voice, her case would have begun the process of letting a jury armed with all the facts decide whether she was acting in self-defence. Even though her husband was asleep, the question a jury could have been left to decide was whether, given the history, circumstances and perceptions of the defendant, she could reasonably have believed that she could not preserve herself from being killed by her husband except by killing him first. However, the primary interest must always be that of the individual woman on trial. It will be rare that a woman who is offered a plea to the lesser offence and the likelihood of a non-custodial sentence will choose to go on with a fight.

The case histories abound. In 1979 judges in the Appeal Court rejected the appeal of June Greig, who received a life sentence for killing her extremely violent husband, saying she could surely have taken another course of action.

Carol Peters was convicted in February 1992 of murdering her husband. In November 1990, after years of domestic violence, she fought back for the first time. He died of stab wounds but also bore terrible injuries inflicted with a hammer. Her mouth was so damaged that she could not eat after her arrest and for many days drank through a straw. The history of domestic violence was minimised in the defence of Carol Peters for fear that its full disclosure would arm the Crown with the powerful weapon of motive. This has been a recurring theme in such cases: until recently psychiatrists knew little of the dynamics which were at work.

Carol Peters's story of the violence she experienced is classic, starting with minor assaults and escalating so that she had to receive hospital treatment on two occasions. Her life was wretched, made bearable only by the presence and love of her children.

The trial concentrated almost entirely on the night of the killing, when her husband's behaviour was especially bizarre and violent, possibly exacerbated by a sleeping drug, temazapan, which was found in his bloodstream. In very large doses temazapan can induce paranoia and disinhibited conduct. When interviewed by the police, Carol's account of the events of that terrible night and her own behaviour varied at different times, but this was explained by a psychiatrist as being consistent with an experience of extreme trauma, after which the memory renders up recollection only in piecemeal form. Despite a well-fought defence and an exemplary summing-up by the judge, the jury convicted. Carol Peters is serving life imprisonment.

It has been maintained that any change to the present law would create a 'charter' for battered wives, the 'licence to kill' theme which was effective in damning Sara Thornton. This attitude has beleaguered the system. In 1983 Lord Wheatley in the Scottish case of Mabel Patterson passed a life sentence after she was convicted of murder, saying that there were so many wives subjected to rough treatment that it would be dangerous to establish a precedent for them to take the law into their own hands. However, juries in other countries have no difficulty in applying the law justly, with no consequent rush of manslaying.

Justice is likely to remain a lottery while so much depends on the woman's fulfilment of society's expectations. One of the factors which undoubtedly affects the outcome of murder trials is, as always, the persona of the woman in the dock. It is my view that this is what really determines the outcome. Women who conform to the conventional image of the cowed victim fare better than those who come to trial angry that they are being blamed for what ultimately took place.

As in rape trials, women on any kind of charge frequently experience irrelevant questioning which discredits them as women in the eyes of the jury. In Sara Thornton's case, efforts were made to find a motive for the killing aside from vengeance. It was suggested that she stood to gain financially, had had an affair, and lived an unorthodox life, all of which apparently justified the Crown's asking her why she wore no knickers and whether she occasionally smoked cannabis. Ordinarily assertive and lively, Sara became totally demoralised in her marriage to a drunken violent man. However, by the time she came up for trial her confidence was returning. She cavilled with prosecuting counsel, drew distinctions when she answered questions, and had all the disadvantages of a now rational person attempting to speak about a period of irrationality. To a jury she probably seemed too feisty and in control to be a victim. She also articulates a complaint that is made with growing frequency by women, that they are infantilised by lawyers, who fail to recognise their intelligence and do not listen to their views about the conduct of their cases.

In March 1992, whilst the furore around Sara Thornton's conviction was still at its peak, another battered woman was tried for stabbing her husband, not once as had Sara, but seventeen times. Acquitted of murder on the grounds of provocation after testifying to her husband's violence and rape, she was given a suspended sentence of eighteen months. This was seen by the press as evidence of the law's lack of bias. Elizabeth Line, however, had been a nun before her marriage, and was a pious, long-suffering woman who endured sexual as well as physical abuse.

In 1984, 65-year-old Pamela Megginson was convicted of murdering her 79-year-old lover, Alec Hubbers, with a champagne bottle. They had begun living together in 1970. She was a well-educated middle-class woman whose husband had left her; he was a rich and successful businessman, separated from his wife but not divorced. They had an expensive lifestyle with a house in Hampstead and a flat in Cap Ferrat, for which Hubbers met the bills.

Hubbers became infatuated with a Frenchwoman half his age some months before his death. Although this was not the first of his additional women, Pamela Megginson realised that this was an affair of a different order when she flew to join Hubbers in Cap Ferrat and found that he had sold the flat to his new mistress and intended to live with her. Mrs Megginson described how 'churned up and humiliated' she felt, and in a long statement to the police told how after a 'ghastly quarrel' over dinner they went back to the flat. 'I got into bed with him and had oral sex which he always wanted. I was doing it partly because of routine and partly because I wanted my position back.' As she began making love to him, he pushed her away and told her she was not as good as his new love, nor as beautiful. 'He was shouting, "I don't want you. I only want her." I lost my head and went completely crazy. I reached out of bed for the champagne bottle we had for lunch and hit him a number of times.' Afterwards, she went straight back to England and told friends what she had done. The events led to a nervous breakdown.

At her trial, prosecuting counsel Michael Worsley told the jury,

'She lied and she fled. We see a woman with old age ahead of her – just around the corner – her financial security fading away in front of her very eyes, being taunted while they are in bed having some sort of sex and going, as she put it, completely crazy.' He emphasised to the jury that they would have to decide whether the killing had taken place while she was in a jealous rage or whether she knew quite well what she was doing. This woman knew that 'she was being supplanted and was in the course of losing the financial security she had got [from Hubbers]'. He alleged that, without Hubbers's financial support, Mrs Megginson's income would be only a few hundred pounds a year, whereas she would be a beneficiary on his death.

The line between murder and manslaughter can be very fine, but the consequent sentences can be vastly different. For murder there is only one possible sentence, and Pamela Megginson got it. Yet at the time her case was compared with that of Doris Croft, a very gentle, well-loved soul who killed the publican with whom she lived when she discovered he was having an affair with someone else. Doris was not sent to prison at all.

Pamela Megginson appealed, but her conviction was upheld by the Court of Appeal. The view taken by Their Lordships was that the taunts about her sexual performance, the rejection of her in preference for the younger woman and the totality of the deceased's conduct did not amount to provocation. Apparently a 'reasonable woman' would not have lifted the nearest item and struck her errant partner. This is a strikingly different assessment to that of the reasonable man, who is 'grossly provoked' if his sexual performance is called into question.

It can, of course, be misleading to make comparisons, because facts which appear similar can be subtly distinctive, making all the difference in the world in a criminal case. However, the odiousness of making comparisons can also be used as an excuse by those who function within the legal system to excuse gross discrepancies in approaches to cases. Alec Hubbers's daughter was in court for the trial of her father's mistress, and she watched the jury's reactions:

I could feel the atmosphere turn against her. The jury were all working-class and before them was a woman who'd never done a day's work, had all the advantages, staying with a man who mistreated her for what could only have been financial reasons. They obviously took a dislike to her.

In fine-line cases those sorts of feelings about a defendant count for a lot. Pamela Megginson did not have the demeanour of the female victim. Mistresses have a special burden to carry, and have to be very downtrodden indeed if they are to overcome their moral handicaps. Doris Croft, on the other hand, was every bit the victim, and the system worked for her.

The conclusion that emerges from the case law and press coverage is that, whatever drives you to do the old man in, you must be as clean as a whistle yourself, with not a hint of mispropriety. If you think about it at all, do not think about it for too long, and wait until he is upright. You have to keep a tidy house, scrub the children, and it helps if you are still proclaiming love whilst holding the bloodstained carving knife.

The deceased, on the other hand, has to be more than adulterous. He has to be violent as well as a womaniser, feckless with money, and just a hint of unpleasant sexual practices could just about swing it.

The press reports say it all:

A wife killed her husband after he told her he loved the dog more than her. Mrs Oates who killed her husband with a spanner pleaded guilty to manslaughter and was sentenced to probation for three years. Her husband was a drunkard and unfaithful but she told the police she still loved him very much. (*Daily Mirror*, 26 October 1976)

A former teenage bride, who shot dead her drunken, domineering husband as he slept, set the gun beside the bed and lovingly placed beside it a white rose she had picked from the garden. She telephoned a close friend and blurted out that it was a weight off her shoulders. 'For twenty years I have not been allowed to smile, laugh or do anything without his approval.'

She was jailed for three years. (*Daily Telegraph*, 25 January 1979)

A devoted wife who killed her husband with an axe in their bedroom was placed on probation yesterday. The judge said it was not in the interests of justice for details to be displayed to the world. (*The Times*, 21 March 1981)

A woman who had been battered for years by her drunken, work-shy, common-law husband, snapped and stabbed him to death with a carving knife when he kicked the Sunday roast out of her hands. Weeping and whispering, 'I am very sorry,' the woman who had worked all hours as a cleaner was jailed for two and a half years. The Recorder of London said, 'You are a woman with a faultless, hard-working past and are undoubtedly remorseful for what you have done.' (*Daily Telegraph*, 7 June 1988)

There was mercy yesterday for a slave wife who turned on her master. She raised an axe to the brutal husband who had battered her into submission for fourteen years but was placed on probation. Her counsel described her as a wonderful mother to her five children. Her teenage son told the court, 'I would say she is the best mum in the world.' Yet despite all the cruelty she still loved her husband deeply. (*Daily Express*, 14 February 1976)

A wife who stabbed her brutal husband to death walked free yesterday after a court heard she idolised him. (*Sun*, 22 December 1987)

A wronged wife walked free from court after shooting dead her woman-chasing husband. Ex-detective Harold Ruston had affair after affair but forgiving Elsie still loved him. The devoted mother of two finally snapped. (*Daily Star*, 9 November 1978)

My own favourite case is that of an elderly Mrs Prosser, who ran her husband through with a knife after one of many attacks. She phoned the police and, much to the misery of those who acted for her, kicked the dying Mr Prosser in the ribs in the presence of the local constabulary and said, 'I hope he's dead. You can take him up the morgue. I'm glad I did it. I hope I can get some peace now.' Fortunately, the degree of provocation cancelled out Mrs Prosser's apparent callousness and the judge placed her on probation.

Our understanding of psychology and gender differences has developed since the ambit of self-defence and provocation was decided in case law. Like the law on marital rape, those decisions have to be considered afresh in the light of different circumstances and knowledge. The definition of provocation should be tested in a House of Lords ruling as soon as possible.

However, new legislation will ultimately be required, and the opportunity should be taken to consider whether provocation is an appropriate concept to include as a defence within the law at all. It is not available to defendants charged with any lesser crime because it undermines the value of resisting violent responses to insult and offence. What society accepts is that account should be taken of the state of the accused's mind if they kill in despair or when they are profoundly disturbed. In parts of the United States the defence which encapsulates both provocation and diminished responsibility is that of Extreme Emotional Disturbance, which reduces murder to manslaughter. A re-evaluation of the law of homicide could consider a similar defence which would embrace the desperation that can drive men and women to kill.

(Change in the law is not needed only for women. Men also suffer the consequences of the law's limitations. Anthony Cocker, for example, was convicted of murder at his trial in Manchester Crown Court in 1988, on Mr Justice Boreham's direction; in the circumstances of the offence he could not invoke the law of provocation to reduce his offence to manslaughter. Mr Cocker had suffocated his wife, who was a longtime victim of Friedrich's Ataxia, a wasting disease. She had frequently pleaded for him to end her life and eventually lost all will to live. On the night of her death she had wakened him, screaming in pain and distress, begging to be relieved of her misery. No appropriate defence was available to him and he was sentenced to life imprisonment, but the jury was so angry at the outcome that they wrote to the judge complaining that Anthony Cocker had not had justice.)

Like the aftermath of Ruth Ellis's trial, Sara Thornton's case has provided a head of steam for a number of reforms, some of which have support amongst the great as well as the good. Because she did not succeed in getting her charge reduced to manslaughter, the judge could not take into account her tragic circumstances and had no option but to sentence her to life. The mandatory life sentence ensures that a victim of domestic violence who finally fights back gets the same sentence as a cold-blooded murderer. Justice cannot be served according to such rigid prescriptions and it should be a source of shame that in 1991 the House of Commons voted down the amendment to the Criminal Justice Bill which proposed the abolition of the mandatory life sentence for murder. Currently, the length of a life prisoner's sentence is determined in the traditionally secretive British way by Home Office officials, paying some regard to the number of years pencilled privately on to the file by the judge at the time of sentencing. This secretive procedure, which cannot be subject to any challenge in our courts, has been criticised by the European Court of Human Rights.

Until the full exposure of this process, it was practice that criminal advocates never rose to mitigate after conviction in a murder trial; nowadays, however, many of us do raise matters in mitigation which we want to be considered by the civil servants, and ask for them to be included with the transcript.

However, it is important that empowering the judges to distinguish between types of murder is not seen as the way out of the central issue of battered women who kill. Changing the mandatory sentence will provide the court with some way of ameliorating the experience of men and women who are not afforded a defence but who have considerable mitigation for their actions. But if a jury convicts someone of murder, not manslaughter, the judge will be affected by the jury's rejection of the defence, and will sentence with that in mind. It will mean there are still good reasons for a woman to secure a conviction on the lesser charge, not forgetting either the stigma which attaches to a conviction for the most serious crime in the calendar. Sometimes, it is true, the stereotype works in women's favour, but women must be entitled to invoke defences which are available to men, and that means ridding the law of any gender bias.

9

The Unreasonable Woman

A prominent actor in the dramatis personae of the courtroom is 'the reasonable man'. No longer confined to the Clapham omnibus, he is nowadays supposed to be transsexual and multicultural. 'Of course, we all know there is no such thing as the reasonable woman,' was the law lecturer's joke, but that sort of puerility is supposed to be behind us now. In contemporary trials, the judge explains to a jury that the reasonable man can be female. The idea of changing the language seems to have escaped consideration.

The fictional 'man' is introduced into criminal trials whenever juries are asked to consider whether behaviour was reasonable. This occurs specifically in the provocation defence to murder: would a reasonable man have been so provoked? and in self-defence: was the degree of force used reasonable?

It became clear to the courts that a totally objective test did not operate fairly because once the law, for example, stipulated that words could be sufficient provocation, it was clear that some insults touched a rawer nerve with certain people than others. Insults about race, physical infirmity or some shameful incident in the past may make verbal abuse a more powerful weapon if they are true. A subjective component had to be introduced while at the same time keeping some consensus on what was acceptable in a civilised society. The defence could not be made available to the person with a fragile ego who sees insults in the glance of a passerby.

'The reasonable man', in the words of Lord Diplock, 'is an ordinary person of either sex, not exceptionally excitable or pugnacious but possessed of such powers of self-control as every-one is entitled to expect that his fellow citizens will exercise in society as it is today.' The judge in a criminal trial today is supposed to explain that the reasonable man is a person of the sex and age of the accused, having the power of self-control of an ordinary person, but in other respects sharing such of the accused's characteristics as they think would affect the gravity of the provocation.

In the Washington State Supreme Court decision of Wanrow it was held that the traditional instruction to the jury of drawing on the standard of defence acceptable to the 'reasonable man' did not adequately represent a woman's perspective, and consequently threatened to deny a woman equal protection under the law. Mrs Wanrow, whose daughter had in the past been molested by an intruder, shot an unarmed man who tried to enter her home. The court acknowledged that 'in our society women suffer from a conspicuous lack of access to training in and the means of develop-ing those skills necessary to effectively repel a male assailant with-out resorting to the use of deadly weapons'.

In the United States, the judge's direction now has to give special emphasis to the woman's own perceptions of her situation, rather than providing a purely objective assessment of whether the steps she took in self-defence were reasonable.

Although in this country we have already moved away from the purely objective test of the reasonable man, and juries are told that they must not altogether disregard the particular character-istics of the defendant – if, for example, he or she is homosexual, or black, or a vagrant – the reality of some people's lives is often incomprehensible to the court.

In the case of a woman, a judge may in his direction ask a jury to take into account that she has been subjected to years of abuse and that they must therefore judge the reasonableness of her behaviour in that context. But what reasonable person continues to accept repeated beatings? What reasonable person continues to stay with her abuser, does not ring the police, comes to believe her partner is so all-powerful she will never get away from him, thinks killing is the only answer?

Because the reasonable man is supposed to set the public

standard, a professional or expert view is resisted in cases of provocation or self-defence. The Appellate Committee of the House of Lords has expressed the view that the evidence of witnesses as to how they think the reasonable man would react to the provocation is not admissible, since the question is one for the jury. This dictum was *'obiter'*, and therefore challengeable, but within our courtroom culture there is a deep-seated reticence about introducing external knowledge of the kind I have mentioned. The response of normal, reasonable people to abnormal conditions would not be within the knowledge of the ordinary juror, and it should therefore be open to the defence to call a recognised expert to explain the psychiatrically recognised impact of trauma on men and women. Judges always explain to the jury that they should attribute any enduring characteristics of the defendant to the 'reasonable man' – for example, if he is a hunchback his deformity may be the subject of provocative remarks. Surely, if a defendant has a psychological deformity, invisible to the eye but none the less an enduring characteristic, a psychiatrist should be able to testify in court to its existence?

However, the justice system fails women in many cases for reasons other than the constraints of 'the reasonable man' test. One of the aspects of our criminal process which has been highlighted by the recently exposed wrongful convictions is the inadequacy of the Court of Appeal. It is only within the most limited circumstance that cases will be reconsidered, and unless there has been a misdirection on the law or new evidence it is almost impossible to have a case reviewed.

The BBC's *Rough Justice* series looks at cases where there may have been a miscarriage of justice. Few of the cases have concerned women, because the majority of serious crimes involve men, making them more likely to suffer the sorts of miscarriage around which campaigns develop. However, Margaret Livesey has always maintained her innocence of the murder of her son, Alan, and the BBC team tried to reopen her case. She was convicted in July 1979 after a second trial, the first having been abandoned at a very late stage when the relative of a juror became seriously ill. The problem with abandoned trials is that witnesses have time to consider answers to the questions they were asked the first time round, and the prosecution's case has usually been well rehearsed in the papers. There is a risk that people are already establishing their views before they are even empanelled as jurors. Press interest was particularly great in a trial where a mother had allegedly killed her 14-year-old son, especially when it emerged that Margaret Livesey's alibi for the time of the murder was a man with whom she was conducting a secret affair whilst her husband was on night-shift at British Leyland.

According to the Crown, Mrs Livesey arrived home late, having been out with her manfriend, and embarked on a terrible row with her son. During this row, it was claimed, she lost control and stabbed him repeatedly with a kitchen knife that she had used earlier for peeling potatoes. The prosecution then maintained that the defendant attempted to cover her tracks by tying the boy up, cleaning the murder weapon and leaving the house so as to ensure that the discovery of the body was made by someone else.

The allegations were deeply flawed. When the murder came to light, Margaret Livesey was by all accounts in deep distress, but after five days' interrogation eventually said to the police, 'Well, if you say I've done it, then I must have, but I can't remember.' She then began a lengthy confession based largely on knowledge which by this time was shared by most of those investigating and by most of those who had been around after the discovery of Alan's body. She retracted her confession two days later.

Margaret Livesey told the police that she had been having problems with her adolescent son in recent months. Concerned that he was getting into trouble, she had been trying to exercise some parental control; this had placed a strain on their relationship. According to her confession, on this particular night the argument got so heated that it led to a physical struggle. She went into a complete frenzy and stabbed the boy time after time. However, much of what she said was totally inconsistent with the forensic evidence. For a start, the position of the body was not as she described it. Then she maintained that she had put socks over the boy's wounds after the stabbings because she could not bear to see them, but the evidence showed that the stabbing had in fact been done through the socks. Nor was the nature of the stabbings and the absence of blood-spurt staining consistent with a frenzied attack; indeed, the socks accounted for the absence of bloodstains.

One of the most bizarre aspects of the forensic evidence was that four of the incisions were pricks with the point of a knife, including a prick to the eyelid, more in keeping with carefully inflicted injuries than with a struggle. And the boy bore no sign of defensive injuries. Wherever someone has attacked another with a knife, the first things to look for in courtrooms as well as in mortuaries are wounds on the forearms or the palms of hands, where the unarmed victim has tried to fend off the weapon or protect their own face. None of those signs of struggle existed, and the knife which was supposed to have inflicted the injuries had no trace of blood on it, although it had a handle of unvarnished wood which would have been particularly receptive to staining.

Crucial to the whole case was the timing of the death. At the trial, the prosecution claimed that it would have been around 11 p.m. This was deduced from the temperature of the room, which was taken by the scene-of-crime officer; what was forgotten was that the windows had been thrown open because the gas taps had been turned on. Reappraisal of this as well as examination of the stomach contents provided evidence on appeal that the death may well have taken place an hour earlier than was believed at the time.

Margaret Livesey's lover gave evidence that he was with her until after 11 o'clock, and she was at her neighbours' house by 11.10. It is hard to believe that she could have committed the murder and trussed the boy up in a complicated series of knots in such a short space of time. The neighbours described her as completely unruffled and unstained with blood.

However, neither Margaret Livesey nor her lover were believed. There was even evidence at her trial that she had been reported to the NSPCC for abuse of her son prior to his death, and although there was no evidence to support the complaint and it came to nothing, 'no smoke without fire' hints were being made. Clearly this was a defendant who had failed both the mother and wife tests.

If Margaret Livesey did not kill her son, then who did? At the trial the evidence of a mentally handicapped boy, who said he saw

an intruder leave the Livesey house by the back door around
10 p.m., was discounted: the prosecution claimed the boy was
unreliable. Furthermore, in the house there was an unaccounted
for cigarette packet and some cigarette ends. A forensic pathologist
who was called in years later believed that the murder had the
hallmarks of a sadistic and ritualistic homosexual murder, which
would explain the elaborate knots, the teasing pricks with a knife
and many other features. The police had been so convinced that
this aberrant mother was guilty that no forensic tests of the
cigarette packet or ends were ever conducted.

Margaret Livesey confessed, and for most people in the court,
whatever the quibbles over the evidence, that was good enough –
after all, who in their right mind confesses to something they did
not do? What was not sufficiently taken into account was that
this was the confession of a woman who was experiencing a
profound reaction to the monstrous death of her child. Not only
was she filled with guilt over her contentious relationship with
him and her feelings of failure as a mother, but his death had also
exposed her affair and the turmoil of emotions around that aspect
of her life.

It is only recently that we have come to understand that certain
people in certain situations are more likely to confess to crimes
which they did not in fact commit. Sexual discrimination can
actually take its toll in the investigation process. When any person
comes to the attention of the police, they are confronted with an
authority figure who from childhood has been held up as frightening and all-powerful. For women, this can be especially potent,
and their response can be to act submissively and co-operatively.
If they feel guilty, for whatever reason, they may be manipulated
into confessing to intentional killing, whatever the reality. They
may acquiesce to propositions put to them in a leading manner
which distort the truth of what happened. Policemen, trained in
a culture which is not attuned to women's lives, are likely to ask
questions from a perspective quite alien to the experience of
women, imposing their own conditioning on her perceptions.

The record of interview is a crucial part of the evidence. The
jury is given a transcript, if the record has been signed, and they
take it with them into the jury room. Great weight is attached to

the account a defendant first gives to the police, because it usually takes place so soon after the event, sometimes within hours of the incident or, in a murder case, of the realisation that someone with whom they have been intimately involved is dead. Rarely is this going to be their best and most complete account, because of the state they are likely to be in. Yet their answers will be scrutinised, and any slight discrepancy between them and their evidence to the jury will be leapt upon. Inevitably interviews are interrogator-led, and one frequently finds that the defendant's story is told inadequately because the answers reflect the limitations of the questions. If, for example, a woman is never asked whether her husband beat her, she may not mention it at that stage, particularly if she is finding the atmosphere unsympathetic. If she is being required to re-create in answer to questions, blow for blow, a nightmare of violence, she may disturb the sequence or leave out matters which later seem central.

Professor James MacKeith of London University and his psychologist colleague Dr Gisli Gudjonsson have been conducting research into false confessions and how they come to be made. Their work has moved beyond those confessions made under pressure or in response to inducements, to those where the defendant has experienced a short-term mental state triggered by great distress or bereavement, or where their intelligence quotient or psychological make-up put them at risk. Both sexes can be vulnerable. The Blakelock Appeal in March 1992 exposed how Engin Raghip, a man with low intelligence, had confessed to a crime he did not commit. In 1977 Stefan Kiszco also confessed to a terrible crime. He was said to have admitted the rape and killing of a little girl, although he had an alibi for the time of her death. A comparison of his seminal fluid with that found at the scene showed he could not have been the killer, but the shame of his conviction was not exposed until he had spent fifteen years of his life in prison.

The cautionary tales emanating from the research should be included in the training of all criminal lawyers. There is a lesson too about the rigour lawyers should bring to the cases they handle.

One of the factors MacKeith and Gudjonsson have considered is the susceptible personality, the person who adopts the perspective of the interrogator and desires to please. In extremis, and under constant questioning, such people do not measure the consequence of their statements but simply say whatever they think will satisfy the person asking the questions. This was the core of the evidence which Professor MacKeith would have given at the Appeal of Carole Richardson, one of the Guildford Four, had that event not been overtaken by the Crown's own disclosure that police interviews had been improperly conducted.

Carole Richardson's case was the key to that particular miscarriage of justice and, because her alibi was so strong, galvanised much of the support. A friend repeatedly testified that she had been in his company elsewhere when the bombings had taken place. Once those who took up her case accepted that she had been wrongly convicted, the whole edifice had to crumble, because no individual case could be separated out from the others. But the question always remained, why did she confess? The account she gave after long periods of interrogation was inconsistent in itself and at odds with much of the other evidence, even though she 'admitted' her involvement. She was, in the view of Professor MacKeith and Dr Gudjonsson, a classic case of the 'susceptible personality'.

One of the recently disclosed miscarriages of justice concerned a young woman, Jacqueline Fletcher, who was convicted of murdering her baby son. The most damning evidence against her was her confession to the police, made during a six-hour interrogation. She was tested in prison at the request of the *Rough Justice* programme and found to have an IQ of 70, at the edge of mental handicap and equivalent to that of a 10-year-old. Evidence of her low intelligence was not before the trial court. Half an hour into the questioning, Jackie had had a private conversation with a policewoman, after which her language noticeably changed and her vocabulary included professional terminology and references to post-natal depression. She also gave a description of drowning the baby in a manner which proved impossible when a reconstruction was undertaken. However, a pathologist who examined slides of the baby's lung tissue described them in court as waterlogged, an unfortunate expression; what he saw was the body fluid frequently found in the lungs of cot-death babies.

Jackie Fletcher had a tragic history with her children. She had become pregnant in her early teens and had been deemed unable to look after the child, who was taken into care and subsequently adopted. She had another child by the same father, and it was this baby who was found one morning dead in his cot. An autopsy was conducted and nothing at all suspicious was found. The verdict was cot death. It was when her third child was small that she was overheard by a landlady to tell the crying child to shut up 'or I'll do the same what I done to the other!'

It was the view of David Southall, consultant paediatrician at the Royal Brompton Hospital, that Jackie, of limited intelligence and with one baby already taken from her, shared the guilt felt by all mothers who have lost babies through cot death. The grief and sense of responsibility can go on for years.

Jackie Fletcher's conviction was quashed by the Court of Appeal in February 1991, but a case which had a less happy conclusion was that of Beverley Weightman, who was convicted of murdering her only child, a 2-year-old girl. The child had inhaled a plastic bag and suffocated. Mother and child had returned home from a neighbour's house where all had been well. Within forty-five minutes Mrs Weightman returned to the neighbour's with the child dead in her arms. She was hysterical there, and equally distraught later at the hospital.

In a statement to the Coroner's Officer, Beverley Weightman described going to the bathroom to wash her own hair:

> I went into her room and found her on her back on the bed with a plastic shopping bag plastered over her face. Her head was not inside the bag. I rushed to her and peeled the bag off, she was not breathing . . . Ruth kept her toys in a plastic shopping bag but she may have taken another bag upstairs when she was pretending to go shopping. She was fond of playing shopping.

The bag made a 'whooshing' sound when it was removed.

The post-mortem report concluded that the cause of death was accidental asphyxiation. Three months later, in the course of an argument, Beverley Weightman's husband accused her of killing their little daughter, and she agreed. The following day she went to her probation officer and made the same claim, saying voices had told her to do it. In the presence of a senior probation officer she repeated what she was saying and wrote a note to her husband, asking his forgiveness.In turn, she confessed to the police, having declined a solicitor, and, two days later, repeated her confession with a lawyer and psychiatrist present, saying that she had confessed because 'there had been four deaths in the church' which she attended and death was preying on her mind. The fact that she was directly responsible for this other one, she claimed, became too much for her. She also explained that she was in regular contact with young children and was frightened of the responsibility. She denied to the police that she was confessing to focus attention on herself or to seek assistance by roundabout means.

At her trial Beverley Weightman denied murdering her child with the plastic bag. She could not explain why her story changed, nor provide an adequate reason for confessing. The defence sought to call the psychiatrist, Dr Earp, who had been present at the second stage of police interviews, to testify that in his view Beverley Weightman suffered from a histrionic personality disorder, characterised by emotional superficiality and impulsive behaviour when under stress. He called the condition 'La Belle Indifference', a recognised syndrome. Two psychiatrists instructed by the Crown also took the view that she had a histrionic personality. The woman's own probation officer had agreed in cross-examination that she was theatrical by nature and could say things to draw attention to herself. Of the two, the view of a professional psychiatrist would have carried greater authority with the jury, yet it was for this very reason that the evidence was excluded by the trial judge, who said he was 'very concerned lest the jury see it as a suggestion that their function should be usurped by an expert witness . . . Jurors do not need psychiatrists to tell them how ordinary folk who are not suffering from any mental illness are likely to react to the stresses and strains of life.'

While Beverley Weightman is not someone of abnormally low intelligence, and her condition could not be characterised as mental illness, it is hard to imagine that she would be included in the run of 'ordinary folk'. Few jurors would have come across a personality of such an hysterical type as to confess a crime of which they were innocent; the possible vulnerability of certain types of people is not within their normal purview. Mrs Weightman was convicted and, although she appealed, her conviction was upheld on 18 October 1990 on the grounds that the judge was right not to permit the calling of a psychiatrist's evidence where the defendant was not suffering from a mental disorder. She is serving life imprisonment.

The phenomenon of wrongly confessing to crime is not new. On 24 March 1935 Francis Rattenbury was bludgeoned to death with a carpenter's mallet as he sat sleeping in an armchair in his drawing room. Alma Rattenbury claimed that she found him there already unconscious. By the time a doctor and then the police arrived, Alma was extremely drunk, and was making statements to the effect that she had killed her husband. An account of the case appears in a series called *Notable British Trials*, and a revealing passage describes her as a 'highly sexed woman . . . and six years of being deprived of sexual satisfaction had combined with the tuberculosis from which she suffered to bring her to the verge of nymphomania'. We should be grateful for penicillin.

Mr Justice Humphreys' summing up was no more generous: 'Members of the jury, having heard her learned counsel, having regard to the facts of this case, it may be that you will say that you cannot possibly feel any sympathy for that woman; you cannot have any feeling except disgust for her.'

In fact, Alma Rattenbury was a rather dizzy, good-hearted woman married to a man many years her senior with whom she no longer had any sexual life. She had embarked upon a crazy love affair with their 18-year-old chauffeur cum handyman when she was still only 31. Because of their age difference, Alma was assumed to be the dominant partner – which, given her temperament, was probably not the case. It became apparent during the trial that she cared greatly for her husband and that he probably knew of the affair but chose to ignore it because of his own attachment to her. When she found him dead she drunkenly accepted responsibility because she felt guilty and knew what the consequences would be for the chauffeur, George Stoner.

Although Alma was acquitted, she was destroyed in the process, hounded by the press, socially despised, and tortured with guilt about the imprisonment of her former lover and the shame she had visited upon her children. She stabbed herself to death soon after the trial.

Irish trials import particular problems into the courtroom. As with sex and race cases, another agenda operates in addition to that prescribed in every criminal trial. People have strong views which can influence the proceedings and the risk of miscarriage of justice is real. The campaigns arising out of the convictions of the Birmingham Six, the Maguires and the Guildford Four have drawn attention to the powerful feelings which can deny a fair investigation and trial. The convicted prisoners in these cases at least had the support and sustenance of families and close friends throughout their long sentences, who refused to give up the fight on their behalf. Even less fortunate are those prisoners who do not have people on the outside to hammer on doors and write letters to influential public figures. Many women on the inside lose family and friends in the face of convictions, and the shame of imprisonment silences protest even in those cases where there is serious doubt about the outcome.

Judith Ward was convicted of the M62 motorway coach bombing, a horrible explosion which killed Corporal Clifford Houghton, his wife and two young children, as well as eight other British soldiers. She was sentenced in 1974 to twelve sentences of life imprisonment plus thirty years for that and two other bombings. Her father disowned her after her trial. Until her release by the Court of Appeal at the end of April 1992, she was the longest serving woman prisoner in Britain or Ireland for offences connected with the Irish conflict. Like the Guildford Four, the Maguire family and the Birmingham Six, she had never been acknowledged by the IRA as one of its adherents. For years people hardly knew her name, and she received little media attention or campaigning interest over the eighteen years of incarceration. Judith Ward did not campaign or write letters over the years but quietly maintained her innocence. Prison officers and probation officers involved with her had deep misgivings about her conviction, but felt that she became resigned to a course of biding her time in hope of eventual release on parole. She had to settle for a fate she felt she had brought on her own head.

The evidence against Judith Ward was paralleled by that in the Birmingham case. She made confessions which were deeply flawed and in significant respects unreliable and fantastical. At trial her defence lawyers described her as a 'Walter Mitty' character who made claims which were manifestly untrue. Forensic evidence was supposed to show that she had been in contact with explosives. However, the expert was Dr Frank Skuse, also of the Birmingham case, who was forced to resign in 1985 because of his 'limited efficiency'. He used the infamous Griess test for detecting the presence of the explosive nitro-glycerine on swabs taken from Judith Ward's hands. This simple presumptive test was called into serious doubt in the Birmingham case because positive reactions can also be obtained from innocent material such as soap, Formica and the coating on cigarette packets. It is usually followed by a more sensitive procedure called thin-layer chromatography. When the more sophisticated process was applied to Judith Ward's swabs, the results were negative.

While the mental state of women is usually leapt at to explain their aberrations, at her trial the emotional vulnerability of Judith Ward was never allowed to explain her behaviour. This was terror-ism, where different rules seem to apply. She was questioned extensively by police over many days without a solicitor or outside contact. Sixty-three interviews took place, an unbelievable number, and outside the experience of any lawyer I know. Thirty-four of those interviews were not disclosed to those who defended her at her trial, and the jury heard nothing about them. The failure of the crown to disclose this evidence was quite extraordinary. It meant that the full extent of the contradictions in her interviews was never fully before the court. The reason why such a volume of questioning took place was because the versions of events were so ludicrous and did not quite fit the evidence. Judith Ward has described in letters and statements her feelings of exhaustion and her desire for the interviews to end. The confessions she made contained statements which were shown not to be true and names which she could have readily known. There was also invention, which people from her past claimed was typical of the kind of lies she used to tell to glamorise herself.

Judith Ward was born in Stockport, but claimed to people that she was Irish and that her father was Irish, which was not true. Her childhood had been disrupted by her parents' divorce and a period in care had left her lonely and rootless. She went to live in Ireland for a while, and those who knew her there described her as insecure and desperate for attention. She became 'a Republican groupie', romancing that she had had a relationship with an Irish folk hero, Michael McVerry, who had been killed. There is no evidence that she ever even knew him, although she claimed they had a cathedral wedding on a day when he was somewhere else. The Crown knew this story was a fabrication, but according to Michael Mansfield QC at her appeal the trial was conducted as though she were an IRA widow. She also told stories of having a baby by another IRA man, but was never seen pregnant. She had taken to wearing a rather conspicuous Provo-style uniform of military jacket and beret when selling Republican newspapers and hanging around Irish bars. She tried to get a job working for Sinn Fein, but they would not accept her, taking the view that she was unbalanced. On a number of occasions before her eventual arrest she had been taken into police stations by police and whilst in custody had confessed to being complicit in IRA offences; her stories were so obviously absurd that she had been released. When a bomb went off at Euston station, she and another woman who were living rough went to the station and shouted IRA slogans at the police. She was arrested then too, but no one believed for a minute that she was anything other than a sadly disturbed young woman.

Dr James MacKeith testified at Judith Ward's appeal that she was at the time of her confessions suffering from a personality disorder which had developed into mental illness by the time she was charged. The disorder manifested itself in attention-seeking, memory problems, mood swings and depression – a condition of 'hysteria' making her removed from reality. His assessment was based on interviews with her, her family, and people who knew her, but also on police and prison records and all the documentation which has subsequently come to light.

After each account given to the police of her involvement in the bombing, the story would be checked, only to find that her alleged supplier of the explosives was out of the country at the time and that her movements did not fit. They would return to question her further, and, anxious to accommodate them, she would produce a new and equally untenable yarn. Interview after interview was filled with palpably false information.

After she was charged, Detective Chief Superintendant George Oldfield conducted yet another interview with her in which she spoke of participating in helicopter manoeuvres with an IRA flying corps over the Yorkshire moors, a fantasy so absurd that the officer expressed in a report at the time that he had reservations about her veracity. He had written that he would be 'extremely reluctant to rely on her . . . Her mood changes from day to day, hour to hour and minute to minute.'

The medical officer at Risley prison, where she was held on remand, prepared a pre-trial report (which juries do not see). It said: 'Ward cannot be described as a very truthful person in that she has changed her story to me several times . . . She is a most difficult person to evaluate. At times she is feminine and well-mannered. At other times she is rough, foul-mouthed and coarse.' In the months just before trial Judith Ward was so mentally ill she attempted suicide twice; the defence lawyers were never informed.

Someone who is unstable could, of course, be responsible for terrible crimes, and it could be argued that they are particularly eligible candidates for suspicion. However, it was the view of a Detective Sergeant in the Royal Ulster Constabulary who knew her that it was 'total nonsense that the IRA would have trusted a person with the mentality of Judith Ward. She was not a stable person.' A wealth of material pointing to her instability was available to the prosecution but never put in the hands of the defence. The inexplicability of this situation is still a source of bewilderment to the legal profession, and was described by her lawyer at the appeal as a dereliction of duty.

Dr Gisli Gudjonsson, the clinical psychologist, also gave evidence in the appeal. His tests on Ms Ward showed she was abnormally suggestive and prone to confabulation, filling in gaps in her memory with fictional material.

When giving evidence at the appeal, Dr MacKeith said that it would not have been reasonable to expect the jurors in her trial to be conscious of Ms Ward's mental state. The full body of interviews showed clearly how disturbed she was, but the jury and defence were never availed of that information, having heard less than half the possible evidence. The lawyers were putting together a jigsaw with most of the pieces missing. It is a scandalous indictment of the prosecution that such non-disclosure could ever have taken place, especially when expressions of concern about the woman's reliability were already in the minds of some police and expressed in their reports.

Michael Farrell, a staff journalist on the *Irish Press* and a respected writer, interviewed a woman who claimed that she had planted the M62 bomb; the detail of her account led him to believe that it was decidedly more credible than any of the multiple stories proferred by Judith Ward.

Judith Ward was not a woman likely to evoke much empathy when she came to trial. From her own mouth she was a Republican supporter and her behaviour, unless explained psychiatrically, marked her to many as an enemy of the state. During the course of her case the bomb at Guildford exploded, a factor which it would be hard for a jury to ignore. The temptation to say 'better safe than sorry' and to convict in that spirit is especially strong in cases where public safety is an issue.

Her case added to the catalogue of shameful conduct in Irish cases, but it also raised important concerns about vulnerable suspects. Even if interrogators do not use threats or physical violence, hostile and aggressive questioning by men can be particularly oppressive to women, especially if they are psychologically fragile. This is not pleading kid-gloves for the weaker sex. The research of psychiatrists working in this field indicates that the personalities most likely to admit offences they did not commit tend to be passive in the face of authority and anxious to avoid confrontation. The way most women are socialised inevitably means that they are particularly susceptible, the more so if they have lived with an authoritarian man.

On 4 June 1992 Judith Ward's convictions were quashed by the Court of Appeal as unsafe and unsatisfactory; the judges, in an excoriating judgement, made clear their disgust at the non-disclosure of important evidence by the Crown, a doctor in the prison service and the scientists in the case.

Because so few women are involved, the investigation and trial of serious crime is not designed with them in mind, and little consideration is given to the impact of conventional policing methods and trial procedures on women. There should be greater use of women police officers in primary roles where women are accused of crime; and officers should be trained in good interrogation practices, creating an awareness about the inherent risks. The presence of solicitors should be required before any questioning takes place, and statements made in their absence should be inadmissible, without any judicial discretion to allow them to be included later. This should be an absolute right, since research by the Lord Chancellor's Department disclosed as many as twenty-two different ploys used by police to prevent access to a solicitor under the present rules. It should be a requirement that any incriminating admission must be repeated in front of the accused's lawyer before it becomes admissible and that interviews should be video-taped. The courts should also be much less resistant to the inclusion of expert evidence when an accused may have a vulnerable personality. Above all, no conviction should be possible on uncorroborated confession evidence alone.

As yet, the non-disclosure of evidence to the defence in a number of the miscarriage of justice cases has remained a mystery: it is as though a veil is being drawn over those parts of the events. The code of professional conduct for barristers must make it clear that the defence have a right to see all the material in a case, and if evidence is being withheld because the security of the state would be put at risk by disclosure, the defence should be told the nature and ambit of the evidence so that a challenge can be made in court to the decision to hold it back.

It was a source of great sadness to many women and men who have made a special study of women and crime that the Royal Commission on Criminal Justice drew up its terms of reference without any special consideration of women's needs and experience within the system. The assumption as always is that the law is neutral. It cannot be insignificant that women, though such a small percentage of serious offenders, have been a real presence in the acknowledged miscarriages of justice; Carole Richardson, Annie Maguire, Judith Ward, Jacqueline Fletcher or that three of those women made confessions.

Central to any reforms must be a review of the working of the Court of Appeal. The limits which are placed on the kind of cases which can go to appeal should be removed, and much wider criteria introduced.

Many of the cases which have come back to haunt the system were heard at appeal, and the judges often went through the farce of knitting together new evidence with that which was presented to the original court, and trying to imagine what impact the totality would have had on the jury. Judges should not have been playing the role of jurors, any more than they would allow experts to do the same thing, and the cases should have been sent back for retrial.

A Tribunal for Miscarriages of Justice should also be established, accountable to Parliament and with members who are in the main non-lawyers. The membership would have to change with some regularity to prevent case-hardening. The court would be able to review cases referred from any source and would commission its own investigations, having the power to subpoena documents, such as police files, and to summon witnesses. It should also have the power to quash convictions.

Without such a radical innovation the risk of serious miscarriages of justice will remain; the price is always liberty.

10

She-devils and Amazons

In almost every culture and every period of history, a she-devil emerges as an example of all that is rotten in the female sex. This Medusa draws together the many forms of female perversion: a woman whose sexuality is debauched and foul, pornographic and bisexual; a woman who knows none of the fine and noble instincts when it comes to men and children; a woman who lies and deceives, manipulates and corrupts. A woman who is clever and powerful. This is a woman who is far deadlier than any male, in fact not a woman at all.

Contemporary moral panic has focused on the discovery of child sexual abuse on an extensive scale, and has brought accompanying allegations about covens, satanic ritual and the devil's work. Satanism or witchcraft is given as the explanation for depravity and torture, with accounts of children being subjected to all forms of sexual abuse including rape, buggery and bestiality, and stories of babies being sacrificed.

Some of the accounts are probably true, but it should also not be surprising that those who are profoundly damaged by their experiences give disturbing and distorted accounts of their abuse, especially when complicated emotions such as personal guilt are involved. Nor should it seem strange that the pretence of super-natural powers is claimed by the perpetrators to obtain silence and submission. And it should be understandable that there will be occasions when social workers and supporters of the victims, who are emotionally drained by the terrible demands of the job, have difficulty standing back from the evidence. There is some support for accounts of cultish behaviour in a number of cases, but no physical evidence to support any stories of babies being killed and eaten. Hysteria is difficult to control once inflamed, and becomes a distraction from the central problem, which is the prevalence of sexual abuse within families. At the end of the seventeenth century the Salem witchhunt in New England led to trials of 141 people; nineteen were hanged and one was pressed to death in an effort to exorcise the evil spirit.

The current stories invariably revolve around cases where women have played a central role. Since the perpetrators are often related to the children, their names quite properly escape publication, so as to prevent identification of their victims. However, because of the degree of secrecy about the trials, and because the people involved remain anonymous and shadowy, our innermost fears are again aroused; we seek an explanation of some sort, even if that explanation becomes irrational and absurd. Women who allow wholesale abuse of their own children, even if they had in their turn been abused, are women deemed unworthy of the name. They join the likes of female Nazi torturers Ilse Koch and Irma Griese. They can only be 'witches' or 'servants of the Devil'.

Other courtroom allusions are often classical. Such women are gorgons, sirens, harpies; Medusa is invoked, and Circe the seductress. Literature is rich with comparisons: Lady Macbeth, Lucretia Borgia, Messalina. Witches and Salem and all the hellish ghosts of the past rise to haunt the trials, conspiring to make woman central to the human fall from grace.

The perversion of the human spirit that underlies crimes of desperate cruelty invokes an atavistic desire to punish those who inflict such pain, not just on the victims, but on the scarred families who are left to mourn. It is all too easy to characterise women criminals as victims, because so many of those who go through the system have themselves been at the receiving end of criminal behaviour. However, the inhumanity of women can be as terrible as any. Men enter the pantheon of monsters more often than women: one thinks of John Christie, Peter Sutcliffe, Denis Nilsson. But those convicted of killing who do not belong to the dominant culture are more likely to be mythologised. Until his successful appeal, Winston Silcott, who was convicted of murdering PC Blakelock, was subjected to wilful demonising by the media, much of which was blatantly racist: the Black Beast of Broadwater Farm, the Evil Warlord, the Dark Demon. There were unsupported suggestions that he was a pimp, a drug dealer, a black Fagin who operated gangs of young criminals around London. And the imprisonment of Myra Hindley has come to stand for more than simple punishment for an abhorrent crime: her continued incarceration symbolises our fear of returning to a more primitive past. In an increasingly secular world, a woman like Myra Hindley is the vessel into which society pours its dark secrets: like a war criminal, such a 'she-devil' is a reminder of what is horribly possible.

Myra Hindley is the embodiment of all that is unnatural in women. Yet if you ask people under 40 what she actually did, they are uncertain, apart from a hazy appreciation that children were killed and that the case had sadistic sexual overtones.

It is impossible to fathom what corruption or disturbance of the human spirit can account for the horrible crimes Ian Brady and Myra Hindley committed, and no lawyer is going to be able to provide the answers.

The investigation began in October 1965 when David Smith, the brother-in-law of Myra Hindley, informed the Manchester police that he had been witness to the savage murder by Ian Brady of a 17-year-old youth. On the information he provided, the police went immediately to the address of Ian Brady and Myra Hindley and found the boy's dead body cleaved by an axe. Brady maintained at his trial that the boy was homosexual and that he had picked him up with Smith to 'queer roll' him for money, and that the death resulted accidentally when the boy struggled.

In a notebook discovered in the house was a list of names, including that of John Kilbride, a 12-year-old boy who had gone missing two years before. The police sensed that they might be dealing with a complex investigation and scoured the couple's property for information of John Kilbride's whereabouts. They found a quantity of photographs taken on the nearby moors, and with the assistance of a neighbour's child the location of a number of other photographs was identified. A search of Saddleworth moor unearthed the body of another missing child, Lesley Ann Downey, who had disappeared the previous year.

The case began to come together when David Smith also recollected that he had seen Ian Brady remove two suitcases from the house which could not be found. They were discovered in the left-luggage office at the city's central station and contained crucial evidence linking the pair to the body of the little girl. Days later, the body of John Kilbride was also found on the moors.

The contents of the cases included books on sexual perversion, coshes, photographs of Lesley Ann naked, and a tape-recording of her screams, pleading not to be subjected to whatever was happening. The voices of Ian Brady and Myra Hindley are clearly audible, remonstrating with the little girl, telling her to shut up and to co-operate. The child is threatened and told to put something in her mouth. The playing of that tape in the court did more than any other piece of evidence to secure the convictions.

At their trial in 1965 at Chester, Myra Hindley was presented by both Brady himself and the prosecution as his faithful lieutenant. In the popular press she was described as his sex slave, and there was little doubt at the time that, while her role was criminal and appalling, she was not the prime mover in the murders. Yet as the years have passed she has moved to the centre stage. Brady's psychosis is long since established, and he is now serving his sentence in a penal institution for the mentally insane. The mad dog is safely caged; whatever power he once wielded, he is now, we are told, a pathetic, demented specimen.

Not so Myra Hindley, whose survival and persistence in seeking parole is seen as a testament against her. Her academic success and her support from prominent campaigners like Lord Longford and Lord Astor serve only to compound public perceptions and to put paid to any suggestion that we are here dealing with a psychiatric case.

Dreadful crimes challenge belief in fundamental goodness, and if there is no understandable motive, such as jealousy or greed or a response to some form of provocation, we cannot comprehend them. We are disturbed at our failure to categorise the conduct, beyond accepting that it falls well beyond the bounds of moral acceptability. We are happier cataloguing the deed as a result of madness, because we do not then have to deal with the troubling concept of wickedness. Madness, for all its elusiveness, is a label which gives us comfort in the face of inexplicable behaviour. Yet there is ambivalence about how it is used. The public want murderers convicted as 'murderers' rather than madmen if they have killed in cruel and vicious ways; they want lunacy to be diagnosed after the magnitude of the crimes is recognised, not before. The catharsis of public condemnation has to be ritually experienced.

In the case of Peter Sutcliffe, the Yorkshire Ripper, the judge felt that the issue of the accused's sanity should be tried by a jury. It would have been wrong for a decision about the state of Sutcliffe's mind to have been resolved by a cabal of lawyers and medical men, even if their opinions were completely sound. Public involvement in such decisions is crucial, because it maintains a balance between the *vox populi* and the law. If it had been decided that Peter Sutcliffe was not guilty by reason of insanity and he had been sent to Broadmoor, a secure hospital, under section 60 of the Mental Health Act, the public would have felt aggrieved. That a serial killer who had stalked women, attacked them, sexually assaulted, mutilated and killed them, and also put all women in fear of their lives, should not carry the label murderer would have seemed like an affront. In fact, the jury decided that he was not criminally insane, but since his initial incarceration he has been transferred to Broadmoor in recognition of his deep psychopathy.

Many lawyers in the Temple felt that the trial was a show put on for public consumption; they thought it was an abuse of the process, as Sutcliffe's psychiatric state should have been recognised. Psychiatrists of considerable reputation were publicly undermined, but it was subsequently shown, by his move to a mental institution, that what they were saying was true. It is all too easy to make fun of a defendant's descriptions of hallucinations or divine injunctions to commit crime, but psychiatrists with a wealth of experience do know when they are dealing with a psychopath. Although the jury had no hesitation in deciding that in their view Sutcliffe was not criminally insane, that does not necessarily mean they doubted his madness. They wanted an acknowledgement of his wickedness and were unable to contemplate returning verdicts of not guilty. I have no doubt, however, that the jurors who listened to the rollcall of Sutcliffe's violence ultimately found it reassuring that his crimes could be attributed to some deep-seated mental abnormality which did not defy diagnosis.

There is a conflict between seeking an explanation for the inexplicable in madness and an unwillingness to allow madness to become an excuse. When we ask ourselves, how could someone do that to another human being, to an innocent child? we want someone to make the behaviour intelligible to us. We hoped that psychiatry might have all the answers and that evil might be rendered obsolete, but the medical profession is not as magical or all-powerful as we like to believe. Explanations for deliberate acts of criminality are sometimes not available; although these occasions are comparatively rare, there are motiveless crimes with no suggestion of diagnosed disease of the mind. And, of course, if they are denied by those charged with their commission, no insight comes from the offender.

Evil as a concept is resisted by some people, but the majority do accept the idea of evil and want punishment for its perpetrators. Sexual depravity as a component in killing heightens our revulsion, and our inability to understand becomes the more pressing if children are involved. However, countless men have been convicted of revolting crimes, beyond the imagination of most people – raping and mutilating, torturing and killing, severing and dismembering – in a nightmare of atrocities that make one long for the simple bullet in the head or the knife wound. These men fill the pages of penny dreadfuls and chambers of horrors, but few of them are remembered by name.

We feel differently about a woman doing something consciously cruel because of our expectations of the 'gentle', nurturing sex. At Myra Hindley's trial the prosecution played the tape-recording of Lesley Ann Down pleading with her tormentors. Myra Hindley's voice is on the tape, which is still held by police. It defies explanation that someone, especially a woman, stood by and allowed torture to take place. Similarly, Mary Bell, the 10-year-old girl who said she strangled two small children 'for fun', perplexed and terrified the British public because her behaviour contradicted the sugar and spice make-up that little girls are expected to have. Yet in every child's fairy story the delicate heroine is contrasted with a wicked woman who is there to put fear into the hearts of little boys (and girls), a reminder of corrupted womanhood. Wicked witches, old crones, evil stepmothers and ugly sisters leap from the pages in greater numbers even than the giants and ogres. Terror is a man, but wickedness is a woman. These women, who either have a cruel beauty like the stepmother of Snow White or are as ugly as sin, insinuate themselves into positions of power over children and grown men, luring them to danger, plumping them up for a final devouring, cutting them to pieces.

Most police mug-shots are less than flattering, but the photograph of Myra Hindley which is forever used in the press is in a class of its own, and bears little resemblance to the woman. The female who looks out with steely eyes has badly dyed, dishevelled hair and a heavy face. Her mouth is tight and mean. This is a woman to hate.

A female client spoke to me recently about a woman incarcerated with her called Carol Hanson, whom she said was serving twenty years for child murders. The story amongst the prisoners was that she had been employed as a foster mother and had killed the babies in her care. She was supposed to have cut them up and sent the pieces of their bodies through the post to their natural mothers. To the other convicted prisoners, many of whom had had their own children taken from them, she is a pariah. She has to keep away from them for her own safety and has hung a notice on her cell door saying she killed only one child.

I was interested in this woman because, if she had committed crimes against children, why was her name unknown to us? What made Myra Hindley so different? I had great difficulty in tracing reports of the crime and eventually found out that she had been convicted of murder in circumstances very similar to those of Myra Hindley, but bearing no relation to the prison mythology of cutting up babies.

Carol Hanson and her husband Michael were convicted in 1970 of murdering Christine Beck, who was 10 years old. Michael Hanson, a soldier, was also convicted of unlawful sexual intercourse with the child. The court had heard evidence of 'sex games' played regularly by Mrs Hanson and numerous children aged between 11 and 15. At least five of them had been sexually assaulted. The Crown's case in relation to the death was that, as part of 'some form of perverted sexual pleasure, Christine was sexually assaulted, partially strangled and then stabbed twice through the heart with a flick-knife'. The defendants blamed each other, Carol saying that the killing happened when she was downstairs, unaware of what was going on.

My client described Carol Hanson as someone who had become 'noncified', an elaboration of the prison term 'nonce' which is used for sex offenders. She explained that the woman was now a broken creature, despised by all the other inmates. This is not true of Myra Hindley, who has had her share of physical attacks and rejection but has survived intact. If punishment has not bowed her, the public expect guilt and remorse to achieve the same effect. That is what separates Myra Hindley from other women offenders, and still gives her the status of high priestess of wickedness.

In 1986 the Moors Murders case was reopened when Ian Brady was said in the press to have confessed to reporters that he had also killed two other young people, Keith Bennett and Pauline Reade. In the prison interviews with the police which followed this disclosure, Ian Brady refused to help, but Myra Hindley admitted that they had also been murdered. She described the unbearable pain of confessing to crimes of such enormity, but wanted the whole thing to be laid to rest for herself and for the families. Her years of imprisonment had provided ample opportunity for self-analysis and introspection, and she was able to describe the fierceness of her passion for Ian Brady, who had such a powerful hold upon her at the time, but her attempts at explanation only fuelled the cynicism of police and public. The lucid explanation that Myra Hindley herself puts forward to explain (but not excuse) her involvement in the killings – that she was then a naïve young girl totally in the thrall of a complex, experienced man – misses its mark because of the very coherence with which it is expressed. From the knowledge of her as she is now, the public find it hard to extract a sense of the woman that she was then.

An obsessional quality, which she still seems to possess, is clearly revealed in the personal diary that Myra Hindley kept when she first met Ian Brady at their place of work. The entries are a catalogue of childish desperation for him to show some interest in her, and since they were not written for public consumption and were penned before the spiral of degradation was under way, they support her contention that she was deeply immature. But it is hard to see beyond the strength of character and force of will which she now exudes in middle age to her essential personality. Her recent confessions of guilt in relation to the original charges and the further admissions of two additional murders were hard to interpret as genuine repentance, and appeared rather as part of calculated machinations to get herself released. Press revelations of her lesbian relationships in prison have further stoked the fires of abhorrence.

There have been virtually no female serial killers, although in a recent case in the United States two gay women were convicted of killing repeatedly and cold-bloodedly in the commission of successive petty robberies. The popular press, needless to say, blamed their deviance on their sexuality.

No case has emerged, however, where the killer is a lone female operator, who stalks successive, unfamiliar prey. Despite efforts by Hollywood to create movies on those lines, there seems to be no female Boston Strangler or Yorkshire Ripper. The nearest women have come to this systematic taking of life are when women carers, such as nurses or keepers of old people's homes, kill their charges, or bizarre instances like Mary Beth Tinning, an American, who gave birth to nine babies in fourteen years and killed them all, year after year.

Men who commit multiple crimes are usually involved in a misogynistic power-play deriving from a deep-rooted anger against women, often directing their perverse rage at women they perceive as bad. The blame for the criminality of the serial killer is frequently put on his maternal relationship or lack of one. Interestingly, the experience does not seem to operate in reverse, with powerless women seeking indiscriminate vengeance against men. The physical imbalance between men and women might again be a factor here, but why do we not see women with access to guns mowing down their oppressors at random?

On the few occasions when women have played a role in serial killings, as in the Moors and Manson murders, they have functioned as hand maidens to a master. This is not the same dynamic as the battered wife who submits or colludes because of her own passivity in the face of violence. These are women in the power of strong-willed men who kill to express their scorn for humanity, men who see themselves as superior and are empowered by exacting the ultimate price from their victims. Some women feel strangely flattered at being chosen by such men, as though they had been singled out from the ordinary run of womankind.

There are people whose sexual make-up seems to require a relinquishing of personal will; it implies never having to face moral responsibility for sexual indiscretion or having to accept guilt if your deviance becomes criminal. It may be that at that time in her life Myra Hindley needed Brady's sexual control just as much as he needed a witness to his atrocities, and that they then became welded together by their mutual knowledge.

No one should be surprised at Myra Hindley's reconstructing of the past. We all do it, and the enormity of her shame must require some delusion. But every attempt she makes to explain her acts only feeds the view of her as a devious, manipulative woman. Her own gender is especially repulsed by her crimes.

The idea of contemporary witches may seem laughable, but the treatment of women suspected of crime is often manifestly different. The Lindy Chamberlain case in Australia became a *cause célèbre* for a mixture of reasons, one of which was undoubtedly that the person at the centre of the allegations was a woman and a mother. The Chamberlain family had gone on a camping holiday to Ayers Rock, which is to Australians what Stonehenge is to the English. The parents had with them their two young sons as well as a newborn daughter, Azaria. Lindy Chamberlain put the baby to sleep in its basinette and had only just rejoined a group of campers when a cry was heard and she flew back to the tent. Her story remained consistent from the outset: seeing a dingo (wild dog) emerge from the tent, she ran in to the baby, but it had disappeared, snatched, as she assumed, by the animal. There was blood spotted about in the tent and a search by campers and subsequently by the police discovered no infant, nor any remains. The couple were interviewed repeatedly by the media, and after their initial grief displayed a calmness in the face of questioning which they attributed to their religious faith as Seventh Day Adventists. They explained that they had accepted the baby's death as part of God's great design and had resigned themselves to their loss.

Some time after the death, the baby's stretch-towelling suit and her vest were found, allegedly in a neat pile. Zoologists testified that, though they had not known a dingo kill a human baby before, they did think it was capable of peeling and shaking a baby out of its clothes. They also believed that a dingo would devour every last fragment of an infant, leaving no debris behind.

Speculation and gossip mounted, and even by the time of the coroner's inquest the couple were being accused behind hands of killing the baby. The problem was absence of motive. The mother showed no signs of post-natal depression, and the baby had seemed to be particularly welcomed because she was a little girl in a family of boys. She was to all appearances well cared for and loved. Why would they do it? There were rumours about human sacrifice in biblical fashion, as though anyone who belonged to a peculiar religious sect might be tempted to surrender unto the Father what was really His. It was even suggested that there were links with the Jonestown mass suicide a couple of years before, when whole families had surrendered themselves to the higher good. The hiss of 'burn the bitch' followed Lindy Chamberlain wherever she went. There were stories that she had dressed her baby in black and behaved strangely, all part of the hatred that the Australian public was developing for her. The family received calls from people who found her composure 'affronting' and accused her of treating the baby's death as 'a big joke'. She was not behaving in the manner expected of a grieving mother.

By the time Lindy Chamberlain stood trial for murder, she was expecting another baby and her pregnancy was obvious to the world. This was seen as an attempt to manipulate the sympathies of the court, although the trial had originally been set down for many months before, when no one would have been aware of her condition. She appeared in the dock with her husband, who was charged with aiding and abetting her after the event. The prosecution case turned on the forensic evidence of a bloodstain on the baby-suit, which a British expert said was in his view the imprint of a small, bloodied hand, a contention which did not withstand cross-examination. Splatters of blood were allegedly found in the well of the Chamberlain's car, but there was evidence to suggest that other substances might have created the same response to the haematology tests. As against the forensic case of the prosecution, an independent witness for the defence said she heard the baby cry out when Lindy Chamberlain was standing in front of her. It was as a result of that cry that the mother ran to the tent, and therefore the baby could not have already been dead as the state was maintaining.

In the theatre of the criminal court, Lindy Chamberlain was a bad witness. She did not disclose the emotional torment which the situation (and public) seemed to demand. She was disgusted and angry with the way the media had treated her, and made no attempt to conceal her feelings. Her anger at the prosecution meant that she came across as a cold, hard-faced woman. She was damned if she was going to give them the show they wanted to prove her innocence, and damned she was as a result.

In this country, the professional rule against speaking to your client when he or she is in the middle of giving evidence is religiously observed, but in Australia there is a slight relaxation, in that whilst counsels cannot talk to the defendant about the content of their evidence, they can discuss extraneous matters such as the client's demeanour in the witness box. John Bryson, who wrote the definitive account of the trial, recorded a conversation relayed to him by someone who was present. Andrew Kirkham, Lindy Chamberlain's counsel, was worried about the impression she was making and warned her against sounding 'like a fish-wife' as she answered the prosecutor's questions. He advised her to hold her temper, not to sound too harsh or angry. He suggested she should try to be more 'demure'. This was a lawyer who knows his trade attempting to squeeze his client into a more acceptable manner; there is no criminal lawyer who has not done the same in his or her time. Lindy Chamberlain's reported response was, 'I am the way I am. The jury will just have to get used to it.' The jury did not, and she was found guilty, although no reason could be found to explain why she might have done it. Benjamin Cardozo, the American Supreme Court judge, recognised this type of problem when he wrote, 'Deep below consciousness are other forces, the likes and dislikes, the predilections and the prejudices, the complex of instincts and emotions and habits and convictions, which make the man, whether he be litigant or judge.'

We should add jurors to the list.

Lindy Chamberlain did not cry. Ruth Ellis did not cry. Myra Hindley did not cry. Real women cry.

After the failure of successive appeals, Lindy Chamberlain and her husband were eventually cleared because the forensic evidence was discredited. But the gender factor was the one that really counted.

In her authoritative book *Women Who Kill* (1991), Ann Jones suggests that moral panics about women and crime coincide with the periods when women make strides towards equality, and that such panics may be a crude and perhaps even unconscious attempt at controlling these advances. She cites the cases of two twentieth-century American examples of the female criminal, Ruth Snyder and Alice Crimmins, in support of this view, placing both historically in times of dynamic change for women. Ruth was tried with her lover Judd Gray in 1927 for the killing of her husband, who had been bludgeoned to death with a sashweight. The couple had been conducting a clandestine affair and the murder had been made to look like a robbery, with Ruth left tied up and some jewellery missing. The sophistication of this plot was somewhat undermined by the discovery that the seductress had simply hidden the supposed proceeds of this robbery under her mattress. When asked about the name of Judd in her address book, she immediately asked if he had confessed.

The attorney who represented Judd Gray went to great lengths to describe the wiliness of Ruth Snyder's character:

That woman like a poisonous snake drew Judd Gray into her glistening coils, and there was no escape. It was a peculiarly alluring seduction. Just as a piece of steel jumps and clings to the powerful magnet, so Judd Gray came within the powerful, compelling, attractive force of that woman. She held him fast. This woman, this peculiar venomous species of humanity, was abnormal, possessed of an all-consuming, all-absorbing passion, an animal lust, which seemingly was never satiated.

Every detail of the adulterous affair was pored over in court, and in the press. There Ruth Snyder was described as having no heart, being a bad woman, a bad wife, a bad mother, who did not even look like a woman. Comment was made on her dyed blonde hair, her 'masculine' jaw and her mouth, which was 'as cold, hard and unsympathetic as a crack in a dried lemon'. Ruth Snyder and Judd Gray went to the electric chair.

In 1967, with the rise of women's liberation, came Alice Crimmins, who was tried for the murder of her two children. Again, Alice did not look like a decent woman, let alone a proper mother: she was a sexy blonde who wore tight trousers and had affairs and, like Ruth Ellis, had been a nightclub hostess. The police officer in the case took one look at her and decided he had his murderess. He took her to the scene where her little girl's body had been found and showed her the corpse. She failed the test by failing to cry, although she did faint. It took him two years to put together a case against her, and it later came to light that this had involved bribing and suborning witnesses.

Alice Crimmins suffered the same fate as Lindy Chamberlain. A campaign of attrition was mounted against her by the press and by the time she came to trial she was angry and defiant. She too was hurt that her grief was not recognised because her manifestation of it did not conform to expectations. Apparently she too was coaxed and cajoled into dressing more appropriately, wearing her hair differently and generally presenting herself in a more acceptable form. However, she was certainly not going to break down in court just for the spectators, which meant that she was seen, as usual, as unnatural and hard. This being the 1960s, she was described by the press as a 'sexy swinger': an example of what freedom for women brought. Alice was convicted on the doubtful evidence of having been seen in a car with a bundle, supposedly a body, and an unknown man. A former lover of little credibility claimed she had confessed to the killing to him, but little credibility is more than none, which was the status attached to Alice's own account. After a successful appeal she was retried and again convicted; another appeal led eventually to her having the conviction reduced to manslaughter.

It is difficult to assess accurately whether Ann Jones' theory about moral backlashes against female advances holds true in Britain. Serious crime by women here is still sufficiently rare to invoke horror whenever it happens, and it is hard to link the outrage to specific periods in history, but a number of notorious cases are remarkably similar in their facts and in the response they evoked to the ones cited by Ann Jones.

Edith Thompson was hanged at Holloway prison in January 1923 at precisely the time when women were being admitted to the professions, having successfully secured the vote. She had been convicted of murdering her husband.

The Crown alleged that the Thompsons were walking home in a dark road in Ilford, Essex, in October 1922, when a figure emerged from the shadows and stabbed Mr Thompson to death. The assailant was later proved to be Frederick Bywaters, a young ship's purser and Edith's lover, once a lodger at her house. From the moment of her arrest, Edith denied all complicity in the killing and insisted that she had no idea that Bywaters was anywhere in the vicinity or had any intention of harming her husband. Bywaters himself confirmed this. However, the core of the evidence against her at her trial at the Old Bailey was her correspondence to the man she loved whilst he was at sea. The love letters seemed to indicate that she was learning about poisons and wanted him to send her something to do away with her husband. The defence were able to show that much of the contents were fanciful, that she was merely using the letters as a means of indulging her fantasies of being free to share a life with Freddy. The autopsy report from a celebrated pathologist, Sir Bernard Spilsbury, proved that her claim to be adding broken glass to her husband's food was a nonsense, wholly unsupported by the findings at the postmortem. The picture that comes clearly across today is of a woman trapped in a loveless marriage to a less than admirable man who physically abused her, but she received little understanding from the trial judge, Mr Justice Shearman, and his bias against her repeatedly filtered into his summing up. The same old judicial formula was used whereby judges absolve themselves from any responsibility for prejudicing a jury when they indicate their own interpretation of the evidence. Mr Justice Shearman invoked this when he chose to assert his view, and followed it with the rider that the final decision was, of course, in the hands of the jury: 'That is for you and not for me.' He was clearly convinced that Edith was culpable of inciting Frederick Bywaters to murder. Even if she was not privy to the fine detail of the ultimate plan or its execution, it was she, as an older woman, who had to be held responsible. His moral outrage on behalf of husbands was obvious, and he was particularly offended by the descriptions of the defendants' great love.

At the end of one of Edith's letters to Freddy, she referred to her husband as having 'the right by law to all that you have the right to by nature and love'. Mr Justice Shearman vented his spleen:

> Gentlemen, if that nonsense means anything it means that the love of a husband for his wife is something improper because marriage is acknowledged by the law, and that the love of a woman for her lover, elicit and clandestine, is something great and noble. I am certain that you like any other right-minded persons will be filled with disgust at such a notion.

His Lordship also suggested that some strange chivalry, rather than an expression of the truth, might account for Freddy's exculpating Edith.

In the press, Edith was portrayed in a covert way as the New Woman: she earned her own living as a supervisor in a clothing manufacturer's, taking home more than her husband, who was a city clerk. She was portrayed as a flapper, who liked to go to a show in the West End and have a port and lemon with her girlfriends. She showed little interest in having children. Was this the kind of woman society wanted?

Poor Edith went to the scaffold amidst some public concern about her conviction. Horrible stories were told in the press alleging that she disintegrated emotionally at the point of hanging, that she fought, kicked, screamed and protested her innocence to the last, and that five warders had to hold her down as she was carried to the gallows. It was even suggested that 'her insides fell out'. As late as 1956, during the death penalty debate, the then Home Secretary denied these accounts, but accepted that she had to be given sedatives before the hanging. Recent investigations into the case suggest she may have been pregnant at the time of the hanging, but her Home Office file has been withdrawn without reason and is no longer available to the public.

The trial of Ruth Ellis took place in 1955 at a time when women, having been shooed back into domesticity after the war, were being portrayed in advertisements and on the radio as the core of the modern nuclear family. There had been a general outcry against the collapse of morals due to the pressures of war, and calls had gone up for the re-establishment of 'traditional values' – always bad news for women. Ruth Ellis served as a perfect example of the consequences of female venality, and the double standard relating to sexual behaviour was never questioned. It was one thing for David Blakely to hang around nightclubs picking up hostesses, but quite another to be that hostess. And while it wasn't altogether decent for Blakely to slap Ruth Ellis about, had she not an illegitimate child and a daughter by a failed marriage whom she did not even look after? She failed society's expectations on all fronts. The only criticism made of David Blakely was that he gave her false encouragement, letting her believe that they might have a future together. Leslie Boyd, who was the chief clerk at the Old Bailey at the time, described Ruth Ellis in his reminiscences as cold and calculating, an evil example of womanhood.

One of Britain's 'swinging sixties' cases took place at the High Court in Aberdeen. On 2 December 1968 Sheila Garvie, who was 34, and her lover Brian Tevendale, who was 22, were sentenced to life imprisonment for the murder of her wealthy farmer husband, who had disappeared in mysterious circumstances the previous April. Not until August was the decomposed body of Maxwell Garvie found by the police in an underground tunnel some miles from his farm. During the trial it was said that Mrs Garvie had wined, dined and loved with Tevendale in the knowledge that he had bludgeoned and then shot her husband to death in their own home while her three young children slept. She was described variously by counsel as Lady Chatterley, Lady Bountiful and Lady Macbeth.

As with Edith Thompson, it was suggested by the Solicitor-General, who was prosecuting, that because of her age Sheila was ultimately responsible for the crime. Particular exception is taken to women having young lovers. 'Is Mrs Garvie the real brains behind the crime? She had everything to gain by its successful completion, she would get rid of a husband with whom, in her own words, life was hell . . . Do you think she is resourceful, cool, business-like?' The sordid life to which she was subjected by her husband was described by Sheila Garvie during the trial in some detail, no doubt in an attempt to counter the automatic disapproval it was anticipated the jury would feel about her affair with a younger man. The Solicitor-General was then able to describe her defence as a double-edged sword, on the grounds that 'it may show you she would have a very strong motive to seek her husband's destruction'. This is a Catch 22 situation which faces many women on trial who try to expose their husband's rotten behaviour.

Where Ann Jones' theory has most potency is in the legal response to women who are depicted as 'women's libbers'. For a while the theory that women's expanded horizons led to more female crime had some currency, but examination of the data showed that women were no more criminal in the 1960s and 1970s than they had ever been. The numbers of reported cases has increased in the last thirty years but is consistent with more effective policing of the kinds of crime traditionally committed by women, largely offences of dishonesty.

As well as witches, we have amazons: women who have most seriously confronted the male authority of the court are those whose offences emanate from their political beliefs. In the last twenty years we have seen many more waves of political women coming before the courts, and involved in anti-nuclear campaigns like the women's peace camp at Greenham Common, or feminist demonstrations such as Reclaiming the Night and Women's Right to Choose on abortion. These public campaigns echoed the suffragette campaigns of the beginning of the century. The response of the court has changed remarkably little, and women today voice very similar criticisms of the patronising and paternalistic nature of the system.

The operation of the criminal justice system in public order cases always produces feelings of anger. The mass-processing involved in dealing with so many cases arising out of the exercise of political freedom inevitably creates a sense of injustice. In most circumstances the response of the court is no different whether you are male or female, but some other component does come into operation when the demonstration is actively organised by women for women.

In the early days at Newbury Magistrates Court, where the Greenham campaign cases were tried, the celebratory atmosphere of women coming together demanding peace penetrated the courtroom. The magistrates were perplexed and unsettled by the motley collection of women who appeared before them: women of all classes, ages and marital status, gay women, nuns, mothers. I always remember being instructed to appear for a group of peace women. After making the legal argument in relation to the right of way and not succeeding, I was instructed to withdraw so that the women could make their own political statements. I stayed to watch, and it was quite extraordinary to see the way in which the traditional regimented courtroom procedure was changed. One after another, the women gave forceful explanations of why they were involved. Their large numbers together in the dock meant that they were not intimidated and were able to express themselves freely in what is normally an inhibiting male theatre. They gave each other encouragement and support.

Apart from the male magistrates and a few police officers, the only other man in the court was the court interpreter, who was there to translate the incantation of the Japanese Buddhist nuns. He had learned his Japanese in a prisoner-of-war camp and he entered into the spirit of the event as few interpreters do. Instead of sounding like the speaking clock, he charged his translation with some emotion and enthusiasm, and spoke with deep feeling about the horror of war. The women were all found guilty, but my last memory of the courtroom was of a great festival of kissing and hugging, with the little interpreter getting his fair share of the affection.

However, this female insurrection had to be contained, and a decision was made to separate the women so that only one or two were tried at any one time in the courtroom. The variety of the women involved was soon homogenised by the popular press into the 1970s stereotype of the political woman in dungarees, spiked hair, non-matching earrings and no trace of lipstick. The legend was created that this or that woman was a man-hater, an iconoclast with no respect for the institutions, a woman who abandoned her responsibilities of home, hearth and children to haunt the perimeters of legitimate male activity in defending the realm. The antagonism towards the Greenham women was soon tangible in the courtrooms; in the most minimal of obstruction cases, questions would be asked about whether women had children and who had been caring for them at the time of their arrest. No miner on a picket line would ever be asked to account for himself in this way.

Women who enter the political arena are either mythologised or marginalised. Greenham moved from being portrayed in the press as legitimate peace campaigning to a side show, and eventually a freak show. This process of marginalisation was completed in the courts. However, contemporary politics threw up a different kind of she-devil.

The trial of the Price sisters in 1974 for bombing the Old Bailey court was the first of a number of cases, alleging acts of terrorism, against women involved in Irish republicanism. The surprise and sense of horror that women were playing a prominent role ran right through the trial and the publicity which surrounded it. The headlines on 11 September 1973 blazoned the significance of their leading roles: 'DOLOURS BOSSED THE IRA BOMB SQUAD' (*The Times*); 'THE TERROR GANG WAS LED BY A GIRL CLAIMS QC' (*Daily Mirror*) – and she was 'a pretty 23-year-old redhead' to boot, according to the *Sun*.

The terrorist woman is a new category of female offender, in that she challenges the pathos of so much female crime. Her attack upon the state is dual, assaulting the institutions both directly, in bombing attacks, and indirectly, by confronting the traditional role of woman as a cornerstone of established society. Some women criminologists perceive a 'unisexing' of terrorists, with women activists being denied their gender. I have always found the opposite, that in fact women involved in terrorist trials stimulate enormous prurient interest. Their womanliness is described in detail, with accounts in the press of the clothing they wear and their appearance in the dock.

There seems to be a sexiness about the combination of women, so long as they are young, and power: possibly the idea of a bossy, pretty woman like Dolours Price summons up repressed sexual feelings about dominant women. The words 'cold', 'calculating' and 'ruthless' are often juxtaposed with 'attractive', 'vivacious' and 'pretty'. The men involved in these cases – police, lawyers, judges and reporters – are titillated by images of the armalite rifle in feminine hands, but they are also fearful of its implications. Running through most of the cases of IRA activity involving women is a sense of horror that women should use the very attributes which make them so appealing to men to undermine their guard.

In the Price sisters trial in 1974, evidence was given that Dolours was asked by police about a photograph in which she was seen smiling in the company of a British soldier. It was maintained that she flirted with the army to get information, ruthlessly exploiting her charms. According to press reports she had 'fluttered her long natural eyelashes' at army officers.

Being duped by men is one thing, but to be taken in by a woman particularly rankles with men. Judges frequently become exercised that women provide cover for activities which are traditionally seen as within the province of men, presenting as half of a married couple, as Martina Anderson did in the Brighton bombing conspiracy, or as half of a courting couple for the planting of a bomb, as was alleged against Carole Richardson in the Guildford bombing trial. It was alleged by the prosecution that when Marion Price was being interrogated after being arrested for the Old Bailey explosion and was asked about other possible bombs, she looked at her watch at 2.50 p.m. and smiled. At 2.44 p.m. a bomb had exploded in Great Scotland Yard. Her image as an ice-hearted maiden was reinforced by the claim that she was known as the Armalite Widow because of her reputation as a crack shot against the British army. Whether this was because she made widows out of military wives, or was a woman no longer dependent on a man, or was as deadly as the Black Widow spider was never made clear, but one was left in no doubt that this young woman was lethal.

Women like Ulrike Meinhof and Gudrun Ensslin, who led the German Baader Meinhof group of urban guerrillas, Bernardine Dohrn and Kathy Boudin of the American Weather Underground, the Angry Brigade women, Anna Mendlesson and Hilary Creek, or Patty Hearst, have all provoked more interest and speculation than their male comrades. All were educated, middle-class women who became involved at the extreme end of the radical politics which grew out of the anti-Vietnam war movement. However, it was their sexual liberation, rather than their class analysis, that seemed to interest the male voyeur.

This response may have been influenced by some of the cultural images which were prevalent at that time, in the late 1960s and the early 1970s, images of leather-clad Diana Rigg in *The Avengers* or 'Pussy Galore' in the James Bond films, physically able to floor men without losing any of their sexual charms. These women also functioned alongside men, introducing exciting possibilities about what they got up to sexually, in contrast to women-only politics like Greenham Common, which are at best boring and at worst involve sexual activity that few want to hear about.

The domination imagery is interesting because it has to stay on the right side of the narrow line between attractive sado-masochistic fantasies and the fearful domineering form of control. Evidence was adduced against Dolours Price that she had ordered Paul Holmes, a co-conspirator, to take the considerable risk of going back to prime the Scotland Yard bomb when he had forgotten to do so. The impression given was of a woman who expected manliness of her men, a challenge that few can resist. But the dividing line is very narrow. The seductiveness of powerful women is mesmerising but also frightening because of the unspoken notions that such power is won at the expense of men, and that powerful women consume and destroy. The need to show who is master (the same dynamics which underlie domestic violence) are played out publicly in the courtroom, as women are reminded of their proper place.

The theatrical convention, from Jean Genet to Monty Python, in which the judge indulges his fetish for sado-masochism with some beautiful, scantily clad domitrice spanking him in the wings of the court, has its roots in the complicated relationship between sex and guilt, punishment and power. These elements charge the atmosphere at the trials of political, independent women, and as a result subtle and insidious inferences undermine the proceedings. There is no difference in the way women are sentenced – the courts cannot be criticised for inequality on that score – but the sense of alarm that they should be involved in such warlike activity infects the rhetoric of the courtroom. In summing up to the jury, or in sentencing, judges almost unconsciously single women out for comment. When Martina Anderson and Ella O'Dwyer were sentenced after the Brighton bombing trial in 1986, the judge made a special comment about their cold-heartedness. On the evidence, they were no less feeling than their male co-accused, but of course 'caring' is not the province of men.

However, although the IRA women invoke complicated responses, their commitment is understood. The calculated nature of their offences means they acquire the 'bad' rather than 'mad' label, but their motive is appreciable. The support they receive from their own community helps them maintain dignity and self-esteem, and they are acknowledged as a special category of prisoner within the penal population itself. They may be perceived as a monstrous regiment, but they do not fill the nightmares of the public in the way that Myra Hindley and child abusers do.

11

Courtly Gestures

Women are not going to settle for a legal system that does not listen to them or take account of their lives, and the system is becoming wise to that fact. Women have gone through the stage where they did the adjusting; now it is time for the institutions to change. The symbol of justice may be a woman, but why settle for symbols?

When judges were first challenged about gender bias they refused to recognise there was a problem. Indeed, many women did too. They could not see that change had overtaken our political and social institutions – that male behaviour which was once considered acceptable is no longer so, or that what was deemed chivalrous or courtly is now patronising. Conversely, we hear male judges, in relation to women lawyers and defendants alike, asking why they are so aggressive. 'Why can't they act like women? Why must they act like men?' In fact, they are acting like lawyers or independent human beings.

'Gender bias' includes bias against men, and there are cases, particularly those involving child custody, where this certainly applies. The difference is that the majority of men in court are stereotypically viewed as powerful, credible and independent. The men who do invoke stereotypical assumptions – homosexual, black, Irish, Arab, vagrant, gypsy, unemployed – can suffer as women do.

My focus has been on women throughout this book. However, the failures I am seeking to describe are about more than sexual bias, racial prejudice or a narrow class perspective. I have sought to show the legal processes which produce injustice and the mind-set of lawyers and judges which allows the law to be reproduced in an unfair way. The crisis in the law concerns an institution which is incapable or unwilling to adapt to a different order: a system unable to recognise its purpose and its own failings. I hope I have demonstrated that while the law is in a lamentable state it can be changed; it can be challenged and is being reformed in some degree. However, what is needed is a much more profound and systematic reconstruction.

We have reached an extraordinary impasse, for example, in sentencing policy: the prison system is in crisis because of over-crowding yet the judges continue to sentence as though oblivious to the fact, or its serious implications. The compartmentalising of different sections of the criminal justice system – police, prisons and the courts – means that devising a coherent law enforcement or penal policy can be undermined by lack of co-operation between the parts. There is small point in introducing a progressive police policy on domestic violence if the courts do not reinforce it, nor is there any sense in the penal system working to maintain family relationships, if those same relationships play little part in the considerations of the court.

Reviews of the prison system often neglect women, because they make up such a small part of the whole and because there are rarely disturbances in the female jails. However, given their limited size and the varied nature of the population in women's prisons, it should be possible to try out new initiatives amongst women first, such as small satellite units instead of the few large prison institutions which currently exist. In hostel-type units women could have their children with them on a more prolonged basis and gain work experience where appropriate. The increased numbers of small prison units would mean less dispersal to remote parts of the country, something that has a fatal impact on many relationships.

Before any woman with a child is sent to prison the burden should be upon the court to obtain full information on the impact of separation upon the child and reasons should be given for rejecting an alternative to incarceration. Once that process had begun the same arguments could then extend to men coming before the courts, but a start should be made with this small proportion of defendants and the effects monitored.

Not all judges by any means are dyed-in-the-wool reactionaries: they too can suffer from stereotyping. There are signs of movement. Judges are becoming sensitised to the arguments about accountability and are seeing the need to present a more human face to the public. Sleeves are being rolled up and efforts made to reach the people. All practitioners have their own favourites who epitomise good judgement, intellectual honesty and humanity. Chief amongst the good guys must be the three Lord Justices of Appeal, who did not shrink from the task of apportioning responsibility for the outrageous miscarriage of justice which took place in the case of Judith Ward. Lord Justice Woolf, who looks set to be the next Master of the Rolls, is on everyone's list. He is one of the few judges who has publicly expressed real concern about the system and is suggesting methods for improving it. Most of the judges currently sitting at the Old Bailey are fair and conscious of how people really live. There is a clutch of fine judges in the higher courts, and the consensus amongst lawyers in a law journal straw poll in May 1992 was that one of them, Sir Leonard Hoffmann, was the most respected judge on the bench. The latest batch of recruits to the House of Lords is liberal and inspired. There is also great hope that the new Lord Chief Justice, Peter Taylor, will set a different tone.

A new generation of men are now taking their place on the bench, with different views about the world. They are more used to working alongside women as colleagues and come from more varied backgrounds. The English Bar has been renowned for its integrity and high level of professional competence, but this new generation had a particular dedication to their clients and a special commitment to the meaning and quality of justice. It was this generation which first challenged the orthodoxies of the Bar, setting up new chambers which organised democratically, and challenging the attitudes in conventional sets. They have largely been responsible for a political shift, albeit slight, within the Bar Council, and for the shaping of a less entrenched profession. It is claimed that the apotheosis of this group will be the class of

'68, with their very different views about social mores and class divisions. They will surely make some difference, it is said, when and if their time really comes.

However, there is no cause for celebration. The fact that there is some change shows that movement is possible, but if judges are left to their own accords this shift will be marginal, destined to solidify like lava. Many judges remain blinkered and arrogant. Just as can happen to children in care, hospital inmates, long-term prisoners and mental patients, they become institutionalised, dependent on known forms and reluctant to contemplate change. The power of the system to turn any free spirit into a conforming replica of those who went before is considerable, and it is often not long before the great new hope on the bench begins to look very like the old vintage.

In *The Bar on Trial* Robert Hazell highlighted a problem which starts at an even earlier stage:

> There is one other way in which the conventions and traditions of the Bar affect the development of the law and its institutions, and that is by ensuring that barristers who challenge the conventions do not reach positions of importance in which they can influence matters. Outwardly the Bar has a reputation for tolerance . . . but this tolerance can only exist within clearly defined limits. Most barristers are conformist by training, if not by temperament, and for those few who are not, the ceremonies, rules and patterns of behaviour in the Inns soon ensure that they pay proper respect to the ethos and traditions of the Bar which are inculcated into them by their elders.

Even the good ones succumb to tunnel vision; the life seems to induce complacency and the system becomes an end in itself. They do see that the very notions which are idealised by the law deserve examination. The ideal of objectivity, for example, is a masculine value which has come to be taken as a universal one. Often when the law fails people it is not because of some lack of objectivity but because judicial objectivity has meant a denial of the female or black or working-class experience. There is a systematic exclusion of other perspectives. Insisting on equality, neutrality and objectivity is not to insist on judgement by the values of men of a particular class. It is, therefore, important that truly universal values are created.

In fairness to judges, the judicial role has become more difficult at a practical level, because courts are so much busier. Management is required to get through the list, and the pressure is considerable. Judges are also isolated and receive very little feedback. The people they mainly mix with socially are their own peers, who do not see them doing the job. In David Hare's play, *Murmuring Judges*, an elderly member of the judiciary responds to the suggestion that judges are 'out of touch' with the claim that he and his brethren are very familiar with common folk since they see them in court every day. (A familiar utterance at the Bar.) Coupled with this isolation is the enduring characteristic of judges: they are in charge and wield great power over people's lives. They are not used to being challenged and it is hard for them to accept questioning of their function as creative.

Part of the remedy for the law's failings must be reform of the judiciary. First, we have to find more accountable ways of making appointments. The current method of taking soundings amongst the present incumbents as to who should join their ranks means that the potential for cloning is overwhelming: existing judges effectively appoint new judges. In a television programme in April 1992, Lord Bridge, a newly retired member of the Law Lords, agreed that when selecting a new judge they looked for chaps like themselves; there has to be a very conscious effort to break that mould.

A Judicial Appointments Commission is essential to any renewal by introducing outsiders to the decision-making process but there is fierce opposition to this proposal, not least by the Lord Chancellor and new Lord Chief Justice. It should include members of the legal profession, solicitors and barristers, judges and legal academics, but also a significant number of lay representatives. Such a body would work with the Lord Chancellor in considering appointments. The criteria should be made public. Elizabeth Sydney, a clinical psychologist, has just completed some research for the campaigning organisation, Justice, which shows that a job specification could easily be created which would stipulate the necessary qualifications and skills that any prospective judge should have. Formal applications should be made after advertisement and there should be a proper period of full-time training.

For the Higher Court, the Court of Appeal and the House of Lords, there should be public notice that someone is being considered, with the opportunity for public debate on the appointee's track record, declared opinions and background. At the moment we operate a fiction for public consumption that none of these things matters, when in fact it is acknowledged privately within the profession that prospective candidates who are deemed too progressive are unlikely to be considered for preferment. Not many human rights lawyers appear on the secret list which circulates among the judicial fraternity for their comment. One of the strange things at the Bar is the belief that only people on the left are political. When I was a pupil barrister I remember being advised sternly by a senior member of the chambers not to mix politics with a career at the Bar. He was a Conservative MP.

It is essential that the bench should reflect the diversity and richness of our social landscape. New blood refreshes the parts otherwise not reached. For example, women educate men for the most part about sexism. Men then educate other men.

A Canadian lawyer was in Britain when the rituals of the opening of the Law Courts took place at the beginning of the legal term. All the Law Lords and the Judges of Appeal and the High Court processed in their robes with full bottom wigs and knee breeches and silk stockings. He was shocked that this full display was so barren of women, having become used to the near equality of numbers in his own country.

The process of women becoming judges and reaching the top of the legal profession cannot be left to chance or the passage of time. Positive action has to be taken to get women on to the bench in real numbers, and that will only be achieved by removing blinkers about what constitutes merit and experience. Most women lawyers, who can manage a home and a reasonably successful career, can manage a court. When asked what skills are required for judging, male barristers always cite intelligence, judgement, integrity and 'standing' (this apparently is still measured in the Lord Chancellor's Department by reference to earnings and word on the grapevine) but rarely mention patience, open-mindedness, balance or courtesy.

At least 30 per cent of women are needed in the practising profession and on the bench before tokenism ceases to function and a real difference is felt. Currently 19 per cent of practitioners and 4 per cent of the bench are women.

The Lord Chancellor may maintain that there are insufficient women of the right experience greatly to increase female representation at this stage, but if that is true he should initiate fast-tracking of very able younger women. I question the assertion that there are not enough women when I know competent, talented women who are not getting on to the Bench. Women at the Family Bar resist the present training structure because, rather than drawing on their expertise, they are expected to start sitting as judges in criminal courts where they have not set foot for 15–20 years. It is a ludicrous way of drawing in new personnel and smacks of the notion that the criminal courts are a good nursery for tomorrow's judge.

Another source of new blood can come from within the legal profession. There are many senior women solicitors who have never been considered and who would not dream of suggesting themselves. Women often do not have a career plan and have to be encouraged to think of sitting but they should also start asserting themselves and making their own claim on these appointments. Solicitors, male and female, could provide an enormous pool of potential judges but they have to be urged to think of judicial appointment if they have established busy, lucrative practices. However, many would find the idea of public service inviting.

I have always supported the extension of rights of audience, enabling solicitors as well as barristers to act for clients in courts at every level. In the interests of consumer choice it is a crucial development, but it also means the breaking of the charmed circle which binds judges and barristers, often contrary to the interests of justice.

Currently potential judges – barristers and the occasional solicitor – begin their judicial career by sitting on a part time basis for one month a year as an Assistant Recorder. Counsel whose practices have involved commercial contracts and trust deeds and who have barely set foot in a criminal court are given this meagre training on the basis that any reasonably sensible lawyer is capable of conducting a simple criminal case in a judicial capacity. This means that any competent solicitor should have the same potential.

Peeling away the mystique is very important if we want to encourage a wider intake. The cases dealt with by these novice judges are not very serious, and there is training on the conduct of a small trial and on sentencing. After acquiring some experience, an assistant normally receives an appointment as a full Recorder, which again requires that they sit for at least twenty-eight days in each year. Part-time sitting is supposed to equip lawyers for eventual appointment to the circuit or High Court bench.

At the moment, the earliest age at which judging can begin is 35 but it is much more usual that the lawyer is in his or her 40s or even 50s. There is no valid reason why judges should not begin this training at 30. Women with young families, for example, may be particularly interested in using this time for acquiring judicial skills, sitting part time in the lower courts. The resistance to reducing the age is based on a view of the world from the far end of the telescope, where the ageing judges who currently run the show look down on someone in their early 30s as a mere child.

The Lord Chancellor's Department is keen to encourage applications from women and members of the ethnic minorities. But the encouragement has to be more active, and the reasons why candidates fail to come forward in these groups analysed. Those on the outside of exclusive networks feel uncertain about attempting to join: functioning on your own in a court seems an intimidating prospect and joining the white, male club is not inviting.

The entry of women would be easier if the job were attuned to more realistic living arrangements. Circuit and district judges are locally based, but the grander office is that of High Court judge; these are the people who set the judicial tone. On appointment they receive a knighthood. Rather than basing High Court judges in a particular part of the country, they are all centrally located in London at the Royal Courts of Justice, but those who deal with criminal cases travel to the different circuits for stretches of a month or two at any given time. Sometimes, if they are handling a long trial, they may spend many months away from home.

During these periods they live in special judges' lodgings (rather grand houses with a cook and butler and other staff). Currently, £1.4 million per year is spent on maintaining judges' lodgings. It is not a life that can easily be combined with the care of a family. Most of the men have wives who make it all possible, having sacrificed their own careers, while their chidren usually are at boarding school.

The wives of High Court judges are expected to travel the country to attend functions on their husband's arm, which is rarely easy if they themselves have a professional life. They are exposed to all the wretched snobberies of the Bar, with pecking orders as to whose wife is allowed to leave the dining room first. There are older judges who take the wives of new incumbents to one side to advise them on their behaviour when they go to stay at judges' lodgings, often suggesting that wives are not welcome at breakfast.

However, for the majority of women, for men whose wives have demanding careers, or who themselves wish to be involved actively with their children, it is an unacceptable lifestyle which urgently needs to be changed if the people who take office are not to remain unrepresentative and remote from the changing world. It is perfectly feasible to appoint local High Court judges and to restructure the court system.

Effective judicial training is another vital reform. In relation to women in the United States, there is now a National Education Programme to Promote Equality for Women and Men in the Courtroom. However, the mention of continuing education touches a raw nerve amongst British judges, who refuse to accept they need formalised instruction. Our own Judicial Studies Board (so called in an effort not to engage with any neurosis on the topic) is run by the judges themselves; apart from providing a weekend residential course to launch the new judge, it holds the occasional seminar on the impact of legislation and changes in sentencing powers. Little is said about attitudes.

A revolutionary change did take place with the introduction of the Children Act 1991 where contact was initiated between judges and professionals in other fields in an unparalleled way: paediatricians, psychiatrists, social workers and others with important experience to share attended seminars with judges to talk about the problems in cases affecting children. We now have the Ethnic Minorities Advisory Board, chaired by the dauntless Mr Justice Brooke, carefully raising the sensitive subject of race with new judges. The benefits are bound to be considerable.

There are many other areas where such schemes are needed, for example on gender issues, management skills, criminology, forensic science. A Judicial College should be established to maintain well-structured education with sustained input from outside the profession: there is no major industry which does not provide special opportunities to acquire new skills to senior management. The initial training should be much more rigorous and over a period of months, not days. Nor should training be confined to judges, but should be extended to magistrates and all lawyers who practise in the courts. As well as initial preparation for new judges, there should be in-service training at regular intervals. Opportunities to look at the work of social agencies, legal reform and the workings of foreign jurisdictions could be provided within sabbatical periods, allowing judges to get off the bench and breathe a different air. Why should our judges not spend the occasional term as a visiting tutor at a university, where they might impart some of their knowledge and also have the starch taken out of their own ideas?

I am also firmly of the view that there are special skills which advocates should be required to learn when handling child abuse cases and mental health cases. The way in which vulnerable witnesses are cross-examined is often unacceptable; the assumption that techniques which work with armed robbers should be used in sensitive cases is ludicrous. Legal aid in cases involving children should only be available to those barristers and solicitors who are certificated to handle such trials. To obtain the additional certification the lawyers should be required to take specialised courses.

The Bar is already having discussions about continuing learning for the profession but is meeting some resistance from practitioners who can see no advantage for themselves; a sure way of compelling practitioners to acquire new skills is to preclude them from remuneration if they do not have them.

At the same time as these reforms are introduced, there should be a concerted effort to widen the intake into the legal profession. We are still seeing too narrow a class of student and the whole legal profession would be enriched by having greater diversity and experience within its midst. (This, alas, is unlikely to happen soon, since it is closely related to education and according to A. H. Halsey in *Decline of Donnish Dominion* (1992), there has been no increase in the percentage of working-class children entering university in the last thirty years.)

In the barristers' profession there is currently a bottleneck, with too many students, too few pupillages and even fewer tenancies available in sets of chambers. As soon as there is a run on space the old covert mechanisms for nepotism are likely to come into play, as has happened with the scholarship scheme mentioned in Chapter 2. If the chambers themselves finance the training of the next generation of barristers the nature of the intake will not change. Selection for the Bar has always been based disproportionately on connections and financial resources rather than on ability. To remedy this, grants for pupillage have to be centrally distributed by the Bar and chambers should be given incentives to look at less conventional candidates. There should also be public funding available to ensure that students from non-traditional backgrounds are able to undertake the vocational training course for the Bar and the solicitors' side of the profession. Many local authorities will not pay for this stage of legal education, and students without private means are excluded. Any review of students shows that financial considerations are still a major inhibitor for those from less than privileged backgrounds, and the process of self selection keeps out those from working-class homes.

The Inns also provide scholarships, but here an examination of awards suggests serious gender and ethnic differentials. The key to change would be for women and members of the ethnic minorities to be included in scholarship-giving committees. All the selection committees, appointment boards, offices, the Lord Chancellor's Department, the Judicial Studies Board, the Law Commission, the Inns of Court, the Law Society, the Bar Council, have to review their ways of working, and should have at least 30 per cent women as well as members from the ethnic minorities.

The Bar will and should survive so long as it provides specialist

legal services to the client, but its justification has to be grounded
in expertise. The time has come to call it a day for ridiculous
practices like compulsory dining. These tribal rituals induct young
lawyers into modes of behaviour which are exclusive and objectionable. They are the product of a particular class experience
which starts in the public schools, and they force anyone who is
an outsider by virtue of sex, race or class to conform to their
paralysing and inward-looking ethos. Tradition is invoked to
maintain vested interests and social reproduction ensues. Every
profession has the odd dinner to create professional bonding but
it is ludicrous that we are still so wedded to this schoolboy ritual
and the tradition of the High Table.

One of the fictions which must also be laid to rest is that the
profession comprises both the bench and the Bar. A judge is no
longer a barrister, but a salaried official of the state, with different
interests and concerns from practising lawyers. The role of the
Inns should be completely overhauled, democratised and reduced
enormously, with the judges on the sidelines rather than governing
a profession to which they no longer belong. The Benchers who
govern the Inns comprise many judges, and the average age of the
membership is 65. There should be direct election of executive
Benchers, and if necessary the Inns should be brought under
statutory control, like the Universities of Oxford and Cambridge
and the solicitors' branch of the profession.

The sacred cow of judicial independence is used as an excuse
for isolationism, complacency and remoteness. No one would
contest the idea that judges should be independent, free from
political pressure and distant from the government of the day. It
is essential that they have security of tenure, irremovable unless
they become mentally unstable or corrupt. However, judges are
political – not just in the personal way that we all are, holding
views on governance and the state of the nation, but in the implications of their decisions for social policy, prison administration,
the Treasury; they are even more overtly political when the issues
before them involve resolution between competing rights. They
claim that insulation is a means of preventing political compromise, but it is, in fact, the aspic in which their conservatism is
preserved. A close examination of those with whom their lordships

are expected to dine on their circuit rounds, the Lord-Lieutenants and the High Sheriffs and the police chiefs, inspires neither envy nor confidence.

The new Lord Chief Justice, in the spirit of openness, indicated his desire to create better links with other parts of the criminal justice system, such as the police and the probation service and prisons. Indeed he attended, as a silent observer, a seminar held by Liberty, on the miscarriages of justice. Why not more active contact with other bodies which offer a critique of the system, like the Howard League for Penal Reform, NACRO, the National Association of Women's Organisations and the Commission for Racial Equality?

The mystification which surrounds the law has in the past protected barristers and judges from scrutiny. They have been able to hide behind their regalia and ritual. Too grand to be doubted, they have until now escaped the close gaze of the people, but a more demanding and educated populace is no longer content to accept the circus – it is demanding bread.

A day in court is enough to convince most men and women that the legal system is a foreign country, where the language and pomp serve only to obscure, engendering a sense that the events are hardly connected with those who are most affected. In 1970 Sir Morris Finer (quoted in *The Bar on Trial*) sought to persuade the Bar to change its ways but it has taken over twenty years before, under threat of reform, it has begun to listen:

> Consumer-orientation may be a provocative phrase to use to the profession, but we need much more of it. The lawyer's consciousness of his inner rectitude – a phenomenon which afflicts the Bar more peculiarly than it does the solicitors' branch – is no substitute. It is apt, indeed, to communicate itself to the lay public as an aloofness, or worse still, a pomposity which they find hard to bear.

In the training of young barristers, greater store is being set on putting the client at ease and trying to ensure that they appreciate the issues and the procedure.

Victim Support, an organisation which supports the victims of crime, has made enormous headway with its efforts to reduce the terror for witnesses by negotiating with courts for better facilities, providing a knowledgeable volunteer as a support, taking the victims into courtrooms to familiarise them with the room and the box in which they will stand, and explaining procedure. Witnesses are often uncertain whether the prosecutor or the defence counsel will ask the questions first. However, it is still early days for these initiatives, and the impact could be even greater if the impetus for making the courts accessible were taken up by all parts of the system.

Many defendants as well as victims need support. They would welcome the opportunity of sitting close to their representative so that they can communicate more readily, rather than remaining in isolation in the dock. Defendants frequently do not have a clue who is who and the distinctions between barristers and solicitors escape them. (The public often believe barristers are solicitors with a few more years' training, an illusion which barristers are happy to maintain.)

Televising the courts would be a different way of significantly reducing the mystery of what goes on in the Halls of Justice, although the spectacle of the Kennedy-Smith rape trial in the United States was convincing testimony of the need for caution on introducing such a move. Sexual offences provide such potent material for the prurient and voyeuristic that the admission of cameras would have to be regulated with careful guidelines.

The medical and teaching professions have already gradually lost much of their mystique through greater public awareness and criticism: it is no bad thing that a new value system is created for professionals. Authority and status should not come from a job title or a fancy costume but should emanate from the way in which the job is performed. People are entitled to knowledge about the processes to which they are exposed: professionals need to have their authority challenged if it is used inappropriately.

The hype which surrounded the media announcement that barristers' wigs might be abandoned met with terror in certain ranks of the legal profession. Large numbers of barristers are wooed to the fancy dress because of the very mystique it introduces; the abolition of the wig, gown and wing collar will undoubtedly be resisted in some quarters. (A survey showed that 70 per cent of criminal barristers want it retained.) But the arguments for keeping it, which stress dignity and authority, are snares. It is as though the costume is some sort of legal corset or scaffold, required to sustain the edifice. The judges in the House of Lords wear no stuffed shirts or horsehair, yet the show still goes on. In wardship proceedings involving children, robes are never worn and the quality of justice has not been undermined: indeed, it has greatly improved.

Another argument for the retention of wigs is that the judges and the barristers benefit from the anonymity afforded by a uniform. It adds to the illusion about the neutrality of the law. If judges are dressed in an abnormal way they are not ordinary men who might have human frailties and prejudices. It is a pretence which simply adds to the whole fictional quality of the court. Judges need to be seen as real, as professionals doing a particular job. Wigs and regalia and dining may seem irrelevant eccentricities of the system, but it is these obsolete adhesions which hold the structure in place; their removal enables essential cultural change.

Commercial lawyers who have to compete in international markets and function alongside bankers and industrialists have been among the first to recognise that the uniform of old, far from enhancing their image, is more than faintly ridiculous, and unsuited to modern commercial litigation. The great news was that none other than the Lord Chief Justice wanted to see the wig resigned to the dressing-up box, and it is to be hoped that no compromise is devised whereby the wig and gown are confined to the criminal courts, where instilling fear is still considered a good thing. In my view, what goes for the bankers should go for the bank robbers. The real reason is professional pride and rivalry: some barristers want to keep the wig because, once it goes, so does a major artificial distinction between barristers and solicitors.

The reforms of the legal profession which began in the Thatcher years brought the winds of the marketplace into the profession: professional clients such as accountants could have direct access to a barrister without incurring the cost and involvement of the solicitor as intermediary; barristers could publicise their specialities and solicitors would be given rights of audience in the courts. The new philosophy – that monopolies had to be broken and competition should dictate the terms of engagement – achieved, for rather different reasons, some of the changes I believed were crucial to a modern legal system.

It became clear to the Bar Council, for example, that survival in this new competitive climate meant addressing some of the criticisms. But changes should not be driven by public relations advisers, who see the value of 'cosmetic' changes on race and women whilst remaining sensitive to the traditionalists' desire to preserve the status quo, as near as damn-it to before. The legal establishment is often concerned that something should be seen to be done: appearances have priority over substance.

In 1988, I wrote to the then Chairman of the Bar asking the Bar Council to set up a committee to look at the position of women. I wanted them to address some of the concerns of women as part of the general public, who felt the law and legal system were failing them. I was told that the senior men considered there was no problem. At last, at the beginning of 1992, a committee was set up after a positive vote at the Annual General Meeting. The job of monitoring for discrimination and encouraging women is underway. The change was possible because of the energy of young women, largely members of the Association of Women Barristers, and enlightened men, like the two recent Chairmen of the Bar Council, Anthony Scrivener QC and Lord Williams QC. Sadly, there are women in influential positions who take no interest in improving the lot of their own sex and they often oppose change more forcefully than any man. But the profession has to lead the way on issues like discrimination if the public is to trust it; policy changes without supportive attitudes are meaningless.

These changes will in themselves create a cultural shift, but redressing the injustices of the system requires a change which would radically reform not just the body politic, but the body legal, namely a new constitutional settlement, including a Bill of Rights. If our law were predicated on a notion of rights and 'entitlement', so that people automatically saw the court as a protector of what was theirs and the law as their instrument, the change in the legal atmosphere would be considerable. A Bill of Rights is not like a new law. It is above the law and it belongs to civil society. It puts into writing our hopes for the principles by which a society should govern itself. It does not therefore place power into the hands of judges so much as place a power of a cultural and ideological kind into the hands of citizens. It makes judges in some respects answerable to us. A Bill of Rights is a source of empowerment for people, but it would also mean the lawyers would be trained differently and would think in a fresh way. Our methods of practising would be different and the judges would have a new approach to their task. A Bill of Rights is now an essential step in making the courts part of our country rather than the courts being some foreign (alien) place. The women, mothers, black people and immigrants who suffer at the hands of the law have no claim upon it. An unwritten constitution and unwritten principles are part of the male elite world where the chaps are the ones who know what is going on. In order for people such as I have written about in this book to have a claim on the law, they must be able to claim their rights, and to do so they have to know what those rights are. Unless our rights are written down we might all be reduced to a choice of submission, resentful defiance or a winking collusion.

The present spirit of reform has opened the doors to ideas which would have caused mass hysteria only a few years ago; the gap between the two branches of the profession, solicitors and barristers, is closing, and the consumer's requirements are becoming the priority. The law can be dragged into the twenty-first century, but to do so it has to discard a culture and tradition so turned in upon itself that its members cannot understand why it is alien to so much of the population. Now is the time to restore public confidence, by renovating the whole ethos and springing the trap of history and culture in which the legal world has, for so long, been caught.

Index

Adams, Hargrave L., *Woman and Crime* 18–19
Adler, Zsuzsanna 127
Ahluwalia, Kiranjit 203–4, 206
AIDS 153, 154
Alliot, Mr Justice 121
Anderson, Martina 260, 262
Archer, Jeffrey 65–6
Archer, Mary 65–6
Ashley, Jack 206
Auld, Mr Justice 210

Back, Peter, QC 143
bail, refusal of 165–7
Baldwin and McConville 161
Barnett, Sharon 100
barristers
    racial background 43, 164, 189
        women 177–8
    social class of 13, 43
    taking silk 58–9
    tenancies 44, 273
    training 266
        dining 36, 37–40
        Inns of Court 35–40
        pupillage 40, 42–4, 273
    wigs 13, 51, 277
    women
        discrimination against 44–6,
            49–51, 52, 54–63, 141
        over-identification with
            client 50–1
        racial background 177–8
        rape trials 134–6
'battered woman syndrome' 93, 94–5

see also domestic violence
Beckford, Jasmine 89
Bell, Mary 245–6
Berlins, Marcel 53
Besant, Annie 27
'beyond reasonable doubt' 3–4
Bill of Rights 279
biology 23–4
    diminished responsibility 103–4
    menstruation 24
    pre-menstrual tension 24, 104
    pregnancy 24, 102–4
Birchell, Ronald 110
Birmingham Six 5, 8, 233, 234
Bisla, Rajinder 205–6
Black, Dr Dora 79
Blake, George 10–11
Blakelock Appeal 228, 241–2
Booth, Margaret, Mrs Justice 58
Bordes, Pamella 142
Boreham, Mr Justice 220
Boyce, Christabel and Nicholas 106–8
Bracewell, Joyanne, Mrs Justice 58, 61
Brady, Ian 242, 243, 247, 248, 249
    see also Hindley, Myra
Bray, Chief Justice 136
Bridge, Lord 267
Bristow, Mary 108–9
Brooke, Henry, Mr Justice 189, 272
brothels
    keeping 148
    legalisation 153–4
burglary, rape in course of 117–18
Butler Sloss, Elizabeth, Lord
    Justice 58, 61

Index

Byrne, Mr Justice 70

Calladine, Joan 206–7
Campbell, Duncan 76–7
Camps, Frederick 122
Cantley, Judge 76
Cardozo, Judge Benjamin 252
Carlen, Pat 73
Carman, George, QC 9, 142–3
Cassell, Harold 110–11
Caufield, Mr Justice 65, 116
Cave, Bertha 57
Chamberlain, Lindy 249–52
children
  battering of 88–90
    mother's complicity in 89–90,
      95–8
  custody of 25–6, 27
  killing of 95–7
  of prostitutes 151–2
  sentencing, gender bias 77–8
  separation from mother 78–81, 264
  sexual abuse 97–100, 240–1, 272
    by women 98, 100–1
Children Act 1991 271–2
clerks 55–6
Cogland, Monica 65–6
confessions
  false 7–9, 227–39
    susceptible personality 229
Corder, Fran 100
corroboration rule 116–18
court procedure 12–15
Criminal Justice Act 1991 80
Crimmins, Alice 253–4
Croft, Doris 218
Crowe and Cove 161
Cunningham, Dr Jack 44

damages 27, 142
  for rape 27–9, 116, 122
Davies, Mr Justice 142
Davies, Anwyl, Judge 79–80
Dean, Judge 111
Denning, Lord 8, 173
Deutsch, Helene, The Psychology of
  Women 121
diminished responsibility 103–4, 190,
  191, 200, 210
  pre-menstrual tension (PMT) 24,
  104

Diplock, Lord 222–3
domestic violence 82–8, 212–13
  'battered woman syndrome' 93,
    94–5
  children
    battering of 88–90
    killing of 95–7
  cumulative 200, 201, 202, 206,
    209–10, 223
  expert witnesses 92–4
  police and 83–5, 87, 264
  race and 175–6
drug offences 178–85
  sentencing 184–5

Ebsworth, Mrs Justice 58
Edwards, Dr Susan 147
Ellis, Ruth 190–9, 256
Emery, Sally 96
Erskine, Henry 48
Ethnic Minorities Advisory Board 272
expert witnesses 15, 92–4

Fairbarn, Nicholas 121–2
false confessions 7–9, 227–39
  susceptible personality 229
Fennell, Mr Justice 136
Finer, Sir Morris 275–6
Flannery, Peter 87
Fletcher, Jacqueline 229–30, 239

Garvie, Sheila 256–7
Gayle, Colin 149–50
Gebhard, Paul H., Sex Offenders: an
  Analysis of Types 121
Green, Alan 147–8
Greenham Common
  campaigners 258–9
Greig, June 214
Griffith-Jones, Mervyn 70
Grunwick dispute 174–5
Gudjonsson, Dr Gisli 228–9, 236–7
Guildford Four 5, 8–9, 229, 233, 237
  see also Richardson, Carole

Hale, Sir Matthew 130, 139
Hanson, Carol and Michael 246–7
Hare, David, Murmuring Judges 267
Harman, Mr Justice 53
Harris, Jean 208
Hartley, Ruth 97

Index

Havers, Mr Justice 198–9
Hazell, Robert, (ed.) *The Bar on Trial* 54, 266, 275
'heat of the moment' principle 198, 201
Hedman, Sally 96
Hill, Anita 159
Hindley, Myra 24, 192, 242–3, 245–9
Hoffmann, Sir Leonard 265
Hoggett, Brenda and Atkins, Susan, *Women and the Law* 117
Homicide Act 1957 103, 191–2
homosexuality
  age of consent 158
  lesbians 155–8
Hood, Roger 162
Hooson, Lord 48
Horn, Andrew, *The Mirror of Justice* 56–7
Hughes, Sally 60
Humphreys, Christmas 193
Hutchinson, Lord 70

immediacy principle 198, 201
immigrants, vulnerability of 185–6
imprisonment, gender and 22, 33, 264
infanticide 102–3
Inns of Court 35–40, 273

Jackson, Susannah 79–80
Jones, Ann, *Women Who Kill* 252–4
Jones, Janie 143–4
Jowett, Mr Justice 170
judges 4–9, 265
  background of 29–30
  gender bias of 141, 263
  independence of 274–5
  Judicial Studies Board 189, 271
  jury and
    directions to 3
    warnings to, corroboration 117
  police and 6–9, 10, 163–4
  rape trials 11, 120–1
  reform of judiciary 263–272
  women 58, 60–1, 268–9
Jupp, Mr Justice 120–1
jury
  'beyond reasonable doubt' 3–4
  composition of
    challenging 187

racial background 173, 174, 187–8
  women 53–4
  criticisms of 9–10
  judges and
    directions to 3
    warnings to, corroboration 117
  rape trials 122
Juvenile Courts 77–8

Kanter, Dr R. M. 60
Keith, Lord 130–1
Kennedy-Smith rape trial 127–8, 276
kerb-crawling 146, 148
Kiszco, Stefan 5, 228

Lady Chatterley's Lover trial 14, 69–70
Lane, Elizabeth, Mrs Justice 57–8
Lane, Geoffrey, Lord Chief Justice 1–2, 8, 180, 188
language, gender bias of 52–3, 222
Lavallee v Regina 93–4, 95
Lawton, Sir Frederick 70, 84
Lees, Sue 111–12
Leonard, Mr Justice 121, 204
lesbians 155–8
  stereotyping 157–8
Line, Elizabeth 216
Livesey, Margaret 224–7
Lombroso, Cesare and Ferrero 20

McGrail, Joseph 205
Mackay, Lord Chancellor 30, 70
MacKeith, James 228–9, 235, 237
Maguire family 5, 233, 239
Makanjuola, Adebola 185–6
manslaughter *see* provocation; self-defence
marital rape *see* rape
marriage
  'the good wife' 65–70
  rape in 25, 84, 112, 130–3
    implied consent 131–2
  women's rights and 25–6
Married Women's Property Act 1870 26
Married Women's Property Act 1882 26
Meah, Christopher 28
Megginson, Pamela 216–18

Index

mens rea 129
mental states 208–9
  abnormality of mind 191, 202, 204
  fugue state 201–2
  'La Belle Indifference'
    syndrome 231
  M'Naghton rules 191
  see also psychiatry
mercy killings 191
Miles, Lorraine 116
Miskin, Sir James 108
M'Naghton rules 191
Moors Murders *see* Hindley, Myra
Morris, Lord, of Borth y Gest 212
mothers
  black 172–3
  child-battering, complicity
    in 89–90, 95–8
  prostitutes as 151–2
  sentencing of 23
    imprisonment 78–81, 264
  stereotyping 74–5, 172–3
Mozart Seven 173–4
Murphy, Lionel 53
Mylavagnum, Tanoo 177–8

Narayan, Rudy 189
Neil, Andrew, libel action 141–2
Nussbaum, Hedda 86

Oakley, Ann 166
O'Donnell, Kevin Barry 9–10
O'Dwyer, Ella 262
Ognall, Mr Justice 120
Owen, Mr Justice 97, 132

Pankhurst, Christabel 57
Patel, Jayanti 90–1
Patterson, Mabel 215
Payne, Cynthia 140, 143, 144–5
Peters, Carol 214–15
Pickles, James, Judge 70–3
Piggot report 1989 88
police
  domestic violence and 83–5, 87, 264
  'good character of' 170–1
  judges and 6–9, 10, 163–4
  misconduct 6–9
  procedures 2
  racial stereotypes 163, 168, 171–2

Police and Criminal Evidence Act
  1984 2, 7
Pollak, Otto, *The Criminality of
  Women* 20
Pollock, Sir Frederick, *Essays in the
  Law* 35
Ponting, Clive 11, 76–7
Poole, Susan 96–7
pre-menstrual tension (PMT),
  diminished responsiblity and 24,
  104
pregnancy 24, 102–4
  sentencing and 72, 184
Price, Dolours and Marion 259–60
probation 22–3
prostitution
  brothel-keeping 148
  living off immoral earnings 151
  motherhood and 151–2
  rape and 148–50
  social class and 148
  soliciting 146, 152
provocation 106–10, 190–1, 196–200,
  210, 222
  cumulative 202, 206
psychiatry
  gender and 23
  Mental Health Act sections 156
  opinion as to state of mind 208–9
  rape victims 114–16
  treatment as condition of
    probation 100–1
  see also mental states

Queen's Counsel, becoming 58–9

R v Aston and Mason 95–6
R v Ratcliffe 205
R v Riley 123
R v Simbodyal 49
race
  of barristers 43, 189
    women 177–8
  court process and 163–4
  discrimination in legal system 11
  domestic violence 175–6
  drug offences 178–85
  living off immoral earnings 151
  police attitudes to 163, 168, 171–2
  rape and 137–8, 169–70
  sentencing and 161–2, 165–6, 177

Index

stereotyping
  Asian women 174–5
  black women 168–9
    domestic violence 175–6
    as mothers 172–3
Raghip, Engin 228
rape
  AIDS and 136
  buggery 138
  burglary, in course of 117–18
  consent 111–13, 114–15, 122–3,
    129–30, 131–2
    mental state 114–16
    self-defence 123
  'contributory negligence' 11
  corroboration rule 116–18
  credibility 118–19, 123
  damages for 27–9, 116, 122
  'date' 134
  marital 25, 84, 112, 130–3
    implied consent 131–2
  as offence of violence 134
  previous sexual relationships 22,
    124–7
  prostitutes 148–50
  race
    of defendant 137
    of victim 137–8, 169–70
  rape trauma syndrome 127
  sentencing 120–1
  stereotyping 21, 137–8
  trans-sexuals 138
  victims' character 32–3
  women barristers and 134–5
Rattenbury, Alma 232–3
'reasonable man', the 222–4
Renshaw, Michele 71–2
Richardson, Carole 9, 229, 239, 260
  see also Guildford Four
Robinson, Mary 63–4
Rossiter, Amelia 207–8
Rough Justice 224, 229
Rougier, Mr Justice 136

Sainsbury, Pamela 209–10, 213–4
St Clair, Lindy 152
Sanderson, Tessa 142–3
Scotland, June 213
Scott, Frederick 96–7
Scrivener, Anthony, QC 80, 278
Scutt, Jocelynne 53

Sealy, Dr Philip 127
self-defence 129, 191, 206–8, 210–12
sentencing 74, 264
  Criminal Justice Act 1991 80
  drug offences 184–5
  gender and 22–3, 33
    juveniles 77–8
  imprisonment 22, 33, 78–81
  mothers 23, 78–81
  pregnant women 72, 184
  probation 22–3
  race and 161–2, 165–6, 177
  rape cases 120–1
serial killings 248–9
Sex Disqualification (Removal) Act
  1919 57
sexual abuse see children
sexual harassment 158–60
Shearman, Mr Justice 254–5
Sheldrick, Dr E. Carol 98
Silcott, Winston 241–2
Silverman, Dr Gerald 116
Skuse, Dr Frank, pathologist 234
Smellie, Eric 162
Smith, Joan, Misogynies 149
Snyder, Ruth 252–3
social class 153
  of barristers 13, 43
  prostitution and 148
  stereotyping 29
solicitors, right of audience 269
Southall Black Sisters 176
Spilsbury, Sir Bernard 254
stereotyping 106
  the 'good wife' 65–70
  lesbians 157–8
  mothers 74–5, 172–3
  racial 165, 177
    Asian women 174–5
    black women 168–9, 172–3
    rape 137–8
  social class 29
  women
    lawyers 50
    race 168–9, 174–5
    rape 21, 137–8
    as victims 106
Stevenson, Prue 157
Stevenson, Sir Melford 120, 192–9
Stonehouse, John 68
suffragettes 24

Index

Sutcliffe, Judge 117
Sutcliffe, Peter 113–14, 244–5
Swaffer, Yvonne 110
Sydney, Elizabeth 267–8

Taylor, Dr Pamela 97
Taylor, Peter, Lord Chief Justice 51,
    206, 265, 275
Tchaikovsky, Chris 78–9
terrorist crimes 259–62
Thomas, Judge Clarence 158–9
Thompson, Edith 254–6
Thompson, Elizabeth 154–5
Thornton, Sara 201–3, 206, 215–16,
    220–1
Tisdall, Sarah 75–7
tokenism 60–1, 269
Toner, Barbara, *The Fact of Rape* 128
Tumin, Stephen, Judge 79
Tyler, Karen 207

Victim Support 276

Walker, Dr Lenor, *The Battered
    Woman's Syndrome* 94
Ward, Judith 233–8, 239, 265
Weightman, Beverley 230–32
Welldon, Dr Estela, *Mother,
    Madonna, Whore* 99
Wheatley, Lord 215
Wild, Judge 111
Williams, Gareth, QC 278
Williams, Glanville 133–4
    Textbook of Criminal Law 121–2
Willoughby, M. J. 204
Wilson, Bertha, Mme Justice 93–4, 95
witchcraft 25
Wood, Peter 108–9
Woods, Brian, Judge 72
Woolf, Lord Justice 265
Woolf Report 1991 80
Worsthorne, Peregrine 141–2
Wyatt, Pauline 204–5

'Yorkshire Ripper' case
    see Sutcliffe, Peter